Action as History

British Idealist Studies Series 2: Collingwood

1: James Connelly, *Metaphysics, Method and Politics*
2: Marnie Hughes-Warrington, *'How Good an Historian Shall I Be?'*
3: Stein Helgeby, *Action as History*

www.imprint-academic.com/idealists

Action as History

The Historical Thought of R.G. Collingwood

Stein Helgeby

ia

IMPRINT ACADEMIC

For Rebecca and my parents

Published in the UK by Imprint Academic
PO Box 200, Exeter EX5 5YX, UK

Published in the USA by Imprint Academic
Philosophy Documentation Center
PO Box 7147, Charlottesville, VA 22906-7147, USA

ISBN 0 907845 576

A CIP catalogue record for this book is available from the
British Library and US Library of Congress

www.imprint-academic.com/idealists

Contents

Preface vii

Introduction 1

Chapter 1:
Activity and Philosophy 27

Chapter 2:
The World as Process 47

Chapter 3:
Thought and Logic 63

Chapter 4:
The Logic of Question and Answer 77

Chapter 5:
Moral Philosophy and History 101

Chapter 6:
Duty and Individuality 121

Chapter 7:
The Historical Object 139

Chapter 8:
Knowing the Historical Object 159

Chapter 9:
Historical Self-Consciousness 187

Chapter 10:
Historical Civilisation 207

Bibliography of works cited in the text 223

Index 233

Preface

R. G. Collingwood (1889-1943) was one of the clearest writers of philosophy in English, yet most interpretations of his work start by trying to decipher a mystery. For some, the mystery is what Collingwood meant by a particular theory. For many others, the mystery is how such a clear writer could hold confused or muddled views. My problem is different — how to see the clarity of view in the clarity of language. This is, necessarily, to seek to dissolve many of the mysteries.

Collingwood was the twentieth-century philosopher who most closely pursued the dual line of thought that history is the activity of historians and the activity of historical agents. His work can be understood in terms of four related themes: tradition; time and place; a rationale for being concerned with history; and, a project or aspiration.

In my view, Collingwood belonged to a tradition that included Vico, Hegel and Croce. According to this tradition, reason is present or immanent in history through human action. For Croce, who, prior to Collingwood, provided the most recent restatement of the tradition, human deeds, expressions, accomplishments and practices showed the working of reason in its many forms. Historical rationality was founded upon the ways in which self-conscious human beings acted, rather than upon the structure of concepts or the working of extra-human forces. The immanent reason tradition provides a way of understanding and anchoring the theory of agency within a broader world-view. Collingwood's version of this theory was intended to overcome many of the problems bequeathed by earlier thinkers, and to provide an account of history and an ideal for action.

Collingwood's thought emerged from a nineteenth-century culture in which historical studies and historical ways of thinking were pervasive, popular and politically significant. His career developed in a period that saw the emergence of professional academic history, to which he made a significant contribution as a practitioner and theorist. He pursued the problems of the character of historical thought and knowledge across the fields of theory and practice throughout his working life.

On Collingwood's view, history is a universal aspect of action present in each and every act, and this provides the rationale for the philosophy of history. In this context, academic practices are important because they show standards of historical thought at their most developed; nevertheless, a philosophy of history cannot be restricted to academic themes. As Collingwood developed this concern with history as a universal aspect of action, he came to see that our self-knowledge and freedom to act are fully dependent on our historical reason.

I see Collingwood's philosophy of history as aspiring to provide the grounds for a rational faith in the possibility of solving human problems. He sought to secure and deepen modern faith in reason, progress, civility and the malleability of human institutions, and thereby to deepen practice on each of these dimensions. The relevance of his thought to contemporary understandings of history and action lies in this broad project.

Reflection on historical practice provided Collingwood with a theory of knowledge; his moral philosophy provided him with a theory of the object of history. The sense of purpose in Collingwood's philosophy of history was sustained by the close linkages he saw between these areas of philosophy and between historical practice and practical action.

Although each of these four dimensions — tradition, time and place, rationale and aspiration — features in this study, it is primarily concerned with what I have called his rationale and project or aspiration. I draw on, state and restate, Collingwood's published and unpublished work to follow the development of his concepts of action and history. This means that the same issues recur throughout the study, but in different guises and with new and changing implications. In some cases, statement and restatement occur in the same chapter. In other cases, these take place between earlier and later chapters. My goal, then, is to move towards an understanding of Collingwood, rather than to presume it can be presented and then criticised. As, in the course of investigating a range of themes, I come to understand the concepts of action and history, the study draws towards a focus on modern historical consciousness and civilisation.

* * *

I am deeply indebted to David Boucher, who has been invaluable to me as a source of material, information, advice and support since this study began as a thesis at the Australian National University. I would also like to thank Bill Craven for his thoughtful and encouraging supervision of the original thesis and David Boucher and Keith Sutherland for the opportunity to revise it in this form. The Australian National University and the Trustees of the R. G. Collingwood Society provided financial support during the preparation of the thesis; passages from this study have appeared in print in the Society's journal.

In common with other scholars, my understanding of Collingwood's thought has been greatly enriched by the availability, and subsequent publication, of many of his manuscripts. I am grateful to Teresa Smith for allowing me to use these manuscripts. Colin Harris and the staff of the Modern Papers Reading Room at the Bodleian Library were unfailingly efficient in allowing me to read the papers deposited there. The Oxford University Press allowed me to search and utilise their archives, and I am grateful to Peter Foden, Jenny McMorris and Magda Seaton for their help. The Oxford University Archives also gave permission for me to use the material in their possession.

My warmest thanks go to Rebecca for bearing with me while I revised this study.

Introduction

Historical consciousness is common across Western cultures. This is a study of what is involved in that consciousness. The meaning and implications of modern historical consciousness are examined through an account of R. G. Collingwood's thought on moral philosophy and history.

The existence of a way of viewing our place in the world that emphasises contingency, context and process is of inherent interest. The interest is heightened because the historical way of viewing the world may appear to compete with others founded on natural science and technology. One aim of these prevalent conceptions is to enhance control over circumstances, including human activity. Where an historical outlook appears to offer no more than understanding or wisdom, a study based on perceived regularity and law holds out the prospect of manipulation.

To see solely a conflict between historical and scientific conceptions of the world is, however, too simplistic. The scientific manipulation of nature, or the various attempts to offer a social science that permits the manipulation of people, themselves aim to achieve human ends that are situated in history. Rather, it would be better to say that human ends develop in, and are accepted or rejected through, history. The relationships between history, natural science and technology are complex and varied. Collingwood, for example, argued that natural science is dependent on historical thought to understand observations and theories. Understanding what history is must therefore be a requisite to understanding what nature is.[1]

To the extent that Western cultures share an historical consciousness, this is something over and above the existence of a moderately successful competitor in a contest for intellectual dominion. Viewing the world historically is part of our self-conception. If a concern

---

[1]   R. G. Collingwood, *The Idea of Nature*. Clarendon Press, Oxford, 1945. p. 177.

with subjectivity is one of the defining characteristics of modernity and, in particular, of much philosophy from Descartes to Hegel and beyond, how we understand subjectivity is fundamental to what we are. Collingwood detected the rise of a new form of history in the nineteenth and twentieth centuries, meaning principally the emergence of a new activity or way of understanding the human past. He argued that the development of history in his own time represented a new stage in the development of human capability. This study will show how Collingwood's concept of history permitted such a conclusion.

The underlying idea of the study (and which I take to be Collingwood's), is that to give an account of history is to give an account of action, and to give an account of action is to give an account of history. Neither idea can be stated in isolation, but each is dependent on the other. Neither idea is stated once and for all, but each develops. Each idea reflects, but also gives form to, a conception of the world where the primacy belongs to activity and process. Historical consciousness is self-awareness of this world and of what is possible within it.

Historical consciousness permeates our culture, but it does not do so in a single, simple, way. Rather, it takes many forms in different areas of life and thought. Not only are there differences between ways of thinking historically, some of which use narrative and others which eschew narrative, but there are also fundamental differences between those who emphasise persons and their deeds and those who see history as a product of more structural and impersonal elements.

In academia, the historical approach can be seen across several disciplines. In philosophy, it has been maintained that the deep distinctions between philosophers are between those who conceive the world and thought about it historically, and those who hold a view of eternal truths which has its origins in Ancient Greece.[2] In the philosophy of mind, many have come to see mind not as a 'natural organism', but as a grouping of capacities. On this conception, mind 'is a product of human history and artifice.'[3] In academic history, a wide range of movements has broadened the scope of histories to cover people and issues that were previously neglected. In recent decades, history from below, gender studies and feminism, race-studies, post-colonial history and the analysis of popular cul-

[2]   Richard Campbell, *Truth and Historicity*. Clarendon Press, Oxford, 1992. p. 412.
[3]   William Lyons, *Matters of the Mind*. Edinburgh University Press, Edinburgh, 2001. pp. 251-252.

ture have each contributed to showing that all human beings and societies are historical, and that they are historical in the most fundamental aspects of their being. Within archaeology, strong arguments have been put for renewed links between archaeology and history; processual and structural approaches to archaeology have been criticised in the light of approaches that emphasise individual human agency.[4] In literary studies, the issues of historical production and context have assumed great significance. While some theorists have sought to dispense with authors and their intentions in favour of textuality, there have also been moves to restore contingency and complex relations to particular literary studies.[5]

Outside academia, narrative histories, novels and films flourish, though broader intellectual developments have stimulated a great diversity of approaches, styles and subjects. The daily newspaper and electronic media coverage of politics, sport, the economy and culture supply episodes in a number of narratives, together with the commentary that connects them. Television soap-operas and drama series focus most explicitly upon deeds and motives, their interest depending upon the internal logic of relationships and characters together with the influence of external developments upon that logic. In countless forums, but particularly over food and drink, gossip gives narrative form to the deeds of friends and acquaintances. Each of these cultural manifestations represents a form of historical consciousness. It is, however, possible to see each form of historical consciousness as pointing to a more general and deeply rooted feature of humanity. Alasdair MacIntyre, for example, has argued that histories that are narrative, intentional and situated comprise the 'basic and essential genre for the characterization of human actions.'[6] On this view, the structure of narratives lies not simply in the fantasy of writers, but in the way that human lives are lived.[7]

Academic practices are important when they show standards of thought at their most developed, but an account of historical consciousness that was limited to academic themes would be significantly deficient. Yet, simply acknowledging diverse forms and uses

---

[4] Ian Hodder, *Reading the Past: Current Approaches to Interpretation in Archaeology. Second edition.* Cambridge University Press, Cambridge, 1991. See also Ian Hodder, *The Archaeological Process: An Introduction.* Blackwell, Oxford, 1999.

[5] For example, see Robert Dixon, *Prosthetic Gods: Travel, Representation and Colonial Governance.* University of Queensland Press in association with the API Network, St. Lucia, 2001.

[6] Alasdair MacIntyre, *After Virtue: A Study in Moral Theory. Second edition.* Duckworth, London, 1985. p. 208.

[7] Ibid. p. 212.

of historical thinking would also be inadequate. If historical thought and practices are part of our culture, what would our culture be like if it became more thoroughly and consistently historical? Collingwood's argument was that our self-knowledge and freedom to act are fully dependent on our historical reason. If that is so, then a change in historical consciousness must involve a change in how we can act. The bold, tantalising and provocative possibilities of this idea may seem to merit rapid rejection.

There is no shortage of studies of Collingwood that state, and then dismiss, particular arguments. As with other thinkers who typically write dialectically, and who change their perspective and shift the meaning of terms through constant re-working, Collingwood offers up relatively little when studied in that way. An alternative is to seek ways to bring out the plausibility of Collingwood's key ideas about moral philosophy and history. Rather than engage too quickly in criticism it may be fruitful to establish what Collingwood's views were, how far particular criticisms depend on particular expositions of those views and whether such criticisms would hold under other plausible reconstructions of his views. Criticism proceeds on a surer foundation when it originates in the attempt to understand a writer's views.

In his outline for *The Principles of History*, which he intended as his life's major work but did not finish, Collingwood gave a characteristically bold statement of his intent

> III. The main idea here is that history is the negation of the traditional distinction between theory and practice. That distinction depends on taking, as our typical case of knowledge, the contemplation of nature, where the object is presupposed. In history the object is enacted and is therefore not an *ob*ject at all. If this is worked out carefully, there should follow without difficulty a characterisation of an historical morality and an historical civilization, contrasting with our 'scientific' one. Where 'science' = of or belonging to *natural* science. A scientific morality will start from the idea of *human nature* as a thing to be conquered or obeyed: a[n] historical one will deny that there is such a thing, and will resolve what we are into what we do. A scientific society will turn on the idea of *mastering* people (by money or war or the like) or alternatively *serving* them (philanthropy). A[n] historical society will turn on the idea of *understanding* them.[8] [*sic*]

In *An Autobiography*, Collingwood famously proclaimed that '[t]he chief business of twentieth-century philosophy is to reckon

[8]   R. G. Collingwood, *The Principles of History: and other writings in philosophy of history. Edited with an introduction by W. H. Dray and W. J. van der Dussen*. Oxford University Press, Oxford, 1999. p. 246.

with twentieth-century history.'[9] He had earlier argued that the great task of twentieth-century philosophy was to provide a 'reasoned conviction that human progress is possible and that the problems of moral and political life are in principle soluble.'[10] The role of a philosophy oriented towards history was to provide such justification and conviction.

It is necessary to expand upon Collingwood's statements in order to understand them. In particular, Collingwood's argument in the outline for *The Principles of History* turned on his idea of historical knowledge. For Collingwood, historical thinking does not stand outside its object. In that sense, history has no 'object' at all in the sense in which natural sciences stand outside their objects. History is an activity, or act, which involves the historian in performing other actions. Specifically, the historian enacts that which constitutes or differentiates the original acts he is studying — their thought element. For the historian, knowing the action means performing the action again, and thus his act of knowledge is of practical importance to his life; by understanding the past he has become different to what he was before.

Historical knowledge is never merely theoretical, but always practical in the sense of self-creation.[11] From his doctrine of self-creation, Collingwood thought that there would follow certain ideas about civilisation. Historical knowing is important as a kind of acting which permeates all other activities. As his account in *The Idea of Nature* suggests, Collingwood thought that this was not simply a special feature of historical thinking, but also of natural scientific thought. Collingwood contrasted the present 'scientific' ways of thinking and the civilisation built upon them with the historical approach and the kind of civilisation which would emerge in a social community where historical thinking was as fundamental as the scientific approach is today.

---

[9] R. G. Collingwood, *An Autobiography*. Oxford University Press, London, 1939. p. 79.

[10] R. G. Collingwood, 'The Present Need of a Philosophy', *Philosophy*. Volume IX, No. 35, July 1934, pp. 262-265. p. 264. (This letter to the editor of *Philosophy* is reprinted in R. G. Collingwood, *Essays in Political Philosophy. Edited with an introduction by David Boucher*. Clarendon Press, Oxford, 1989. pp. 166-170.)

[11] Michael Hinz has argued that self-creation is fundamental to Collingwood's account of metaphysics. See Michael Hinz, *Self-Creation and History: Collingwood and Nietzsche on Conceptual Change*. University Press of America, Lanham, 1994. Hinz approaches the question of self-creation in history through metaphysics, whereas I approach a similar set of issues through the theory of action, which I take to be more central to the broad range of Collingwood's concerns.

The natural scientific approach was said by Collingwood to generalise about 'human nature' and to develop rules by which to approach human behaviour. Collingwood presented a similar argument in his moral philosophy, where he identified 'regularian', rule-based thinking, where the rules govern 'human nature'. We submit behaviour to rules, and conquer others so that they obey our rules rather than another set. We influence behaviour by finding keys to making that behaviour conform to our ideas of what it should be. Money provides incentives for behaviour that follows one of the rules of 'human nature'. War is a device for gaining our ends by enforcing conformity. The obverse of mastery is service, where we submit ourselves to obeying a certain set of rules existing in society. Collingwood pointed to philanthropy as the most highly developed form of such service, because it is the highest form of submission of the self to a community embodying a particular set of rules.

As with all thinkers who portend a coming civilisation, Collingwood was particularly sketchy on the subject of 'historical civilisation'. His principles of historical thinking preclude the idea that we could predict the future. We can talk about the coming civilisation only in so far as it already exists in a nascent form in our own times. Collingwood clearly thought that historical thinking had reached an advanced state of development in his own time, and it ought therefore to be possible to discern some of the features of the civilisation built upon historical thinking. In his last work, *The New Leviathan* (1942), Collingwood emphasised the rational and dialectical ways in which agreement can be reached between people who start out from different positions. In *The Principles of History*, Collingwood intended to emphasise the way in which we must relate to other people on the basis of their acts, and their acts must be understood.

On my reading, therefore, Collingwood's 'historical civilization' is one in which agreement between people is reached by each enacting the thought of others in an attempt to comprehend views that are initially outside each other. By, in this sense, sharing the same acts, people become other than they were. The emphasis in an historical civilisation would be on the individuality of situations and problems, and on the rational processes by which solutions are found to those individual problems. An historical civilisation will be one of discussion and mutual effort, where the aim is to replace disagreement with a more comprehensive view. In such a civilisation, each person exists not to be mastered but to be understood. This form of liberalism emphasises the critical reason of free agents; each recognises the other as free.

Collingwood's brief picture is a philosophical interpretation of certain elements that already exist within our present civilisation. Collingwood supposed that such values would continue to be realised even during the crisis years of the 1930s and 1940s. Yet, even the most optimistic enthusiast for Collingwood's vision could say only that the historical civilisation remains a future to be attained rather than a present already achieved. It is clear, however, that an historical civilisation as Collingwood envisaged it could not be brought into existence by engineering or design. Rather, an historical civilisation could come about only if people understood themselves to be self-creative persons in individual situations, pursuing individual solutions to individual problems.

It will be clear from even this brief summary that the concepts of action and of history carry a heavy philosophical burden in Collingwood's thought. Arriving at or understanding these concepts is fundamental to making sense of his broader vision. On Collingwood's view, history is a universal dimension of action present in each and every act. Action, for Collingwood, constitutes the human past, present and future. It is a practical as well as theoretical concept. History, then, involves understanding the human past in a way that enables a grasp of the present and, in some defined and important way, shapes the future.

For Collingwood, historical thought is an activity that plays a constructive or reconstructive role in understanding the world. The constructive theme has been common in discussions of history from F.H. Bradley to Croce, Collingwood, Oakeshott and Foucault. In many cases, an emphasis on the activity of historical thought has led to scepticism about historical knowledge, but in writers such as Croce and Collingwood the argument formed the basis for an account of history as knowledge. Nevertheless, the one word 'history' has both epistemological and metaphysical dimensions, where the metaphysics of history involves a theory of the object that historians study. Collingwood's theory of historical knowledge was inseparable from his account of the object of history. While his account of historical knowledge is relatively well understood, his account of the character of the object of history is less frequently discussed. By implication, improving our understanding of Collingwood's account of one must lead to a better understanding of the other.

Collingwood argued that history, as an object for study, is a process of human actions. It was his account of human actions that led him to the view that history involves freedom and the capacity for progress. Such views are controversial in the context of more recent trends in the philosophy of history to place particular importance on epistemological issues, and neglect or dismiss metaphysical considerations. A strong unease about the possibility of a metaphysics of history also arises in the context of the dominant role played for much of the past century by the philosophy of language, which has tended to reject, or at least to constrain, any form of metaphysics.

On a thoroughly sceptical epistemological position, the only historical process is that of the historian constructing history. Any talk of history as an object, rather than about the historian's thought, is simply illegitimate. Yet the idea, underlying many such criticisms, that each historian works in an historical situation, presupposes the existence of historical processes, and therefore implies that we can give some account of them. We require metaphysical inquiries to show how the world must be in order that we can study in the ways we do. If this is so, then any philosophy of history must investigate the general features of history as an object and this metaphysical inquiry must be involved in the account of historical knowledge.

General notions about history are involved in every judgement an historian reaches about various acts or occurrences. An epistemological investigation of specific historical works will bring out that an historian has made certain assumptions and judgements in the course of his inquiries. The metaphysical investigation of his works will examine the relationships between the various elements in his conception of history, particularly their logical priority and their mutual coherence. Metaphysical investigations of this sort can show the tensions between various elements of an historian's underlying conception of the past, and therefore whether his approach to history can be sustained or must be altered or transformed in some way.

The sceptical epistemological position on history can be turned to produce a view such as I take Collingwood's to have been. Since the mind of the historian is active in historical thinking the minimum metaphysics of history is an account of action. Any more complex metaphysics of history will be based upon a theory of action. This does not mean that all discussion of structures or entities such as classes will be illegitimate, but it does render illegitimate any entity that cannot be expressed as an action or a complex organisation of actions. But these are, at best, criteria for metaphysics, rather than an account of the metaphysics of history. We need to look beyond the criteria towards theories that would meet them. As an example, one account of the requisite type (which will provide a useful reference for this study) is Jose Ortega y Gasset's idea that radical reality takes the form 'I am I and my circumstance'. That formula represented Ortega's reworking of Descartes' *cogito*, based on the criticism that the act alone is the unmediated datum of thought in the act of living, and that such living is a radical reality, prior to any Cartesian doubt.[12] In this study, we will need to examine whether Collingwood had a similar theory.

Criticisms of the possibility of a metaphysics of history may be drawn from philosophy of language, but it is also possible to see how much the philosophy of language and the metaphysics of history have in common. Michael Dummett, for example, has characterised analytical philosophy in terms of the view that, firstly, a philosophy of thought is to be attained through philosophy of language and, secondly, that a comprehensive account of thought is only possible in this way.[13] On Dummett's view, metaphysics is possible, but it must follow from and be consistent with a 'meaning-theory'.[14] On his account, philosophy aims only to give a clear view of the concepts with which we think about the world, and therefore how we represent the world in thought. Philosophy, therefore, starts with the structure of thoughts and takes the philosophy of language as the way to approach thoughts. In Dummett's words, 'there can be no account of what thought is, independently of its means of expression...'.[15]

Language, in Dummett's view, is objective, external to mind, embodies thoughts, is accessible and is governed by the criteria and standards of a community.[16] Much, then, depends on how the boundaries of language are drawn and what counts as the expression of a thought. Collingwood shared the conviction that thought can be accounted for only in terms of language, but he drew the boundaries of language more broadly than is the case in much contemporary philosophy. In *The New Leviathan*, he wrote that '[w]ithout language there is no thought. Without thought, and

---

[12] My account of Ortega's philosophy draws in particular on Antonio Rodriguez Huescar, *Jose Ortega y Gasset's Metaphysical Innovation: A Critique and Overcoming of Idealism*. Translated and edited by Jorge Garcia-Gomez. State University of New York Press, Albany, 1995. See esp. pp. 29, 32, 40, 48.

[13] Michael Dummett, *Origins of Analytical Philosophy*. Harvard University Press, Cambridge, 1993. p. 4.

[14] Michael Dummett, *The Logical Basis of Metaphysics*. Harvard University Press, Cambridge, 1991. p. 305.

[15] Ibid. p. 3.

[16] Dummett, *Origins of Analytical Philosophy*. p. 25.

thought of a somewhat highly developed kind expressible only in a
somewhat highly developed form of language, there is no will.'[17] In
his draft for *The Principles of History*, Collingwood wrote of how
'every action has the character of language: every action is an expression of thought.' Thought that has been expressed is language —
broadly conceived to include gesture.[18] In *The New Leviathan*,
Collingwood maintained that language is speech, but it is also 'any
system of bodily movements, not necessarily vocal, whereby the
men who make them *mean* or *signify* anything.'[19] Meaning, therefore,
belongs to forms of human activity that can be embodied in both linguistic and non-linguistic actions. For Collingwood, therefore, consciousness and language develop together through 'the mere
"register" of feelings' to conceptual and propositional thought, and
then to reason as 'demonstrative discourse'.[20]

Collingwood's account of language and thought shared many of
the elements that have motivated the philosophy of language over
the past century. Collingwood, however, developed a more general
account of the objectification of thought. On Collingwood's account,
thought is objectified in action, and an account of action is an
account of the metaphysics of history. Thought is objectified in history, where history encompasses both linguistic and non-linguistic
expression. This clearly placed Collingwood within a tradition that
reached from Vico, through Hegel and down to Croce. A central
insight of this tradition was that there is reason in human history;
history shows an immanent reason.[21] The development of this tradi-

---

[17] R. G. Collingwood, *The New Leviathan, or Man, Society, Civilization and Barbarism.*
      Revised edition, edited and introduced by David Boucher, with 'Goodness, Rightness,
      Utility' and 'What "Civilization" Means'. Clarendon Press, Oxford, 1992. para.
      28.16.
[18] Collingwood, *The Principles of History.* p. 49.
[19] Collingwood, *The New Leviathan.* para. 6.
[20] Ibid. paras. 6.41, 6.58, 6.59.
[21] An opposing view would be that reason, if it existed at all, had nothing to do
      with history or, alternatively, that reason did relate to history, but had nothing
      to do with what human beings did, but only (for example) with what God did.
      The idea that reason is imposed upon past actions by the mind of the historian is
      an incomplete and inconsistent version of this theory. The idea that reason is im-
      posed on history asserts that some people — historians — possess and exercise
      reason, but does not recognise the sense in which every agent is an historian,
      and therefore neglects how every act involves reason. A consistent version of
      the immanent reason theory would say that all acts involve reason, and would
      go on to argue about the character of action and the relationship between his-
      tory and action. On such a view, historians exercise reason because they are
      agents; the kinds of history reflect the kinds of reasoned action, and these de-
      velop in the historical process.

tion and of its rivals may be seen through Collingwood's eyes in *The Idea of History*.[22]

The idea that thought is objectified in history can be expressed in a variety of idioms, and is by no means foreign to more recent thought. Donald Davidson, for example, has developed an account of language that centres on learning and language acquisition in situations that 'triangulate' between two or more agents and a shared world. Words and meanings have what Davidson has sometimes referred to as a 'natural history', but can be properly described as a social and human history, which determines them. Language learning involves stimulus and observed repetition, and interpretation is continuous. Thought emerges only through such triangulation. Indeed, Davidson has cited Collingwood as holding a very similar view to his own in arguing that the discovery of the self is possible only with the discovery of other minds and a shared world.[23] A similar point was also made in a very different idiom, Ortega's view that 'I am I and my circumstance' — self and circumstance are dependent on each other in 'my life'.

If language can be analysed only in relation to situations that involve Davidson's triangulation of self, others and a shared world, a focus on narrowly defined linguistic entities is an abstraction from such circumstances. The focus of analysis of language ought properly to be on the situations in which thought and language develop and on the relations that constitute such situations. Similarly, the problem of interpretation is too narrowly defined if it is expressed solely in linguistic terms. An act undertaken without linguistic expression raises a problem of interpretation simply because it is an act. That is, the problem of interpretation arises just in so far as an act is intentional and particular, involving self, others and a shared world, rather than because it is expressed through, or can be translated into, linguistic terms. But the situations in terms of which interpretation takes place are historical — they are dated and located

[22] R. G. Collingwood, *The Idea of History. Revised edition, with Lectures 1926-1928, edited with an introduction by Jan van der Dussen.* Clarendon Press, Oxford, 1993.

[23] Donald Davidson; *Subjective, Intersubjective, Objective.* Clarendon Press, Oxford, 2001. p. 219. Davidson quoted R. G. Collingwood, *The Principles of Art.* Clarendon Press, Oxford, 1938. p. 248, where Collingwood wrote that 'the child's discovery of itself as a person is also its discovery of itself as a member of a world of persons.' From the next paragraph, Davidson quoted Collingwood's view that 'The discovery of myself as a person is the discovery that I can speak, and am thus a *persona* or speaker; in speaking, I am both speaker and hearer; and since the discovery of myself as a person is also the discovery of other persons around me, it is the discovery of speakers and hearers other than myself.'

within specific circumstances. To the extent that such situations are also described or understood in mental terms, they form part of human history. If we continue to hold that thought requires language and communication, understanding language to understand thought implies understanding history.

Prior to Collingwood, various forms of the tradition that thought is objectified in history, and history has an immanent reason, had encountered a number of difficulties. At some point, the various accounts of the world fell apart into distinct spheres such as Providence and human history, or human history and nature, or the logical and the temporal, and the conceptual and the actual. Depending on how these tensions were resolved, further tensions might arise between the emotional and the rational. Collingwood's focus on the mutual dependence of history and action was a way to overcome such difficulties.

The principal tension in the immanent reason tradition has been between human history and some form of conceptual or logical history. This was particularly pronounced in Vico, and reached an extreme form in Kant and Hegel. Vico saw man as the maker of the civil world, the world of the 'gentile' nations. On his account, the maker can truly know that which they have made. Behind this principle there lay, as Isaiah Berlin pointed out, the scholastic doctrine that to know something fully is to know it through its causes.[24] As people have made the civil world, Vico held that the principles of nations could be rediscovered in the nature of the human mind.[25] Language, myth and custom could be studied as a history of ideas, revealing the metaphysical stages of development of the human mind. Vico attempted to discover the 'ideal eternal history, traversed in time by the histories of all nations, in their birth, growth, perfection, decline and fall.[26] Nature, by contrast, was not made by people and so could be known truly only by God. But human his-

[24] Isaiah Berlin, *Vico and Herder: Two Studies in the History of Ideas.* Chatto and Windus, London, 1980. p. 13.
[25] Croce argued, in a book translated by Collingwood, that knowing what you have made through its causes, in Vico's sense, 'is an ideal repetition of a process which has been or is being practically performed.' Human beings may have full knowledge, therefore, only of that which they have themselves brought about, and they know it by repeating the process in their own minds. Benedetto Croce, *The Philosophy of Giambattista Vico.* Translated by R. G. Collingwood (1913). Reprinted by Russell & Russell, New York, 1964. p. 5. This interpretation of Vico prefigures Collingwood's account of historical knowledge, to be discussed in later chapters.
[26] Giambattista Vico, *Vico: Selected Writings. Edited and translated by Leon Pompa.* Cambridge University Press, Cambridge, 1982. p. 206.

tory, too, showed Providence at work, for though people made the nations, the mind that created the nations was superior to that of human beings with their limited ends. Mankind was moved in its creativity, in its intelligence and choice, and particularly in its emotions, by religion and Providence.[27]

If human beings and Providence are both elements in history, what is the relationship between them? If Providence is fully outside history, why does it become involved in finite human being? If Providence is essentially in history, how can it also be divine? In Kant and Hegel, similar tensions were ultimately resolved in favour of the conceptual or universal element in history. Kant continued the search for universal laws, and thought that human actions only appeared to reveal a free will. For Kant, the laws that governed human actions were those of nature.[28] A special philosophical study of history, supervening upon empirical histories, would reveal a 'history with a definite natural plan for creatures who have no plan of their own.'[29] Yet it was only in the movement of history that Kant saw the possibility of mankind creating 'a new "nature" which embodies a moral and human meaning.'[30] Although history obeys the laws of nature, it culminates in mankind imposing a 'system of rational ends upon the causal system of nature.'[31] Kant reached his conception of history only by abstracting from empirical history. He therefore left unresolved the issue of how empirical history and rational history could be reconciled.

With Hegel, the endpoint of his philosophy favoured the logical or universal, but its origins held the promise of reconciliation between these elements and actual or empirical history. Hegel's entire philosophy can be seen as a philosophy of history, in the sense that his various philosophical works showed the movement of consciousness as being fundamentally historical. For Hegel, the whole world revealed reason at work within its various forms. There were logical structures behind the phenomena of nature as well as those of human history. Nature and history were, nevertheless, quite distinct because they had different logical structures. Movements of nature were repetitive and cyclical, while the movement of consciousness

[27] Ibid. pp. 265-266.
[28] Immanuel Kant, 'Idea for a Universal History from a Cosmopolitan Point of View', in Immanuel Kant, *On History. Edited, with an introduction, by Lewis White Beck.* Library of Liberal Arts, New York, 1963. p. 11.
[29] Ibid. p. 12.
[30] Yirmiyahu Yovel, *Kant and the Philosophy of History.* Princeton University Press, Princeton, 1980. p. 73.
[31] Ibid. p. 134.

14 *Action as History*

was a genuine development from one concrete and determinate form to another. The history of the world was the history of the movement of consciousness through a series of logically structured determinate forms. The movement from one form to the next was necessarily mediated by the movements that had already occurred, so that the self-knowledge of mind was simultaneously the creative force in history and its outcome. In a famous phrase, Hegel described history as 'Spirit emptied out into Time',[32] thereby showing a link between logic and human action, and at the same time leaving open the issue of what specific relationship could exist between the sequence of logical forms and historical events.

Hegel bequeathed to subsequent philosophy the first serious attempt to fully grasp the significance of a world conceived historically, and to the philosophy of history a gap between history studied philosophically and history as the story of finite agents and their deeds. The origins of Hegel's account of history, rather than the final form it took, have been most important in seeking resolutions for the earlier dichotomies. Hegel made the concept of action central to the philosophy of history; in this light, history itself must be both a series of actions and the study of those actions. Hegel recognised that passions, limited ends and specific needs were the 'sole springs of action — the efficient agents in this scene of activity.' Reason was not revealed in history because people were motivated by the ideal of Reason.[33] Rather, in passion and private interests there was a structure which existed initially only as an 'implicit form', made conscious and explicit only through the course of history.[34] Individual actions of finite human beings could advance the development of mind because they had consequences beyond the agent's intentions and a structure beyond their immediate comprehension. Only through passions did reason develop, by what Hegel called the 'cunning of reason'.[35] As he put it in *The Philosophy of Right*, '[t]he history of mind is its own act. Mind is only what it does, and its act is to make itself the object of its own consciousness.'[36] How acts are to be understood, and therefore how mind is to be understood, determines the

[32] G. W. F. Hegel, *Phenomenology of Spirit. Translated by A. V. Miller, with analysis of the text and foreword by J. N. Findlay*. Oxford University Press, Oxford, 1977. p. 492.
[33] G. W. F. Hegel, *Lectures on the Philosophy of History*. Translated by J. Sibree. Bell, London, 1890. p. 21.
[34] Ibid. p. 26.
[35] Ibid. p. 34.
[36] G. W. F. Hegel, *Philosophy of Right. Translated with notes by T. M. Knox*. Clarendon Press, Oxford, 1942. p. 216.

form of much philosophy of history since Hegel.[37] Avoiding the tension between the logical and the actual has meant coming to understand reason in history as the product of the individual actions of finite beings.

Croce set the broad terms for Collingwood's own resolution of the logical and the actual in history. Croce sought the origins of Hegel's philosophy of history in his logic, and developed his own account of history through a criticism of that logic. In Croce's view, one of Hegel's principal advances was his doctrine that pairs of opposite terms are united in one concrete, synthetic, concept. If opposites require one another, they are really aspects of one term, which shows a logical development through various forms. Out of this doctrine came Hegel's emphasis on 'movement' and 'development', and his rejection of merely formal logic in favour of a study of the 'concrete universal'.[38] Croce could not, however, accept Hegel's theory that distinct concepts also have unity. Yet it was out of this set of doctrines that Hegel had derived his concept of an 'ideal eternal history' that must be altogether outside time.[39] By rejecting Hegel's theory on this point, Croce was led to reject Hegel's abstract philosophy of world history in favour of recognising 'the autonomy of historiography', by which he meant the 'history of the historians.'[40]

By treating the concrete universal as the 'pure concept', and abstract, classificatory concepts as 'pseudo-concepts', Croce linked history with philosophy: each dealt with the same kind of concept.[41] History required the logical dimension of concepts in the same way

---

[37] For the Marxists, for example, action should be seen through its logical structure, but that structure should be located in economic action. Marx's theory of history continued to differentiate between the logical sequence and the complications of empirical history. Although Hegel placed the seat of reason in history in the structure of passions, his philosophical history was highly abstract and rational. Similarly, he had drawn a very tight distinction between nature and history. Dilthey, by contrast, rejected Hegel's account of history as being too focused on reason, and tried to substitute for reason 'life in its totality (experience, understanding, historical context and power of the irrational)'. Dilthey thereby reopened the question of how a scientific history is possible and revealed the need for the philosophy of history to deal more explicitly with what constitutes historical acts. See W. Dilthey, *Selected Writings. Edited, translated and introduced by H. P. Rickman*. Cambridge University Press, Cambridge, 1976. p. 195.

[38] Benedetto Croce, *What is Living and What is Dead of the Philosophy of Hegel*. Translated by Douglas Ainslie (1915). Reprinted by Russell & Russell, New York, 1969. pp. 19-20, 27.

[39] Ibid. pp. 86, 93.

[40] Ibid. p. 137.

[41] Benedetto Croce, *Logic as the Science of the Pure Concept*. Translated by Douglas Ainslie. Macmillan, London, 1917. p. 256.

that philosophy required their historical development. Narratives, then, raise, clarify and solve 'philosophic problems'. A new philosophical system shows its value and importance by virtue of the fact that it allows a new interpretation and narration of history.[42] Where Hegel had proposed 'the identity of *philosophy and history of philosophy*', Croce proposed 'the identity of *philosophy and history*.'[43]

Croce had seized upon the element of immanence in accounts of reason, and of reason in accounts of history, since the time of Vico; he attempted to make each theme both more explicit and more complete. From this perspective, Vico's conception of Providence, and Hegel's conception of the cunning of reason, incompletely united the historical and the conceptual. The result was, in Vico, Kant and Hegel, abstract accounts of reason as well as of history. In reality, on Croce's view, it was not possible to separate 'the result from the process or actual acting, in which alone the former is real'.[44] On Croce's own view, there was in history 'no end that has not been realized, as well as it could, in the process, in which it was never an absolute end — that is to say, an abstract end, but both a means and an end.'[45] Ends must be realized in history because there could be no purely transcendental concept or end. Transcendence was a feature of phases in a development that was at once historical and logical. Reason and passion must be related in the same way, not as alternatives but as moments in the one process.

Earlier thinkers such as Hegel had foundered on the relationship between the logical and the actual. Croce pointed to a solution that would lie in developing a more fully immanent conception of reason. Hegel had started from a rich conception of action, with his emphasis on emotion, but his account of reason ended in the overly logical schematism of his philosophy of history, set against 'actual human events'. Croce, however, developed his solutions in perceptive and suggestive essays, rather than in a systematic way. In his account of immanence, Croce also left a significant unresolved problem concerning the relationship between historical processes and nature. Although he held that the so-called history of nature was only a 'pseudo-history', Croce had also maintained that it was possible and necessary to become a blade of grass in order to under-

---

[42]   Ibid. p. 325.
[43]   Ibid. p. 487. (Emphasis in original.)
[44]   Benedetto Croce, *History: Its Theory and Practice*. Translated by Douglas Ainslie (1921). Reprinted by Russell & Russell, New York, 1960. pp. 102-104.
[45]   Ibid. p. 104.

stand its history.[46] In response to Croce's suggestion Collingwood later wrote: 'my scepticism reaches the point of rebellion.'[47]

Collingwood, like Croce, placed the concept of action at the centre of his philosophy of history; he took the 'history of the historians' as his philosophical laboratory. To show that thought is objectified in history, and that reason is therefore immanent in history, is to conceive history and action as jointly dependent, and to conceive action in terms that move from emotion to thought and to logic. History is composed of self-creative actions, differentiated from the processes of nature because they involve thought. Historical thinking has an essential constructive role in the world of action, and historical self-knowledge creates possibilities for further action. Collingwood's thought was systematic in the sense that the concepts of action and history can be traced across the full range of his concerns, but his writings were not systematising in any more obvious sense. He pursued moral philosophy, the philosophy of history and the practice of archaeology in close relationship to each other, although the links between each can be seen only with close interpretation of his work. Each of these areas of concern supported the others and, together, constituted a broader philosophy that encompassed fields such as logic, philosophy of religion, metaphysics, the philosophy of art and political philosophy. To the extent that Collingwood succeeded in developing his philosophy without the problems encountered by his predecessors, we would have powerful tools through which to understand the significance of our modern historical consciousness. How far he did succeed, to what extent his views need to be restated, and what problems might nevertheless remain, is a matter for the body of this study.

To draw out the roles of action and history in Collingwood's thought, it will be necessary to examine the works he published in his lifetime, but also his posthumous publications and unpublished manuscripts. The availability, since the 1970's, of extensive additional unpublished material, has gradually transformed the way in which Collingwood is understood. Much of the earlier scholarship on Collingwood discussed *The Principles of Art* (1938), *An Essay on Metaphysics* (1940, revised edition 1998) and the posthumously edited and published *The Idea of History* (1946, revised edition 1993). Collingwood's *An Autobiography* (1939) was also cited in accounts of his metaphysics and history. These works alone do not show the full range of Collingwood's interests, which we can now see extended across fields as diverse as religion, political philosophy, cosmology, the history and archaeology of Roman Britain, the study of folklore and commentary on contemporary events. Despite the broadening of our understanding of the range of issues that were of interest to him, much of the extensive critical and scholarly work on Collingwood continues to emerge in response to perceived idiosyncrasies, unorthodoxy or paradoxes in his thought. It has been less common to approach Collingwood out of a sense that his concerns relate to more contemporary themes.

Parallels have been drawn between Collingwood and writers as diverse as Vico, Kant, Hegel, Dilthey, Green, Bradley, Croce, de Ruggiero, Gentile, C. S. Peirce, G. E. Moore, Samuel Alexander, Whitehead, Wittgenstein, Dewey, Heidegger, Ortega y Gasset, Ryle, Popper, Oakeshott, Kuhn, Gadamer and Foucault, amongst others. In terms of the common distinction made between Continental and English-language philosophy, John Passmore observed that '[i]n certain, although not in all, respects Collingwood conforms to the Continental rather than to the British philosophical ideal'.[48] In Passmore's view, many of Collingwood's themes are more commonly found in Continental writing, while his style and temper are more at home in the English-language tradition of thought. Important earlier commentators such as Louis Mink generally eschewed the quest for resemblances and resonances because such quests presume that the main lines of Collingwood's thought have already been firmly understood.[49] The breadth of Collingwood's thought means that Mink's injunction should continue to have weight. Nevertheless, not to see Collingwood within the context of a tradition is to miss significant opportunities to understand his goals and problems.

Until at least the late 1950s, interest in Collingwood's thought tended to focus on specific or isolated doctrines within the philosophy of history.[50] In the 1960s and early 1970s several writers attempted to provide broader and more systematic accounts of his

[48] John Passmore, *A Hundred Years of Philosophy*, Second edition. Penguin, Harmondsworth, 1980. p. 302.

[49] Louis O. Mink, *Mind, History, and Dialectic: The Philosophy of R. G. Collingwood*. Indiana University Press, Bloomington, 1969. p. 6. (Reprinted by Wesleyan University Press, Middletown, 1987.)

[50] There is a good survey of the critical reception of *The Idea of History* in W. J. van der Dussen, *History as a Science: The Philosophy of R. G. Collingwood*. Martinus Nijhoff, The Hague, 1981, Chapter 3. A shorter discussion of this theme can be

philosophy. By the 1980s and 1990s there were renewed efforts to reinterpret Collingwood broadly, particularly utilising unpublished material not available to earlier commentators. From an early stage, rival interpretations aligned Collingwood with particular traditions or directions in philosophy. Collingwood's posthumous editor and former student, T. M. Knox, assimilated his thought to idealism.[51] By contrast, Gilbert Ryle, Collingwood's successor as Waynflete Professor of Metaphysical Philosophy at the University of Oxford, presented Collingwood's account of absolute presuppositions as a precursor both to his own criticisms of 'category mistakes' and to his attack on dualisms of mind and body.[52] Ryle's behavioural focus on practices itself informed early studies of Collingwood's work by Patrick Gardiner and W. H. Dray. Each work paid particular attention to historical practices in preference to broader philosophical themes.[53] Alan Donagan, in the first sustained treatment of the broad range of Collingwood's philosophy, painted

---

found in the same author's 'Editor's Introduction' to R. G. Collingwood, *The Idea of History. Revised edition, with Lectures 1926-1928, edited with an introduction by Jan van der Dussen.* Clarendon Press, Oxford, 1993. pp. xxiii-xxviii.

[51] Knox desired to isolate and preserve certain of Collingwood's works or doctrines, and consequently to criticise other work which presented a different view, and this approach lay behind the account of Collingwood's philosophy in Knox's 'Editor's Preface' to *The Idea of History* (1946). Knox tried to salvage *An Essay on Philosophical Method* by denying the apparent relativism and historicism of *An Essay on Metaphysics, An Autobiography* and, to a lesser extent, *The Idea of History.* For Knox, Collingwood's book on method was most clearly identifiable as a mature work in the idealist tradition, with philosophy given an independent role not reducible to history, as in his earlier *Speculum Mentis* (1924). Since the later works did not seem to maintain the old positions, Knox conjectured that Collingwood had undergone a radical change of view during the mid-1930s. Part of the reason for change was supposed to lie with Collingwood's own practice of reflecting chiefly on whatever else occupied him at the time. Another part of his supposed fall from earlier heights was attributed to illness. Knox's speculations about Collingwood's health began what was later termed (by Lionel Rubinoff), the 'radical conversion' hypothesis of his development.

[52] Gilbert Ryle, *Philosophical Arguments: An Inaugural Lecture, Delivered before the University of Oxford, 30 October 1945.* Clarendon Press, Oxford, 1945. pp. 3-4.

[53] Patrick Gardiner, *The Nature of Historical Explanation.* Oxford University Press, London, 1952; William Dray, *Laws and Explanation in History.* Oxford University Press, London, 1957. Dray's book was one of the most important works in subsequent philosophy of history. Dray focused on historical writings for his account, which drew strongly on Collingwood's theory that historians re-enact the thought of the historical agents they are studying. Collingwood, however, had emphasised not historical writing but historical thinking and, in particular, historical research. In an early article, Collingwood had been highly critical of philosophers who reflected on the natural sciences by examining the thinking which was involved, but who examined only the 'finished product of thought, the fully-compiled historical narrative' when they paid attention to history. He

an image of Collingwood that was one of a philosopher moving towards a position like that of Ryle, but hamstrung by his idealist intellectual origins, which prevented him from moving fully in that direction.[54]

Donagan opened up debate about what kind of unity existed in Collingwood's work. There were two broad means by which to express the inter-relationship of doctrines in Collingwood's philosophy. Firstly, it was possible to show the unity of his thought in terms of some central principle or concern within that philosophy. Secondly, his philosophy could be approached through his way of philosophising, particularly his dialectical method. Neither of these excluded the other, but any account was likely to give an emphasis to one kind of unity over the others.

In the 1960s and 1970s, Louis Mink and Lionel Rubinoff saw a unity of principle in Collingwood's published work. Mink took *Speculum Mentis* (1924) and *An Essay on Philosophical Method* (1933) as the keys to a view that mind is an ascending scale of levels of consciousness. Mind develops from pure feeling, through appetite and imagination to desire and perception, and finally to will and intellect. In this development, we move from conceptual thinking, through propositional thinking to rational thought. Corresponding with these changes, experience moves from Art, through Religion, to Science, Philosophy and History as three forms of fourth level, rational thinking.[55] Rubinoff took a similarly schematic view, finding in *Speculum Mentis* a 'master plan' which formed the basis for a highly

---

argued that many apparent differences between natural science and history vanish when 'both are regarded as actual inquiries', and history was not merely a 'dead, finished article.' R. G. Collingwood, 'Are History and Science Different Kinds of Knowledge?', (1922), reprinted in *Essays in the Philosophy of History: R.G. Collingwood* (edited by W. Debbins). McGraw-Hill, New York, 1966. pp. 23-33. See esp. pp. 32-33.

[54] Donagan took seriously, in an extended examination, a range of Collingwood's work, particularly *The New Leviathan* and *The Principles of Art*. In that sense, Donagan inaugurated the serious attempt to show the relationship between various doctrines that Collingwood had propounded. The limitation of his book was that it was only a partially integrated account of Collingwood's thought. In the first instance, Donagan did not analyse the full text of *The New Leviathan* and neglected the essentially political nature of the work. Secondly, Donagan restricted his focus to Collingwood's 'later philosophy', but not to the apparently 'historicist' and 'relativist' elements in his later works. Third, Donagan justified these restrictions by dismissing Collingwood's earlier work, particularly *Speculum Mentis* and *An Essay on Philosophical Method*. Alan Donagan, *The Later Philosophy of R. G. Collingwood*. Clarendon Press, Oxford, 1962. [Reprinted, 'with a new preface and corrections', by University of Chicago Press, Chicago, 1985.]

[55] Mink, *Mind, History, and Dialectic,* pp. 3, 17, 111.

complex schematism in which each subsequent work was shown to fill in a piece of the one puzzle. Under this schema, Collingwood was a 'transcendental historicist', arguing that the process by which historical truth is revealed is historical, but that what the process reveals 'at any given time in history is nevertheless absolute and transhistorical'. Collingwood, then, could be seen in terms of a tradition that included Hegel, Husserl, Rickert, the early Heidegger, Cassirer and E. L. Fackenheim.[56]

Schematic interpretations of Collingwood's work, particularly those that emphasise earlier works such as *Speculum Mentis*, inevitably neglect the dialectical elements within Collingwood's own work.[57] Looking back on *Speculum Mentis* from the perspective of 1938, Collingwood wrote that

> If much of it now fails to satisfy me, that is because I have gone on thinking since I wrote it, and therefore much of it needs to be supplemented and qualified. There is not a great deal that needs to be retracted.[58]

---

[56] Lionel Rubinoff, *Collingwood and the Reform of Metaphysics: A Study in the Philosophy of Mind*. University of Toronto Press, Toronto, 1970. pp. 14, 24, 123, 127, 131-132, 146, 243.

[57] Mink's interpretation, while serving to emphasise the links between various elements in Collingwood's account of mind, ended by drawing boundaries too clearly and stretching connections too tightly. Mink was forced to ignore Collingwood's *Autobiography* and to jettison many of his claims, particularly the proposed 'logic of question and answer'. Consequently, he interpreted Collingwood's 'absolute presuppositions' as a free-standing account of *a priori* concepts, rather than a feature of Collingwood's logic, and sought to argue away the apparent historicisation of philosophy in *An Autobiography* and *An Essay on Metaphysics*. Mink's book importantly attended to Collingwood's concern with both practical and theoretical reason. He did not, however, place as much importance on these issues as Collingwood had in many of his works, including *Speculum Mentis, An Autobiography, An Essay on Metaphysics* and *The New Leviathan*. Nor did Mink consider Collingwood's political philosophy. Rubinoff, like Mink and Donagan, took the philosophy of mind to be the central concern in Collingwood's work. Like Collingwood himself in his later writing, Rubinoff saw the relationship between philosophy and history as central. Rubinoff's complex schematism required him to engage in extended arguments in order to draw links between the various elements of Collingwood's philosophy. Rubinoff paid little attention to Collingwood's practical concerns and political philosophy and, like Mink, did not focus on Collingwood's historical and archaeological practices. Subsequently, in a more recent work, Rubinoff has focused instead on the dialectical nature of Collingwood's thought about history, while recognising the importance of some of his unpublished material, such as that on folklore. Lionel Rubinoff, 'History and Human Nature: Reflections on R. G. Collingwood', *International Studies in Philosophy*. Vol. XXIII, No. 3, 1991. pp. 75-89.

[58] Collingwood, *An Autobiography*. fn. 1, p. 56.

It has since become clear that Collingwood did envisage a series of books, but that *Speculum Mentis* had no part in that series.[59] The relationship between Collingwood's earlier and later work is therefore more complex than can be captured in the idea of a single programme implemented over time. It is now more common to see Collingwood's later works, such as *The New Leviathan*, as representing the latest stage of a personal development. We can see the elements of his later thought emerging and being altered over time. The question, then, is which ideas played the key roles in that process.

Since the 1970s, the availability, and subsequent publication, of many of Collingwood's manuscripts has tended to reinstate the plausibility of his own account of his intellectual development. It has also made it more difficult to argue that any particular view of Collingwood's does not sit with another. It is now clear that Collingwood was able to write *An Autobiography* with his papers around him; he was not working solely from memory, but from documents that can be independently scrutinised.[60] At times Collingwood paraphrased, in different language and with different emphasis, dated papers now available to scholars.[61] Two of the key documents to which Collingwood referred, his 'Die' manuscript of 1928 and some earlier lectures on the philosophy of history, were published in the revised edition of *The Idea of History*. Other important manuscripts mentioned by Collingwood, including a copy of his 'Libellus de Generatione', thought to be destroyed, and a chapter of his unpublished 'Truth and Contradiction', similarly thought to have been destroyed, have also survived and are in the Bodleian Library. Only one important document to which Collingwood drew attention in his autobiography seems not to have survived, or is not

---

[59] The series is described in van der Dussen's 'Introduction' to the revised (1993) edition of *The Idea of History*. p. ix.

[60] It is therefore possible to avoid much of the debate around the 'radical conversion' hypothesis — at least in so far as it is taken to be an account of Collingwood's intellectual development. Instead, we should see the conversion thesis as a means by which certain authors, who recognised that Collingwood sought to develop an integrated philosophy, were nevertheless able to isolate particular works and themes from their accounts of that philosophy.

[61] The first significant study of Collingwood in the light of his manuscripts was van der Dussen's *History as a Science* (1981). Van der Dussen used manuscript material to illuminate Collingwood's development, in particular, to show his historical work, archaeology and philosophy of history in mutual relation. Van der Dussen was able to undermine the 'radical conversion' thesis; to bring in to focus many themes which had lain unexplored (particularly the idea of history as a process); and to throw light on a large range of concepts and controversies surrounding Collingwood's philosophy of history.

readily identifiable amongst his surviving papers. That paper is one he gave on returning to Oxford at the end of the War of 1914-1918, criticising the forms of realism then current.[62]

Access to Collingwood's unpublished manuscripts shows that his work was unfinished not only in the sense that he never completed his projected series of books, but because the systematic elements which were present in his work require further development. The role of a contemporary commentator is, therefore, to see how various themes were implicated across a range of Collingwood's concerns. Such commentary will portray how Collingwood revisited and restated his views in different ways, over a number of years, and in different contexts. Commentary of this type will show that understanding what Collingwood said means understanding how he came to say it. In this way, contemporary commentary can serve to clarify the issues on which Collingwood worked, and contribute to their further development.

The availability of Collingwood's unpublished manuscripts brought into focus the key role of moral philosophy in the development of his views. Neither moral nor political philosophy had received much attention in earlier commentary on Collingwood's work.[63] Collingwood's extensive unpublished lectures and manuscripts on moral philosophy show a strong developmental continuity from the early 1920s to the 1940s. Many of his key concerns in other areas arose from, or were illuminated by, moral philosophy; *An Essay on Philosophical Method*, for example, developed from his moral philosophy lectures of the 1920s. The 1940 lectures on moral philosophy were presented as introducing Collingwood's lectures called 'The Idea of History'.[64] The strength of Collingwood's interests in this area, and the implications for our overall conception of his philosophy, were first brought to notice in David Boucher's *The Social and Political Thought of R. G. Collingwood* (1989), and expanded in editions of his writings on politics and related themes.[65] Boucher's

---

[62] Collingwood, *An Autobiography*. Chapter VI, esp. p. 44.

[63] The notable exception was A. J. M. Milne, *The Social Philosophy of English Idealism*. George Allen and Unwin, London, 1962. Milne discussed several of Collingwood's ideas alongside those of idealist thinkers such as Green and Bradley.

[64] R. G. Collingwood, 'Goodness, Rightness, Utility', in Collingwood, *The New Leviathan, Revised edition*, pp. 391-479. See p. 477.

[65] David Boucher, *The Social and Political Thought of R. G. Collingwood*. Cambridge University Press, Cambridge, 1989; R. G. Collingwood, *Essays in Political Philosophy, Edited with an introduction by David Boucher*. Clarendon Press, Oxford, 1989; R.G. Collingwood, *The New Leviathan. Revised edition*.

work has, for the first time, given systematic attention to Collingwood's moral and political philosophy. Collingwood's thought now appears clearly within a broader historical context of European liberalism. This study takes its lead from that reorientation towards moral philosophy.

In this study, I will follow Collingwood's ideas of action and history into fields such as archaeology, history and philosophy of history. As we shall see, the two concepts illuminate much of his philosophy. For example, Collingwood took action as a primary exemplar of a concept that develops in an ascending scale of forms, where each succeeding form of the concept more adequately expresses its essence. A scale of forms, however, develops only in a process in which gains already made are retained in each and every further advance. Collingwood gave an account of how thought and concepts can develop in his 'logic of question and answer', where each new question in a series presupposes the answers already given in the history of thought about a particular topic. On Collingwood's view in *An Essay on Metaphysics*, every question has a presupposition that allows a question to arise or, in other language, to be logically posed. Some presuppositions, such as that the world exists, are not in fact answers to previous questions, but are presupposed absolutely in each particular attempt to think seriously about the world. The burden of Collingwood's historical survey in *The Idea of Nature* was that modern scientific thinking involves a view that the natural world is in process. In *The Idea of History*, Collingwood showed that modern historical thought involves the view that the human world is created by processes of human action. The distinction between action and other forms of process underlay his distinction between the natural and the properly historical. To give a philosophical account of the concept of action is, therefore, to give an account of the historical presuppositions of current Western thought about the world.

I aim to show that the views I attribute to Collingwood were his, and that the concepts of action and history illuminate those of historical consciousness and historical civilisation. Chapter 1 shows that action was one of a number of closely related philosophical concepts which Collingwood applied across a broad range of fields and at various stages in his development. Action was, however, one dimension of his overall account of the world as process, which forms the subject of Chapter 2. To support the ideas of action and the world as process, Collingwood required an account of thought. In Chapters 3 and 4, Collingwood's logic of question and answer is presented as an account of thought that places the logic of history within the realm of human action.

Chapters 5 to 8 draw out a number of dimensions to history as action. In Chapter 5, I show how Collingwood's moral philosophy and philosophy of history became increasingly aligned. Chapter 6 relates how Collingwood's idea of 'duty' united moral philosophy with history. The concept of duty highlights the need both for a theory of historical knowledge and for a theory of the object of history. The nature of the historical object is discussed in Chapter 7, while Chapter 8 discusses Collingwood's theory of historical knowledge, particularly through his historical practice.

The significance of knowing the historical process is that it gives rise to self-knowledge, and in Chapter 9 Collingwood's accounts of action, history and historical knowledge are brought to bear to characterise historical consciousness. If an historical consciousness is developed fully and consistently, it gives rise to historical civilisation. Chapter 10 concludes the study by examining Collingwood's attempts to characterise such a civilisation.

CHAPTER 1

Activity and Philosophy

From beginning to end, a number of closely related, and even inter-changeable, concepts played key roles in Collingwood's philosophy: activity, becoming, process, action and history. The concepts of action and history, as they were developed in Collingwood's later philosophy, were shaped by his earlier thought about activity, becoming and process; each idea tended to imply the others. This chapter provides a brief overview of the development of Collingwood's thought around such concepts, an intellectual development that also involved the development of the concepts themselves. In that process, Collingwood extended the use of these related concepts into various fields of philosophy. By extending their range and sophistication, he embedded them more deeply in the core of his philosophical approach.

Collingwood's later writings took up and reworked themes that were already present by 1920. His early works did not, however, set a plan for each of the subsequent books, nor did each later work merely fill out one part of the picture unexamined by the others. In his first book, *Religion and Philosophy* (1916), Collingwood began by treating knowledge and experience as activities. This theme was followed through in manuscripts for 'Truth and Contradiction' (1917) and the 'Libellus de Generatione' (1920). By the time he wrote *Speculum Mentis* (1924) and *An Essay on Philosophical Method* (1933) Collingwood approached fundamental philosophical issues systematically through the concepts of action or activity, and this tendency was present in his work to the end of his life.

Collingwood considered his later works as contributions to a number of series; *An Essay on Metaphysics* (1940) was to accompany *An Essay on Philosophical Method*. The *Essay on Metaphysics* sought to show that a particular kind of historical thinking, metaphysics, is necessary to the growth and development of civilisation and science. The dependence of scientific thought on history had been a major theme of *Speculum Mentis* and was reasserted in Colling- wood's posthumously published *The Idea of Nature* (1945). In his unfinished *The Principles of History* (1999), Collingwood was to discuss the concept of history, where history was seen as comprising actions. Both *The Principles of Art* (1938) and *The New Leviathan* (1942) were conceived as related to *The Principles of History*: each was based on an account of mind as activity. In *The New Leviathan*, the analysis of action was extended to a philosophical politics, in which society and civilisation were viewed as activities of mind. In the course of his development, Collingwood gave accounts of logic, the nature of philosophical concepts and truth that reflected a focus on action or activity. His later views on historical metaphysics (which trouble philosophers more than they do historians) similarly developed from an account of mind as action. Collingwood's concerns, in so far as they reflected a focus on action and activity, were consistent, but not identical, from early in his career until his last years.

In *Religion and Philosophy*, Collingwood treated mind and knowledge as activities. He maintained that every human activity simultaneously involves thought and will, or knowledge and action. As he put it, 'mind is what it does; it is not a thing that thinks, but a consciousness; not a thing that wills, but an activity.'[1] *Religion and Philosophy* used this approach as a way of vindicating the intellectual elements of religion against more emotivist and irrationalist approaches. For Collingwood all religious rituals reflected intellectual creeds, and therefore could not survive without a rational basis. Similarly, no activity could be sustained solely by emotion, because emotion is never a separate function of the mind distinct from thinking and willing, rather 'it includes both these at once.'[2] To treat religion as an activity, as Collingwood attempted to do, was to show how it involved thought and will together.

The concept of activity was central to other early works, in which Collingwood began to extend the application of the concept, and to introduce cognate terms. In what remains of 'Truth and Contradiction', Collingwood examined the implications of activity and process for logic and truth. In the 'Libellus de Generatione', he explored the possibilities of an 'absolute' empiricism that resolved all reality into process or experience. Each work dealt with themes to which he

[1]   R. G. Collingwood, *Religion and Philosophy*. Macmillan, London, 1916. pp. 34-35.
[2]   Ibid. p. 10.

would later return in a more systematic manner. The concept of action subsequently shaped Collingwood's philosophy of mind and his account of philosophical concepts. In turn, these ideas were to reinforce his developing thought on moral philosophy and history.

Only one chapter survives of 'Truth and Contradiction', a book manuscript totalling between 60,000 and 70,000 words which Collingwood wrote during 1917. Macmillan declined to publish the book when it was submitted to them, citing the circumstances of the war. According to the idealist philosopher Henry Jones, who read the manuscript for Macmillan and recommended that it be published, the book showed the 'coherence' theory of truth and the 'doctrine of degrees of truth' to be inadequate. It then went on to show a dialectical movement in the fields of art and morality.[3] Because the surviving chapter is one of only a very few documents in which Collingwood gave a sustained theoretical account of truth, and he assigned it an important role in his intellectual development, it merits some detailed description.

In *An Autobiography*, Collingwood claimed that his 'logic of question and answer', which had been a major factor in his rejection of realism and propositional logic, was first developed in 'Truth and Contradiction'.[4] The surviving chapter, Chapter Two, did not deal directly with a question and answer logic, although it is consistent with the idea that Collingwood developed his account of question and answer in a later chapter.[5] Chapter Two of 'Truth and Contradiction' is, instead, a criticism of the coherence theory of truth. Collingwood considered that '[s]o long as we admit the existence of error the coherence test of truth must always be fallacious.'[6] This view was supported by Collingwood's criticism of three 'traditional laws of thought' — identity, contradiction and excluded middle.

Collingwood rejected the 'three laws of thought', which he characterised as that A is A (identity); a thing cannot have contradictory predicates (A cannot also be a contradictory B); and that each given thing is either A or not A (excluded middle). Instead, he asserted

---

[3]   Henry Jones, 'Report on R. G. Collingwood, *Truth and Contradiction*', printed in R. G. Collingwood, *Essays in Political Philosophy. Edited with an introduction by David Boucher.* Clarendon Press, Oxford, 1989. Appendix One, pp. 229-231. Jones commented that: 'All the time he is showing the true nature of Philosophy, and finding that *movement, activity, process* is the living soul of all thinking and of all objects of thought. Having reached his goal I wish he expounded it more fully.' p. 231. (Emphasis in original.)

[4]   Collingwood, *An Autobiography*. Chapter V. esp. pp. 42-43.

[5]   R. G. Collingwood, 'Truth and Contradiction. Chapter 2.' (1917) [Bodleian Library, Dep. 16.]

[6]   Ibid. p. 3.

firstly, that judgements express difference — everything distinguishes itself from itself (A is B). Secondly, he held that two contradictory judgements are equally true — truth doesn't contradict
falsehood, truth only contradicts truth (A is both B and ~B).
Collingwood also maintained that, of two contradictory judgements, both are equally false (A is not either B or ~B). The contrast
between the traditional laws of thought and these contradictory
views was to be reconciled by reinterpreting the traditional laws of
thought on broadly Hegelian lines. The law of identity should be
reinterpreted in light of the idea of identity in difference, and that of
contradiction in light of the activity of criticism. The law of excluded
middle was to be reinterpreted in light of the dependence of truth
and error on each other and the need to reconcile half-truths.[7]

It is, however, Collingwood's positive account of truth, underlying his criticisms, rather the criticisms themselves, that is of interest.
Collingwood's theory of truth derived from a distinction between
'dialectic' and 'eristic' that subsequently became fundamental to his
account of historical civilisation. He observed that judgements are
usually reached 'by something like a debate between opposite
points of view.' On the coherence theory these are contradictory,
such that one is right and one is wrong, one is more coherent and one
less coherent. But the experience of debating a point belies the coherence theory. Why, after all, do we argue? Collingwood thought that
we argue 'in order to increase the comprehension of each by the
inclusion in his own view of that which seeks to contradict it.' At one
stage, Collingwood observed that '[e]veryone who has argued
knows that [in nine] cases out of [ten] the [two] disputants are both
right, or are indeed as a rule defending the same truth.'[8] In *The
Nature of Truth* (1906), the idealist philosopher H. H. Joachim argued
that, despite its imperfections, the coherence theory was the most
adequate conception of truth.[9] From Joachim's argument Collingwood drew the conclusion that

> we cannot distinguish within a theory the true elements from the false.
> Truth or falsehood are attributes not of single isolated judgements but of
> systems of thought, systems in which every judgement is coloured by all
> the others.[10]

---

[7]   Ibid. pp. 1, 14-17.
[8]   Ibid. p. 7.
[9]   H. H. Joachim, *The Nature of Truth: An Essay*. Clarendon Press, Oxford, 1906. pp.
        178-180. The second edition of this book (1939) was edited by Collingwood.
[10]   Collingwood, 'Truth and Contradiction'. p. 11

Collingwood propounded a holism about truth, where truth involves comprehensiveness: '[t]hat truth is greatest or truest which expresses most, which includes most successfully within itself a number of diverse and by themselves conflicting points of view.'[11] Truth is the capacity of a view to actively comprehend diversity and conflict. Our views are transformed through discussion, but it is systems of thought, rather than isolated 'truths', that undergo transformation. Collingwood observed that knowing the truth of 'William the Conqueror won the Battle of Hastings' requires considerable knowledge of William and of the context; every singular judgement depends for its meaning on the system of other beliefs in which it occurs.[12] In turn, every system of beliefs is historical as well as logical. Collingwood used a form of holism to justify and clarify his conception of truth, rather than to undermine truth altogether. For Collingwood, the issue was to show how truth could belong to systems of thought rather than to singular propositions.

If truth and falsity belong to theories or systems, and singular judgements are themselves systems, every system is itself an amalgam or compound of truth and error.[13] Error is just incomplete truth, a theory that leaves 'outside itself unassimilated contradictions.'[14] Conversely, the truth of a judgement may be seen in the

> ease with which it accepts contradiction and undergoes modification in order to include points of view which once it had excluded. Not self-preservation but self-criticism is the mark of a truth; and the enjoyment of truth is not an achievement but an activity.[15]

Put in the form of a slogan, '[t]ruth is not a possession, but an activity.'[16] Collingwood thought that inclusion and transformation are activities that must be carried out continuously. At no point is truth final and unchanging. There is no evidence in Chapter Two of 'Truth and Contradiction' that Collingwood tried to show how, and in what form, different ideas can be included in the one view. As we shall see below, his later idea of the 'scale of forms' can be seen to provide just such an account for philosophical concepts.

The 'Libellus de Generatione' was, like 'Truth and Contradiction', a book-length manuscript to which Collingwood attributed considerable importance in his intellectual development. Unlike 'Truth

---

[11] Ibid. pp. 7-8.
[12] Ibid. p. 11.
[13] Ibid. pp. 11-12.
[14] Ibid. p. 19.
[15] Ibid. p. 13.
[16] Ibid.

and Contradiction', the 'Libellus' was never intended for publication. In *An Autobiography*, Collingwood stated that he set out in the
'Libellus' his theory of historical process as a living past

> making point after point without any attempt at elaboration or explana-
> tion. It was primarily a study of the nature and implications of process or
> becoming. Secondarily, it was an attack on 'realism', showing how the
> *non possumus* of 'realists' towards a theory of history arose from their
> refusal to admit the reality of becoming.[17]

Collingwood's claim to have developed such views as early as
1920 has generally been met with incredulity, and has led a number
of critics such as Donagan to distrust Collingwood's own account of
his intellectual development. Collingwood's claims are, however,
fully borne out by the surviving copy of the 'Libellus'.[18] The
'Libellus' was an exploratory essay, structured around two main
ideas: the traditional realist logic of 'being' and a new logic of 'becoming'. According to Collingwood, the basic failing of the logic of
being was that, beginning from clear distinctions such as those
between the knower and the known, it culminated in an undifferentiated identity, a coincidence of opposites. The logic of becoming or
process solved the problems raised by the philosophy of being and
enabled the traditional philosophical sciences to be reformed in a
way that linked philosophy, history, science, art, religion and moral
action.

Several important themes of 'Truth and Contradiction', such as
the dynamic character of critical thought, were carried through to
the 'Libellus'. Collingwood summarised the point of the essay in the
following terms: '[m]y fundamental doctrine is that reality is becoming, that is to say reality not so much *is* as *happens*, which implies that
the reality of the mind is the process of its experience.' This doctrine
implied Collingwood's total rejection of the concept of 'substance',
together with his rejection of any dualism between mind and its
objects. On Collingwood's account, both mind and object are processes 'and these are not two processes but one process.'[19] In none of
these three works, *Religion and Philosophy*, 'Truth and Contradiction'
or the 'Libellus', had Collingwood yet considered the implications
of this doctrine for general cosmology or the philosophy of history.

In his preface to the 'Libellus', Collingwood related his aims to
those of various philosophical movements since Hume. He said that

---

[17] Collingwood, *An Autobiography*. p. 99.
[18] R. G. Collingwood, 'Libellus de Generatione: An Essay in Absolute Empiricism.
      Written at Skipness, Argyll, July 20-23, 1920.' [Bodleian Library, Dep. 28.]
[19] Ibid. p. 1. (Emphasis in original.)

he followed Hume by criticising realism, and sought to critically reflect German and Italian idealism along with the 'mostly very half-hearted' empiricists of the nineteenth century. Collingwood characterised what he called the 'world of being' as a conception of the world in which 'being' was the fundamental concept, and which could be traced back to the ancient Greeks. Philosophers in that tradition had developed a metaphysics of 'being as such', and based their logic on the subject-predicate form S *is* P. In Collingwood's view, the 'essence' of the world conceived in these terms was 'differentiation' or 'distinction'.[20]

Traditional accounts of knowledge distinguished between the subject and the object, but left unanswered the questions 'what is the subject?' or 'what is the object?'. Collingwood argued that mind conceived in distinction from its object is nothing; the content of the 'mind' must be just the object itself. Similarly, the object as distinct from the mind is also nothing; the content of the object must be, therefore, the subject. The 'cause' of a sensation must be our nervous system as much as it is any external 'object'; to adopt a more recent term, they are co-related. Collingwood found that philosophies tended, at this point, to take *either* the standpoint of the object, thereby eliminating subjectivity, *or* the standpoint of the subject, so eliminating objectivity. By attempting to conceive of the world in terms of a distinction between object and subject, we are left without any differentiation at all, but merely with 'a perfectly rigid static monism'.[21]

In Collingwood's view, the collapse of differentiated concepts into an undifferentiated identity is a logical feature of all opposites. The Aristotelian 'laws of thought', were based on exclusion, on the idea that A is A and not B; but, echoing 'Truth and Contradiction', Collingwood maintained that the assumption of exclusiveness ended in 'the conclusion that opposites coincide.' In practice, it was possible to avoid such collapse by adopting an eclectic approach. Alternatively, both terms could be preserved in a dualistic system, with each term confined to a distinct and limited sphere. Eclecticism and dualism attempted to combine characteristics that could not both exist in the same world, for a world that is physical in part must be physical throughout.[22] Collingwood would not entertain any

---

[20] Ibid. pp. 1-2, 4.
[21] Ibid. pp. 5-9, 10-17.
[22] It may appear that, in this experimental essay, Collingwood had reverted to reliance on the law of contradiction. If so, then we might anticipate a later phase or argument in which contradiction is re-interpreted. We could see Collling-

form of parallelism or interactionism between worlds with quite distinct constitutions.[23]

Collingwood thought that the majority of philosophers were eclectic in some way, and attempted to 'subdivide reality according to some a priori and fanciful scheme'. These subdivisions were subsequently open to criticism because of their pedantic nature. Among those whom Collingwood considered to fall into this trap in some way were Plato, Aristotle, Spinoza, the Scottish philosophers, Hegel and Croce. By contrast, other philosophers, such as Plato (in the *Parmenides*), the Christian mystics and Nicholas of Cusa, had avoided the temptations of eclecticism and the traps of dualism. They had done so by accepting the principle that opposites will coincide, and that absolute distinction and absolute identity will become indistinguishable from each other.[24]

The coincidence of opposites is not, however, total. The process by which opposites come to rest in an undifferentiated unity involves a real discovery; the coincidence of opposites was not known at the beginning. Though A and B may be identical, the move from A to B is not the same as the move from B to A. Collingwood thought that philosophy could wake from its nightmare only in the world of becoming; the price was that this world 'neither contains nor rests upon nor presupposes a world of being'. Nor does it involve any fixed and static 'determinations past which the elements of the world of becoming move'. Having made the concept of 'becoming' central, Collingwood sought to reinterpret many of the traditional concepts and debates of philosophy as phases or moments of a process. At the same time, he continued to criticise philosophies, such as idealism, which gave inadequate accounts of process. In his thought, identity came to refer to the unity of a process through its various phases, while difference referred to the relation of one phase to the next. The fundamental categories of 'change' are, therefore, 'positivity' and 'negativity', and '[e]very determination of this world is a synthesis of these categories'.[25]

In the 'Libellus', Collingwood went on to use the concept of positive and negative phases of a process to reinterpret a broad variety of

---

wood's later distinction between the study of man as mind, by the sciences of mind, and the study of man as body, by the natural sciences (a point expressed in *The New Leviathan*), as such a re-interpretation. On this occasion, however, Collingwood was primarily attributing adherence to the law of contradiction to others.

[23] Collingwood, 'Libellus de Generatione.' pp. 17, 18, 22-23.
[24] Ibid. pp. 34-38.
[25] Ibid. pp. 41-45, 47, 48-50.

themes. In brief form he reinterpreted ideas such as self-identity, good and bad, destruction and creation, permanence and change, freedom and determinism, whole and part, truth and error, subjectivity and objectivity, thought and action, duty and, finally, idea and fact. In the process of reinterpretation, the 'world of being' had to be seen as an answer, given by philosophers such as Plato, to the problem of becoming, as they understood the problem. Knowledge, too, must be a process rather than a state, an activity rather than an achievement.[26] By rejecting the notion that idea and fact could exist apart from each other, Collingwood had undermined the distinction between philosophy and history. In the

> world of becoming...history is philosophy and philosophy history; not as an undifferentiated identity, not, that is, because one cannot see the difference between them, but because they are opposite moments which never exist apart, of which all real thinking is the concrete synthesis. For the fact and its meaning are inseparable, and neither can live or be thought without the other.[27]

By 1920, then, Collingwood saw himself as a critic of realism and several forms of idealism; in this respect, his *Autobiography* proves a valuable account of his intellectual development. His criticisms were grounded in an increasingly radical account of the world, and mind in particular, as an activity or process. This radicalism was already a point of difference between his own views and what he saw as the stultification of forms in the philosophy of Croce (as it was later to be between Collingwood and Oakeshott).[28]

Collingwood turned the dynamic conception of mind into his own map of the major forms of knowledge and experience in his next major book, *Speculum Mentis*. The map would show how it was possible to achieve a modern form of unity between experience and knowledge. The chief obstacle to constructing such a map was the modern conception of art, religion, science, history and philosophy as 'species' of one genus, 'each valid and autonomous in its own sphere but each limited to a single aspect of reality, each constituting

[26] Ibid. pp. 67, 72-73.
[27] Ibid. p. 78.
[28] For Collingwood on Oakeshott see R. G. Collingwood, *The Idea of History. Revised edition, with Lectures 1926-1928*, edited with an introduction by Jan van der Dussen. Clarendon Press, Oxford, 1993. pp. 151-159. See also Tariq Modood, 'R. G. Collingwood, M. J. Oakeshott and the Idea of a Philosophical Culture', PhD Thesis, University College, Swansea, 1984. Modood provided support for the main line of Collingwood's criticism of Oakeshott. For a more general comparison, see David Boucher, 'Overlap and Autonomy: The Different Worlds of Collingwood and Oakeshott', *Storia, Antropologia e Scienze Del Linguaggio*. Vol. IV, No. 2/3, 1989, pp. 69-89.

a single aspect of the mind.' On such a view, for example, art is concerned with beauty, religion with God and science with natural law.[29] Each form of experience involves seeing the world under only one particular aspect.

Collingwood sought to overturn the idea that various forms of knowledge and practice are species of the one genus. Echoing his earlier criticisms, he maintained that, if forms of knowledge and practice are species of the same genus, each way of seeing the world involves assertions about reality that are inconsistent with those made by other ways of seeing. To escape the inconsistencies, it is necessary to become a dualist of some kind. Since, however, forms of knowledge are taken to be species of one genus, logic is an overarching science, and therefore the ultimate form of knowledge. The whole point of conceiving the forms of knowledge as species is, though, to preserve their independence.[30] The view that different forms of knowledge are different species, therefore, collapses on itself. Nevertheless, it is possible to abandon the idea of species and genus, and to avoid dualism. Shifting the focus to mind as activity enabled Collingwood to maintain that there is only one world, and only one object for knowledge. Art, religion, science and history represent a series of errors in the attempt to achieve knowledge; the problems that lead these forms to succeed each other are problems in the one process of trying to know the one object. Each form of experience was shown to succeed the other, but each was reunited in the final form, philosophy.

The second last form in the series was history, overcoming earlier errors. For history, said Collingwood, '[t]he object…is fact as such.' Each historian must struggle and work in order to establish facts; each historian must also seek 'factual coherence'. That is, the historian must question himself about the fit of his facts with everything else that he knows. Collingwood argued that 'fact, as historically determined, is the absolute object' and that the 'mark of the absolute object is individuality, for individuality is concreteness.' In response to the possible objection that historians try not just to state facts but to understand them, Collingwood replied that a fact includes every feature of a specific event together with its context; the objection therefore 'adds nothing' to the definition. A motive, for example, is not distinct from a fact or event, it is 'simply these events themselves as purposed and planned by the agents.' (By the time he wrote *The*

[29] R. G. Collingwood, *Speculum Mentis, or The Map of Knowledge.* Clarendon Press, Oxford, 1924. p. 46.
[30] Ibid. pp. 48-49.

Idea of History, Collingwood would say that there is no difference, in history, between knowing what and knowing why.) History fails, however, to know its own object, for no one can know the whole world of fact. Furthermore, because the parts of such a whole can never be known except in the context of the whole, there is no knowledge of even a part. History, too, seems to fail, but now the failure must force a reconsideration of what constitutes the world of fact. We must see that the world of fact includes both what we know and that we know. Knowledge must change the world of fact. When we know something, because we know it, the 'universe of fact' differs from what we first took it to be.[31]

The world of fact is an object that is altered by being known, and yet it is possible to be in error about it. Collingwood thought that the only candidate for such an object was 'the knowing mind. In this case...an error reacts on the mind itself, and alters its behaviour, which (in the case of a mind) is its nature; for a mind is what it does.' The 'infinite given whole of fact is *the nature of the knowing mind as such*'. Philosophy arms history with knowledge of its true object, while history armed with knowledge of its real object becomes philosophy. The philosopher 'knows what the historian does not know, that his knowledge of facts is organic to the facts themselves, that his mind is these facts knowing themselves and these facts are his mind knowing itself.' *Speculum Mentis* was Collingwood's attempt to map the world of knowledge; the world of knowledge can only be 'the world of historical fact, seen as the mind's knowledge of itself.'[32]

In *Speculum Mentis,* the transition from science to history represented a transition from the world conceived through abstract, classificatory concepts to the world conceived as unique and concrete. Collingwood's next major philosophical book, *An Essay on Philosophical Method* (1933) attacked the idea that abstract classificatory concepts have any place in philosophy.[33] Whereas *Speculum Mentis* described the transition from abstract concepts to concrete universals, *An Essay on Philosophical Method* showed why the concepts characteristic of philosophy are not abstract, and what form they must have instead. Collingwood attempted to show how the species of philosophical concepts overlap in a specific way to create a 'scale of forms', which gives unity to each part. The *Essay on Philosophical Method* intimated that concepts in a scale of forms develop

---

[31] Ibid. pp. 211, 214, 217-218, 231, 241.
[32] Ibid. pp. 241, 295, 309. (Emphasis in original.)
[33] R. G. Collingwood, *An Essay on Philosophical Method.* Clarendon Press, Oxford, 1933.

historically; he would continue his account of thought as an historical system in *An Essay on Metaphysics*.

The key problem Collingwood addressed in his essay on method was how to account for the overlap of philosophical concepts. In empirical science, for example, the species of a genus ideally exclude each other. There are insects, mammals, fish, birds, rocks and so on where no instances of one class are instances of another class of the same genus. But other concepts, such as 'the good' or 'thought', are quite different to the empirical model because they have kinds that overlap each other. The genus 'thought' is divided into judgement or proposition and inference, but a judgement may be an inference and an inference a judgement. As an example, Collingwood used the phrase 'it is raining'. We may infer that it is raining from the noises on the roof. We may also judge that it is raining when we look outside and see the rain. In the same way, the genus 'thought' may be divided into what is pleasant, expedient or right. We may be motivated to act by desire, or by self-interest or duty, but none of these possibilities excludes the other and each is likely to occur together with the others.[34]

Rather than being unusual, Collingwood argued that the overlap of classes was typical of philosophical concepts. He proposed that the species of a philosophical concept overlap with each other in a hierarchical 'scale of forms', where each higher level on the scale embodies the generic essence to a greater degree than the one below. Collingwood found that many earlier philosophers had used a 'scale of forms', including Plato, Aristotle, Locke, Leibniz and Kant, as well as the 'positivists and evolutionists of the nineteenth century'.[35] The scale of forms idea affects issues such as the nature of definition in philosophy, the elements of philosophical judgements, the nature of philosophical knowledge, the systematic character of philosophy and the relationship between theory and experience in philosophy. For example, in light of the scale of forms, to define a philosophical concept is to express its 'whole content' through an 'exposition' of the scale of forms developing both logically and historically.[36] Collingwood's theory of definition advanced upon that of Croce, who had argued that definition is the connection of concepts in answer to specific, changing, problems, because Collingwood had

---

[34]   Ibid. pp. 36, 41-42.
[35]   Ibid. pp. 58-59.
[36]   Ibid. pp. 54, 221-223.

shown how concepts are connected in such a way as to allow change.[37]

In Collingwood's own account of the scale of forms, differences in degree combine with differences in kind, so that each species of a genus not only embodies the 'generic essence in a specific manner' but also embodies 'some variable attribute in a specific degree.' A scale of forms of this type may occur in empirical concepts as much as in philosophical concepts. For example, a 'breaking strain, a freezing-point, a minimum taxable income' all reveal 'critical points on a scale of degrees where a new specific form suddenly comes into being.' A philosophical scale of forms has additional peculiarities that cannot be found in empirical scales. In a non-philosophical scale of forms, differences of degree generally admit of measurement; for example, a substance of the same molecular structure at particular temperatures may be ice, water or steam. Philosophical concepts such as goodness, beauty, truth and pleasantness admit differences of degree, but do not have independent measurable variables like heat. Even when we talk of feeling warmth, '[we] can detect as many differences in kind as [we] can detect differences in degree; and these are not two sets of differences but one single set.' Collingwood's argument was that in philosophical concepts 'differences of degree not merely entail, but actually are, differences of kind.' Feeling heat is, in this sense, a philosophical concept. Some other common concepts which exemplify these characteristics are 'capital and other degrees of punishment', 'degrees of kindred and affinity', a social hierarchy of nobility and gentry, 'degrees of comparison in grammar' and 'university degrees'.[38]

For Collingwood, therefore, there was only one kind of difference in philosophical concepts, which united differences of degree and kind. He also argued that opposition and distinction are similarly united in philosophical concepts. For example, good and bad are both distinct and opposed to each other, for being bad is doing bad, and not just having zero good. Truth and error, beauty and ugliness, 'and all the pairs of opposites that figure in philosophical thought' are related in the same way. Differences between beautiful things are never simply a matter of the one kind of beauty realised to a greater or lesser degree in different objects. Nor are differences in beauty simply a matter of different kinds of beauty.[39] The idea of a

[37] Benedetto Croce, *Logic as the Science of the Pure Concept*. Translated by Douglas Ainslie. Macmillan, London, 1917.
[38] Collingwood, *An Essay on Philosophical Method*. pp. 57, 59-60, 70-73.
[39] Ibid. pp. 75, 77-78.

scale of forms allows us to appreciate the beautiful on its own terms and to criticise lower forms of beauty from the perspective of a higher position on the scale: criticism and exposition overlap.

A philosophical scale of forms has no zero point, for its variable is identical to its essence, while a zero point would mean that there was no essence at all. Since there is no zero point, philosophical judgements are categorical because they always relate to a specific and determinate position on the scale. Philosophical knowledge must, therefore, involve knowing better what, in some sense, we already knew.[40] Each 'philosophical science' can be understood as 'penetrating more deeply than the last into the essence of its subject matter and expressing the nature of the one substance more adequately.' Different philosophies deal with specific forms of the one subject matter, and therefore differ in kind. The same philosophies differ also in degree, because their method and their subject can be more or less genuinely philosophical. Each new philosophy on the scale must include and summarise all previous philosophy.[41] The scale of forms analysis, therefore, gave specific content to Collingwood's earlier argument that truth is a matter of inclusion and comprehensiveness, belonging only to systems.

To make genuine progress in philosophy we must learn what our predecessors were trying to do; like them, we are trying 'to philosophize; but to do it better by doing it differently'. From this perspective

> the entire history of thought is the history of a single sustained attempt to solve a single permanent problem, each phase advancing the problem by the extent of all the work done on it in the interval, and summing up the fruits of this work in the shape of a unique presentation of the problem.[42]

Because the problem changes there cannot strictly be a 'single permanent problem', the terms of which are defined once and for all. Rather, the problem exhibits unity in diversity, for there is unity in the one process, and diversity in its various stages. In this sense, there was no real difference between Collingwood's views in the *Essay on Philosophical Method* and his later criticisms of the realist

---

[40] Ibid. pp. 81, 121, 161. Collingwood argued that philosophical judgements were categorical, and that in philosophy we come to know better what we already knew; he did not directly argue these conclusions from the lack of a zero point on a scale of forms. These conclusions follow naturally and quickly from Collingwood's earlier point and they therefore simplify the task of exposition.

[41] Ibid. pp. 189, 190, 191-192.

[42] Ibid. p. 195.

doctrine of 'eternal problems' in *An Autobiography*.[43] In the *Essay on Philosophical Method* he maintained that each real philosophical system was 'nothing but an interim report on the progress of thought down to the time of making it'.[44] Progress could only be made in light of the 'tradition of philosophy' which, in turn, could only be 'discovered by historical study'.[45] To undertake philosophical work is to understand and criticise a scale of forms that has developed historically and can only be understood historically.[46]

An Essay on Philosophical Method gave particular prominence to metaphysics. Collingwood argued that if something held of metaphysical thought then it held of all philosophical thought

> for metaphysics, even if it is regarded as only one among the philosophical sciences, is not unique in its objective reference or in its logical structure; all philosophical thought is of the same kind, and every philosophical science partakes of the nature of metaphysics.[47]

If each system of philosophy is an 'interim report' and metaphysics is a philosophical science, metaphysics requires a return to its history in order to progress. If philosophy is a scale of forms developing historically, and if, as Collingwood maintained in the *Essay on Philosophical Method*, metaphysics studies the 'existential aspect' of philosophy's subject matter, it must reveal the historical development of concepts.[48] In the language of the 'Libellus', the scale of forms elucidates the logic of 'becoming'. To align Collingwood's earlier terminology with his later practice, in *An Essay on Metaphysics*, Collingwood attempted to reform metaphysics in light of a philosophy of 'becoming'.[49]

Collingwood began his *Essay on Metaphysics* by noting that, for Aristotle, metaphysics was the logically first science. Its place in the

---

[43] Collingwood, *An Autobiography*. pp. 67-68.
[44] Collingwood, *An Essay on Philosophical Method*. p. 198. Collingwood did not seek to force the analysis of the existing state of philosophy into a neat and clear-cut scale of forms. He did, however, maintain that the scale of forms is more than an ideal towards which philosophy should aim. His point was that philosophy in fact tended towards a scale of forms because philosophical concepts have particular characteristics.
[45] Ibid. p. 226.
[46] Rex Martin has suggested that alterations need to be made to the scale of forms before it can be properly historical. See Rex Martin, 'Collingwood's Claim that Metaphysics is a Historical Discipline', *The Monist*. Vol. 72, No. 4, October 1989, pp. 489-525.
[47] Collingwood, *An Essay on Philosophical Method*. p. 127.
[48] Ibid.
[49] R. G. Collingwood, *An Essay on Metaphysics. Revised Edition With The Nature of Metaphysical Study; Function of Metaphysics in Civilization; Notes for an Essay on Logic. Edited with an Introduction by Rex Martin*. Clarendon Press, Oxford, 1998.

system of sciences depended on his theory of universals. In the Aristotelian system, universals formed a hierarchical system. The system was formed by classification or division, and had at its highest point the universal 'being'. All other concepts fell under 'being'. Collingwood's earlier work attacked such 'classificatory' theories, and led to his alternative conception of the scale of forms. Aristotle had also aligned the system of sciences with the system of universals, leaving metaphysics as the science of pure 'being' at the top of its pyramid. In common with philosophers such as Berkeley, Hume, Kant and Hegel, and in implicit opposition to others such as Heidegger (who was not mentioned in the book), Collingwood argued that if there is no differentiation there is no subject matter. Consequently, there cannot be a study of pure being.[50]

From Aristotle, Collingwood also extracted the alternative thesis that metaphysics was an historical study of the presuppositions of other sciences. To the question "How can metaphysics become a science?' The answer is: 'By becoming more completely and more conspicuously what in fact it has always been, an historical science.'[51] Metaphysical statements are true or false statements about history, rather than nonsense statements about pure being as, for example, A. J. Ayer had recently claimed in *Language, Truth and Logic* (1936).

Metaphysics, however, could not be the study of any and every presupposition. Science is an activity of disentangling, arranging, asking and answering questions, and therefore of making and examining some kinds of presupposition. But scientific activity does not investigate all of its own presuppositions. Rather, in every act of thinking, some presuppositions are presupposed absolutely. A pathologist, for example, might presuppose absolutely that 'everything has a cause'. In other words, the pathologist takes causality for granted; he does not attempt to verify the principle and does not discover the principle in the course of his work.[52]

For Collingwood, metaphysics is a study of absolute presuppositions. Absolute presuppositions are not entities, nor are they Pla-

---

[50] Ibid. pp. 6-9, 14-15.

[51] Ibid. p. 77.

[52] Ibid. p. 31. Ironically, one pathologist who read the *Essay on Metaphysics* admired Collingwood's exposition, but thought that Collingwood used 'cause' in a more extended sense than a working pathologist would do in practice. This response can be assimilated within Collingwood's theory if it is taken to mean that a narrow sense of the word 'cause' is investigated by pathology itself, but the more extensive sense of 'cause' is an unquestioned, absolute, presupposition. Letter from H. P. Bayou, 28/6/1940, pasted in at p. 31 of R. G. Collingwood's working copy of *An Essay on Metaphysics*. [Private Collection of Teresa Smith, Oxford.]

tonic ideas; rather, they are ideas that stand in a particular kind of relation to particular kinds of activities, undertaken at particular times. All absolute presuppositions relate to specific, historical, activities of mind. Collingwood described absolute presuppositions as 'catalytic agents which the mind must bring out of its own resources to the manipulation of what is called "experience" and the conversion of it into science and civilization'.[53] Scientific thought does not go on without them. To understand what science is means understanding what science does, and to do that we need to understand what our scientific activities presuppose absolutely. In the past, absolute presuppositions have remained hidden in order to protect the boundaries, domain and status of particular sciences.[54] Collingwood observed that the nineteenth century cry of 'No More Metaphysics' served to protect 'a reactionary science, one which could only be imperilled by a critical inquiry into its foundations.' Reactionary science was protected by philosophical reluctance to expose the particular absolute presuppositions which were being made: '[i]f people became aware that in certain contexts they were in the habit of treating this or that presupposition as an absolute one, they would be unable to go on doing it.'[55] Progress in science, by contrast, requires such presuppositions to be investigated.

Absolute presuppositions can be expressed in language, and in that sense (contrary to some interpretations) they cannot be devoid of meaning, but they are in fact only expressed in, and are only answers to, historical questions. That is, they have meaning in the context of historical thinking; they have meaning in other areas of thought to the extent that those other activities depend upon historical thinking. The only way in which we can know what absolute presuppositions have been made is to analyse particular acts of thinking. Metaphysics must analyse thinking historically in order to find out 'what absolute presuppositions have been made by this or that person or group of persons, on this or that occasion or group of occasions'. Historical thought is needed to establish 'whether absolute presuppositions are made singly or in groups', 'whether different absolute presuppositions are made by different individuals or races or nations or classes...or whether the same have been made' everywhere and at all times.[56]

---

[53] Collingwood, *An Essay on Metaphysics*. p. 197.
[54] In this respect, Collingwood's theory can be seen as anticipating those of later thinkers such as Kuhn or Foucault.
[55] Collingwood, *An Essay on Metaphysics*. p. 96.
[56] Ibid. pp. 43, 47.

Absolute presuppositions can change, in the sense that people
who used to think or act in a particular way, with a particular absolute presupposition, can come to think or act in ways that have different absolute presuppositions. While much attention has been
paid to the idea that absolute presuppositions change 'irrationally',
the basis for such a change can include the inability, on rational
grounds, of particular agents to continue to presuppose an earlier
absolute presupposition or set of them. Collingwood thought that
modern natural science, for example, shared many views about the
presuppositions of natural science with Aristotle, but that it had a
number of presuppositions that were different from those stated by
Aristotle. In particular, Collingwood held that Christian theology
represented an advance in metaphysics because it replaced Aristotle's idea that we discover the existence of the natural world
through our senses with the idea that the existence of this world is
something that we presuppose. The articulation of patristic theology, therefore, removed earlier metaphysical errors and thereby
enabled further progress to be made in natural science.[57]

Because absolute presuppositions can change, Collingwood's
metaphysics has often been seen to imply some form of radical relativism, where the thought of one era or culture may be totally incommensurable with that of other eras or cultures. Firstly, such
objections misrepresent the rationality of the processes by which
absolute presuppositions are identified and become the subject of
scrutiny. They are likely to be replaced not as the result of conscious
attempts to find new absolute presuppositions but through two
kinds of rational process. They may change as a consequence of our
abandoning unsuccessful attempts to continue to think or act in particular ways, where thinking is akin to groping for new solutions.
They may also change as a result of conscious attempts to articulate
them, as in the example of patristic theology cited above. Secondly,
for absolute presuppositions to be different is not to say that they are
incommensurable; the charge of relativism against Collingwood's
theory is laid too quickly. In particular, the idea of a scale of forms
shows how concepts that are opposite to each other can nevertheless
be related to each other in the one progressive scale. Finally, it is an
empirical and not a theoretical issue whether absolute presuppositions do in fact differ. If some concepts occurring in different cultures are unrelated to each other, others may yet be held in common.

Collingwood, then, approached philosophy through concepts
such as activity, process, action or history. In his earlier writings, the

[57]   Ibid. pp. 214-215, 224-227.

concepts of activity or process were most evident on the surface of his works. In his later work, the concepts of action and history predominated. In many respects, Collingwood's later works represented the application of concepts such as action and history to a variety of philosophical problems. History, in particular, became more explicitly central to Collingwood's philosophy. In turn, as we shall see in later chapters, his philosophy of history came to subsume and elaborate upon concepts such as activity, process and action. Why, though, should those concepts play such a significant role in his philosophy? Collingwood did not arbitrarily seize on these key concepts; his uses of them do not represent intuitions that we must either share or reject. Rather, the concepts were significant only within an overall theory of the world as process. As we will see in the next chapter, that theory provides means through which we can understand why activity, process, action and history became so fundamental to Collingwood's philosophy.

CHAPTER 2

The World as Process

A philosophy that conceives of thought as objectified in history needs an account of what sort of world makes such objectification possible. It also requires a theory of thought. This chapter is about the need for such an account of the world, while the next chapter concerns the theory of thought.

Philosophies that focus, by contrast, on language or on the practices of historians may appear to have little need to settle an account of what the world is before they can proceed. Historical practices can be described without waiting for arguments about the adequacy of a particular view of the world to be resolved. There is thus, from this perspective, a question as to why it would be relevant to characterise the world in order to characterise history. Besides the question of relevance, doubts may also arise as to the possibility or legitimacy of providing any account of the world beyond language.

Following Collingwood into such terrain, therefore, may seem simply to highlight a gulf between Collingwood's approach to philosophy and that of many of his successors, who focused more narrowly on language or historical practices. If that is so, it might go a long way to explaining some criticisms that have been made of Collingwood's philosophy of history. Many would find such a gulf to be an argument against Collingwood's philosophy of history. Nevertheless, to avoid the question of what relationship might exist between a focus on historical practice and a philosophy that embeds history in a world of process is to leave each element in that debate under-developed. In particular, it seems that many of Collingwood's most distinctive ideas about history, which attract attention to his work, can be shown to rely on a specific view of the world as process. Understanding those doctrines means understanding his broader conception of the world. Similarly, many of Collingwood's conclusions can be reached by beginning from historical practice; conclusions and practice need to be seen together.

Collingwood carried over into history his focus on becoming — at one time calling it 'the fundamental idea of all history.'[1] Collingwood relied on such a view when he argued that history is not real, but ideal. History is ideal because it is past, not present. Historical thinking, however, can make the past both ideal and actual. If, as Collingwood also claimed, the object of historical thinking is past thought, then historical thinking involves making past thoughts actual. That is, the activity of history involves re-thinking or, if thinking is acting, re-enacting past thoughts. For Collingwood, then, history is conceived as a process with particular attributes that make it past. The theory of re-enactment also requires that a thought that takes place at one point in time, in one mind, can be the same thought as one that occurs in another mind, at another time. To give an account of ideality or of re-enactment we need, therefore, to consider what it is that makes history possible.

We can begin with the practices of history, and see how reflection on those practices gives rise to theories of history. The practice of history includes all the rules, techniques and conventions that enable an historian to undertake their work and achieve a credible conception of the human past. Reflection on such practices can lead to ideas about the purpose of doing history, the adequacy of history in providing knowledge and the relationship between history and other studies. To use terms that Collingwood himself used, such ideas are first-order theories, because they reflect directly on the practice of history. By contrast, theories that reflect on the conception of history and what it involves are second-order theories, and may arise through the interpretation of first-order theories.

There are both realist and constructionist first-order theories of history. Each illuminates history in some way. For example, historical practitioners readily betray a strong strand of realism in their work. In particular, historians are often animated by the conviction that they are investigating the lives and deeds of real people or the existence of particular institutions. Such and such people lived, and we can only study them because they did so. To quote just one recent exemplar, Richard Evans, 'it really happened, and we really can, if we are very scrupulous and careful and self-critical, find out how it

[1]   R. G. Collingwood, 'Oswald Spengler and the Theory of Historical Cycles' (1927), reprinted in *Essays in the Philosophy of History: R. G. Collingwood* (edited by W. Debbins). McGraw-Hill, New York, 1966. pp. 57-75. See p. 74.

happened and reach some tenable though always less than final conclusions about what it all meant.'[2] There is an air of necessity to such
convictions; if someone did not believe this about what they were
doing, they would not be doing history. Animated by such convictions, historians carve out special fields of expertise.

Realist first-order theories of history come in many forms. Notori-
ously, some historians and philosophers of history have seen their
work as finding out 'what actually happened'. By way of example,
'what actually happened' can be set against illusion or deceit. Historians can be seen as keepers of the truth of the past. They may therefore come into conflict with unreliable or mythical stories of the past.
In this sense, history has a powerful moral dimension as 'truth-
telling'. Conversely, an historian who set out to describe 'what actually happened' may self-consciously attempt to replicate one image
of natural science, whereby science is considered free from moral
significance. In yet another interpretation of the same idea, setting
out 'what actually happened' can be taken as a corrective for defec-
tive memory. On this view, history is a way to know about events of
which we were not a part, in places we have never been and at times
before we were born. Finally, there is a view that the dramatic patterns of history are 'what actually happened'. History that finds in
events the signals of broad patterns of change, development or
transformation is about revelation.

Historical practice is not, however, fully realist. Historians also on
occasion betray quite a contrary element in their work. They do this
by imagining past scenes, conjecturing connections and seeking to
augment the power of a story with the qualities of good literature.
Such practices can readily lead to the idea that history is, above all,
literature. They can also lead to constructionist first-order theories of
history, which have been characterised as denying that there is a
relationship between historical work and a real past and emphasising the activity of the historian in forming conclusions by following
certain rules.[3]

Constructionism of some kind has a deal of attractiveness as a theory of historical epistemology and method. For history is the work of
historians, working at specific times and with specific techniques
and interests which they bring to the task. A critic could point out
that claims to historical knowledge are often challenged. Indeed, a

[2]   Richard J. Evans, *In Defence of History*. Granta, London, 1997. p. 253.
[3]   W. H. Dray, *History as Re-enactment: R. G. Collingwood's Idea of History*. Claren-
        don Press, Oxford, 1995. p. 241. C. B. McCullagh, *The Truth of History*. Routledge,
        London, 1998. pp. 43-46.

critic might venture that it is a fundamental feature of historical practice that the human past can be, and is, contested; some would see this as its weakness, and others as a strength in the contribution of history to society.

A number of writers have built their views about history around constructionist ideas. Leon Goldstein put this view most succinctly: '[t]he function of historical research is to constitute the historical past.'[4] It is tempting to adopt such a stance; it captures an important dimension of the discipline of history. The historical past is not simply an imaginary past, but a past given form through a particular kind of labour. Particular elements of constructionist theory therefore present strong challenges to certain first-order realist theories of history. In particular, constructionism calls into question whether any form of realism could hold in history if it required a correspondence theory of truth.

The constructionist suggests that an understanding of the human past does not correlate to a real past; it constitutes it as an object. The fall of the Berlin Wall could have been just another demolition of masonry; what made it the fall of the Berlin Wall was that it was a series of actions understood by agents aware of a particular context and the significance of their deeds. The fall of the Berlin Wall was not, therefore, a non-linguistic entity to which our statements could correlate, thereby making them true. Rather, it was a linguistically constructed entity made by human understanding. Historians of the Wall are therefore able to reveal the understanding that served to construct the entity being studied. This notion, however, seems to restore some of the first-order realist view of history because it falls back on the idea of specific deeds done in specific contexts.

What is interesting about first-order realism and constructionism in history is not whether there are some acceptable forms of each theory or none, but what makes them possible in the first place. First-order realism about history runs the risk of paying insufficient attention to the activity of historians; constructionism is therefore a useful corrective to some forms of realism. On the other hand, without historical practice, there would be no need for, and no interest in, a constructionist theory of history. The question that arises is what it is that gives sense to the constructionist elements in historical practice and, by implication, to constructionist theories. Here the answer seems unavoidable: constructionism as a first-order theory is dependent on there having been a real past. The constitutive charac-

---

[4]   Leon J. Goldstein, *Historical Knowing*. University of Texas Press, Austin, 1976. p. xix.

ter of the mind in historical work is possible only because our minds are real products of real pasts. Critical epistemology of history seems to need realist metaphysics of history. To consider how this is possible, we need to shift the level of analysis to a second level.

Second-order theories of history are concerned with the dimensions of what makes theorising about history, and historical practice, possible. They are, therefore, particularly focused on how history relates to other concepts. If philosophy of history is, as Collingwood suggested, reflection on the problems of history, second-order theory of history is a study that must be concerned with elucidating the nature of history's object. The philosophy of history, therefore, must be concerned with the metaphysics of history. To the extent that the study of history can be said to involve knowledge, the philosophy of history must also explicate an historical epistemology.

The view I will take is that second-order theories of history must be realist in a particular sense and that Collingwood attempted to articulate that realism. Put simply, there is an object for history to study and that object is a particular kind of process. A specific characteristic of process gives rise to history and thus makes historical practice possible. It follows from this view that there are limits to which first-order theories of history and what kinds of historical practice can be fruitfully pursued. Second-order realism is therefore quite different to any realism involved in the practice of history or in first-order theories, although it shapes each alike. The three thinkers who contributed most to this theory of history in the twentieth century were Samuel Alexander, Alfred North Whitehead and R. G. Collingwood. Alongside a methodology, Croce also developed a sophisticated metaphysics of history, encapsulated in the idea of 'history as the story of liberty'. Alexander, Whitehead and Collingwood, however, were more thorough than Croce in relating history to the theory of nature.

Collingwood's understanding of realism was complex and some of his interpretations are not immediately obvious. This makes it difficult to readily define his contribution to realist metaphysics of history. In his writings, Collingwood used the same words in different ways — sometimes in a technical sense, more often with nuances familiar to the broad readership he hoped to reach. He could, for example, vehemently denounce the 'realism' of his Oxford predecessors Cook Wilson and Prichard, but also write a long and positive essay in 1935 to experiment with the idea that all reality is historical. He also developed a distinctive account of the key doctrines of F. H.

Bradley, arguing that the realists had adopted Bradley's fundamental ideas.[5]

In his 1935 essay on historicity and realism, Collingwood took as his starting point the notion that reality is flux. Collingwood argued that Greek thought sought reality outside the flux. By contrast, scientific thought sought it in generalisations or regularities across the flux. For history, however, reality is the flux. History is a way of thinking that makes the flux knowable or intelligible. To understand something historically is to understand just what something was in particular; the French Revolution of 1789 was a specific event, not simply an example of a revolution. Whereas other forms of thought conceive knowledge under the auspices of concepts, generalisation and theory, historical thinking shows that knowledge of the particular is possible. This account lacks, however, a sense of what it is about the historical object that makes for its intelligibility.[6]

Collingwood's realism is more clearly seen through the increasing influence of Alexander and Whitehead on his thought. In the 1920s, while Collingwood developed a conception of activity and a 'logic of becoming', Alexander and Whitehead propounded a cosmology of process based around the tendency of modern sciences such as physics to resolve matter into processes.[7] In his Gifford Lectures of 1916-1918, Samuel Alexander had maintained that '[e]mpirical things are complexes of space-time with their qualities'.[8] Minds and

---

[5]   In Collingwood's view, Bradley had brought to an end the subjectivist or phenomenalist theory of the nineteenth century, according to which appearance was distinguished from reality. On such theory, our knowledge was held to be of appearances rather than of reality. Bradley, by contrast, regarded all appearances as belonging to reality and held that we know reality and not merely appearance. This view opens up the question what features of reality are explored by particular kinds of thought; for example, what are the realities investigated in historical studies? In that sense, Bradley paved the way for the return of metaphysics to the philosophy of history. R. G. Collingwood, 'The Metaphysics of F. H. Bradley: An Essay on *Appearance and Reality*', December, 1933. [Unpublished manuscript, formerly in the possession of Mrs. Teresa Smith, Oxford, subsequently placed with the Collingwood papers in the Bodleian Library, Oxford.]

[6]   R. G. Collingwood, 'Reality as History', printed in Collingwood, *The Principles of History: and other writings in philosophy of history. Edited with an Introduction by W. H. Dray and W. J. van der Dussen*. Oxford University Press, Oxford, 1999. pp. 170-208.

[7]   Collingwood did not immediately admire either Whitehead or Alexander; nevertheless, by the late 1930s he specifically denied that either was a 'realist' of the type he condemned. See Collingwood, *An Autobiography*. Oxford University Press, London, 1939. pp. 45-46.

[8]   Samuel Alexander, *Space, Time, and Deity: With a new foreword by Dorothy Emmet*. Two vols. Macmillan, London, 1966. (First published in 1920.) Vol. II. p. 3.

other objects must be seen as 'co-ordinate members' of the one world.[9] More specifically, mind is 'a set of connected processes which have...the character of consciousness.' In turn, consciousness is a novel kind of quality formed from 'physiological conditions' and which 'has its being in physiological conditions.'[10] Borrowing a term from the philosopher and biologist C. Lloyd Morgan, Alexander argued that '[m]ind is...an "emergent" from life, and life an emergent from a lower physico-chemical level of existence.'[11] In the Alexandrine conception, it was the organisation of space-time which created entities, and the organisation of lower-level forms of existence which created genuinely new levels of existence with new qualities. Mind and matter were not different substances, but emergent features of the one world of space-time.

Alfred North Whitehead, in his Gifford Lectures for 1927-1928, built his cosmology around the concept of 'relatedness' rather than 'quality'.[12] For Whitehead, 'the actual world is process, and...the process is the becoming of actual entities...*how* an actual entity *becomes* constitutes *what* that actual entity *is*'.[13] There could be no place in such a philosophy for the idea of an 'unchanging subject of change' or 'substance'.[14] Describing his system as the 'philosophy of organism', Whitehead asserted that '[t]his doctrine of organism is the attempt to describe the world as a process of generation of individual actual entities, each with its own absolute self-attainment.'[15] Whereas Alexander had used the concept of emergence, Whitehead wrote of 'being present in another entity'. In other words, the synthesis of entities constitutes other actual entities.[16]

Whitehead, unlike Alexander, published work on history, notably in *Adventures of Ideas*, 'a study of the concept of civilisation, and an endeavour to understand how it is that civilised beings arise.'[17] This was also a major theme in Collingwood's own work, particularly in

[9]   Ibid. Vol. I. p. 29.
[10] Ibid. Vol. II. p. 8.
[11] Ibid. Vol. II. p. 14.
[12] Alfred North Whitehead, *Process and Reality: An Essay in Cosmology*. (1929) Reprinted by Free Press, New York, 1969. p. viii. For an account of Whitehead in relation to the broader Western philosophical tradition, see George R. Lucas, Jr., *The Rehabilitation of Whitehead: An Analytic and Historical Assessment of Process Philosophy*. State University of New York Press, Albany, 1989.
[13] Whitehead, *Process and Reality*. pp. 27-28. (Emphasis in original.)
[14] Ibid. p. 34.
[15] Ibid. p. 75.
[16] Ibid. p. 65.
[17] Alfred North Whitehead, *Adventures of Ideas* (1933). Reprinted by Macmillan, New York, 1952. p. vii.

The New Leviathan. Whitehead theorised that civilisation was a process that depended on feelings of

> respect, sympathy, and general kindliness. All these feelings can exist with the minimum of intellectuality. Their basis is emotional, and humanity acquired these emotions by reason of its unthinking activities amid the course of nature. But mentality as it emerges into coordinated activity has a tremendous effect in selecting, emphasizing, and disintegrating. We have been considering the emergence of ideas from activities, and the effect of ideas in modifying the activities from which they emerge. Ideas arise as explanatory of customs and they end by founding novel methods and novel institutions.[18]

The key concepts in Whitehead's account were emergence and novelty and yet it would be possible to criticise him for not allowing sufficiently for these very factors. Dorothy Emmet, for example, was critical of Whitehead's account of process because it did not seem to allow for the emergence of new properties with new powers.[19] On Whitehead's account, processes relate to each other in different kinds of nexus, for example 'Regions, Societies, Persons, Enduring Objects, Corporal Substances, Living Organisms, Events' and the like.[20] Propositions are true if the particular nexus they pick out 'does in reality exemplify the pattern which is the predicate of the proposition.'[21] This form of the correspondence theory leaves history in a peculiar situation. If the past and future are dimensions of one process, and the present and future develop from the past, the theory of truth needs to be particularly focused on problems of history. Whitehead's theory, however, demands the capacity to check the predicate against the reality. Since the past no longer exists, but has become the present, this is, strictly speaking, impossible.

Despite Whitehead's writings on history, Collingwood's own view was that Alexander's theory allowed the greater scope for history. In 1935, Collingwood wrote to Alexander that

> Your world seems to me a world in which evolution & history have a real place: Whitehead's world is indeed all process, but I don't see that this process is in the same way productive or creative of new things (e.g. Life, Mind) arising on the old as on a foundation. W. seems rather to deny that these things are really new at all — at least, he seems to say so pretty explicitly in the little Nature & Life. On that question I am impenitently an Alexandrine. I don't believe that matter is really alive & all that busi-

[18] Ibid. p. 127.
[19] Dorothy Emmet, *The Passage of Nature.* Temple University Press, Philadelphia, 1992. p. 101.
[20] Whitehead, *Adventures of Ideas.* pp. 254-255.
[21] Ibid. p. 313.

ness. I think it's only a dodge to evade the question, how does anything generically new come into existence?[22] (sic)

In his letter of application to the electors for the Waynflete Chair of Metaphysical Philosophy, Collingwood stated that his main interest was in 'the philosophical problems (metaphysical and epistemological) connected with the idea of history (historical process and historical knowledge).' Collingwood said that he would focus on the philosophy of history. In addition, he also proposed that, 'bearing in mind the relation between historical process and natural process, I should try to develop in my own way the metaphysical inquiries concerning nature which have lately been brought into fresh prominence by Alexander and Whitehead.'[23] Reading *The Idea of Nature* in the light of these intentions, it is hard to resist the conclusion that Collingwood found different qualities in each thinker; he was an admirer of Whitehead's analysis and rigour, but he had a deep love for Alexander.

The broad directions of Collingwood's own work had been set well before Whitehead published *Process and Reality*, and probably without reference to *Space, Time and Deity*, yet his contacts with Alex-

[22] R. G. Collingwood to Samuel Alexander, 13 Feb 1935. [Copy in Bodleian Library, Dep. 26.]
[23] R. G. Collingwood, 'Letter to The Electors to the Waynflete Professorship of Metaphysical Philosophy', 22 February, 1935. [Original in Oxford University Archives, UR/SF/PHMM/1; April 1926 - July 1944.] As an aside, this letter was written on Collingwood's 46th birthday. Collingwood provided only one testimonial, from Samuel Alexander. In his testimonial, Alexander placed particular emphasis on *An Essay on Philosophical Method*, which he called 'a work of real philosophical originality and ability', and also drew attention to Collingwood's metaphysical abilities, wide learning and 'literary gifts'. After his election, Collingwood wrote to Alexander that 'the electors were...a good deal tickled that a candidate habitually labelled Idealist should send in, as his only testimonial, one from our Leading Realist'. The two philosophers corresponded for more than a decade on a number of topics, such as the philosophy of art, and Collingwood reviewed various publications by Alexander. In 1938, Alexander was dying, while Collingwood was recovering from a stroke. Collingwood wrote to Alexander that 'I shan't ever be able to write the book which would have shown you how much I am in agreement with you on all the things that really matter; but it has been great fun disagreeing with you about inessentials in the mean time.' The book to which Collingwood most likely referred was a general cosmology in the manner of Alexander and Whitehead, which Collingwood had drafted several years before and upon which he drew for some of his later work. See: S. Alexander, 'Letter to The Electors to the Waynflete Professorship of Metaphysical Philosophy', 11 February, 1935. [Original in Oxford University Archives, UR/SF/PHMM/1; April 1926-July 1944]; R. G. Collingwood to Samuel Alexander, 30.iii.35. [Copy in Bodleian Library, Dep. 26.]; R. G. Collingwood to Samuel Alexander, 24.iv.38. [Copy in Bodleian Library, Dep. 26.]

ander and his reading of Whitehead's work proved a direct stimulus to his own metaphysical thought.[24] In 1933 and 1934 Collingwood worked on cosmology in several notebooks he collectively entitled 'Notes towards a Metaphysic', material from which was later used in *The Idea of Nature*. At the outset, Collingwood thought that his theory 'will, I think, be something like an Emergent Evolution theory: i.e. it will tell how life & mind successively emerge from matter: but without the question-begging term (word, rather) emergence.' (*sic*) Collingwood's approach was to use his theory of method, particularly the scale of forms, to explicate the genus 'reality' through its species 'matter', 'life' and 'mind'. Each must develop out of the earlier forms in the series, and so the major philosophical problem was to give an account of the nisus (or effort towards a higher level) which operates at each level.[25]

Collingwood's account of nisus owed much to Hegel as well as to Whitehead and Alexander. The basic account Collingwood gave was that each form contains ambivalent tendencies, and the tension between these elements results in the development of a 'new specific form.' Such tensions are part of the world itself, and not merely our thought about the world, yet 'the world, in creating minds, has turned itself into something new, something habitable to mind and known by mind.' When new empirical orders of objects come to exist, their qualities affect all of existence; it is the whole universe that develops, and not some part of it developing as a cause of some other part. The appearance of mind is the appearance of historical processes from natural processes, and involves 'the coincidence of logical and temporal order.' That is, in so far as events are historical, they are also logical.[26]

Like Alexander and Whitehead, Collingwood situated history in the context of a world that is real and based on process and emergence, but he differed from each thinker on significant points. Unlike Alexander, whose account was intended to be descriptive of the world, Collingwood's account needs to be seen as metaphysical, that is, as an account of the presuppositions that make thought possible. His argument about the transformation of the whole universe because of the appearance of new orders such as mind was ulti-

---

[24] Collingwood wrote to his friend Guido de Ruggiero on 2 October, 1920, listing new books in the realist vein, and inaccurately referring to Alexander's book as '*Time, Space and Deity*'. [Copy in Bodleian Library, Dep. 27.]

[25] R. G. Collingwood, 'Notes towards a Metaphysic, A', (1933). [Bodleian Library, Dep. 18.] pp. 1c, 6.

[26] Ibid., pp. 8, 14, 65, 69. Part of this material is excerpted in Collingwood, *The Principles of History: and other writings in philosophy of history* (1999). p. 121.

mately an argument for a non-reductive account of mind, within a concept of reality as process. That anti-reductionism was to be fully expressed in *The New Leviathan* in the idea that the distinction between mind and body is in fact a distinction between the sciences of body and the sciences of mind.[27] Unlike Whitehead, on the other hand, Collingwood was not content to treat history as a process much like other kinds. Rather, for Collingwood, the key issue is what kind of process history is. Several years after he wrote his cosmological notebooks, in his 1939 Schema for 'The Principles of History', Collingwood proposed to 'state and expound the concept *of Action (res gestae)'*, and set out to contrast that with 'the conception of *Process* or *Change* and the pseudo-history which that implies.'[28] Collingwood sought to contrast temporal processes with genuine development that is both logical and temporal.

Within his overall treatment of the world as process, Collingwood distinguished two types of process. Firstly, there are law-governed or causal processes, which comprise the field of nature. Secondly, there are will-governed and, in that sense, free processes. The historian is a student of this second type of process; the parts of this process are called actions. Because these processes are processes of thought, a theory of history must see mental life as a process in which the past lives in the present.[29] Both the epistemology and objects of history were illuminated by this distinction. Collingwood's famous statement that '[a]ll history is the history of thought', was a claim about the kind of process that history is and, therefore, about what an historian must try to know.[30]

On Collingwood's terms, the object of history is action, treated as 'events brought about by the will and expressing the thought of a free and intelligent agent'.[31] On this theory, the reason why historians deal with past human affairs is simply that humans are the only

[27] R. G. Collingwood, *The New Leviathan, or Man, Society, Civilization and Barbarism. Revised edition, edited and introduced by David Boucher, with 'Goodness, Rightness, Utility' and 'What "Civilization" Means'*. Clarendon Press, Oxford, 1992. Chapters I and II. A useful comparison is Davidson, who has argued that the limits of the social sciences are not 'natural', but those set 'by us when we decide to view men as rational agents with goals and purposes, and as subject to moral evaluation.' Donald Davidson, *Essays on Actions and Events*. Clarendon Press, Oxford, 1980. p. 239.

[28] Collingwood, *The Principles of History: and other writings in philosophy of history*. pp. 245-246. (Emphasis in original.)

[29] R. G. Collingwood, *The Idea of History. Revised edition, with Lectures 1926-1928, edited with an introduction by Jan van der Dussen*. Clarendon Press, Oxford, 1993. p. 187.

[30] Ibid. p. 215.

[31] Ibid. p. 178.

beings we know to be intelligent agents. It is clear that Collingwood recognised this naturalistic implication of his argument. In his 1936 lecture on 'Human Nature and Human History', he explicitly stated that the 'beginnings of historical life' could be found 'among non-human animals' such as cats. His point was that the 'rudiments of culture' in animal behaviour, such as when a mother cat teaches her kittens to wash themselves, are 'something not essentially different from an historic culture.'[32]

The epistemology of history follows from the character of its object. In Collingwood's view, because the processes of nature differ from the processes of history, our knowledge of nature and of history differ, and the methods of each differ.[33] The key point here is that thought belongs to the process of history in a way that it does not belong to nature but, rather, emerges from it. To try to know history is, therefore, different from trying to know nature. The thought of an historian is itself part of the process of history. The thought of the scientist, on the other hand, stands in an important sense outside the process of nature. As we shall see in chapter 8, developing the epistemology of history means, therefore, expanding upon such distinctions.

I have called the theories of Alexander, Whitehead and Collingwood realist, but they stand apart from many other forms of realism, and the three views are not realist in the same way. The primary difference between the theories of Alexander, Whitehead and Collingwood and some other forms of realism is that they provide reality with a particular content — reality is process in which new forms, not reducible to their components, emerge. This approach is very different to that of, for example, John Searle, who recently claimed that 'external realism' is 'a Background presupposition and not an empirical theory'.[34] Searle's language loosely resembles Collingwood's account of the absolute presuppositions of thought, although the resemblance is primarily one of terminology.

Searle's form of realism amounts to the view that there is an object for our study, but it does not purport to say anything about what actually exists and it does not commit one to a particular epistemology. On Collingwood's view, such a purely formal argument is, however, deficient in an important way, because there is an object of study that must also exist. Specifically, Collingwood took the traditional 'ontological argument' to show that philosophical thought

[32] Ibid. p. 227.
[33] Ibid. p. 217.
[34] John R. Searle, *The Construction of Social Reality*. Penguin, Harmondsworth, 1996. p. 183.

exemplifies that which it takes as its object: its object exists. It is, therefore, not possible to provide a purely formal account of philosophical thought.[35] Instead, the task is to characterise the real object of philosophical thought.

Is it possible to avoid altogether Collingwood's use of the ontological argument, but continue to provide a characterisation of reality as process? Rather than focus on how each philosopher characterised reality in detail, we should ask about the status of such characterisations. When we do so, it becomes clear that the philosophical bases of Alexander's, Whitehead's and Collingwood's theories diverge. Alexander, for example, had a 'natural piety' that gave content to his view of the world and invested it with considerable elegance and beauty. Such a view can be readily admired but is not easy to share. It is, though, possible to see how we could approach such a perspective by building upon particular kinds of intuition. Dorothy Emmet, for example, took up such an element in her own analytical reworking of the idea of process.

Emmet justified a focus on process on intuitive grounds, starting from her conception that the world is 'going on, acting and reacting', and rejecting Bertrand Russell's theory of motion in favour of 'movement as a primitive concept, not as logically subsequent to a function of place and time.' She was not, however, prepared to eliminate substance in favour of process, as Whitehead and Alexander had done. Instead, she argued for substances as constituents of processes, and as 'capable of acting and being acted upon.' According to Emmet, a 'pure process ontology will need to down-grade action, and get rid of agents'.[36] In fact, neither Whitehead nor Alexander had sought to eliminate entities, or agents. Rather, they wanted to account for entities in terms of processes. It appears, therefore, that Emmet may have adopted an intuition about processes, but neglected an intuition about emergence. In this respect, she might reflect an aversion to teleology in much philosophy over the second half of the twentieth century, but revealed the limitations of intuition as a method for philosophy.

A second way to justify a particular characterization of reality is that the view in question is simply that of modern science or modern history. Whitehead, for example, drew extensively on contempo-

---

[35]   R. G. Collingwood, *An Essay on Philosophical Method*. Clarendon Press, Oxford, 1933. pp. 124-133. See also the essay 'The Existence of God', in R. G. Collingwood, *An Essay on Metaphysics. Revised Edition With The Nature of Metaphysical Study; Function of Metaphysics in Civilization; Notes for an Essay on Logic*. Edited with an Introduction by Rex Martin. Clarendon Press, Oxford, 1998. pp. 185-227.

[36]   Emmet, *The Passage of Nature*. pp. 22-23, 43, 49.

rary physical science. Much subsequent philosophy has been concerned with arguments for why the scientific world-view should be preferred to a philosophical one. Collingwood, on the other hand, although he referred to modern science, often did so through the views of others, and referred his own views primarily to modern historical thought.

There are, however, alternative ways to describe the relationship between a view of reality and a field of contemporary thought. One could argue, firstly, that the world-view in question is simply that found in, or abstracted from, contemporary science or history. This, however, seems only slightly more satisfactory than the intuitive method, since it provides a solid foundation for philosophy only in so far as scientific or historical thought have come sufficiently to a halt to merit systematisation in philosophy. A more plausible approach would adopt Collingwood's argument for the existence of absolute presuppositions of thought. On this theory, the role of absolute presuppositions is to enable thought to proceed in particular ways and for particular purposes. This alternative view suggests that the relationship between philosophy and science or history is one in which philosophy identifies and clarifies the basis and limitations of scientific or historical thought at a particular point in time. To characterise reality as process, then, would be to describe an absolute presupposition of contemporary thought; the debate about whether it is so should take the form of a philosophical history of the relevant bodies of thought.

To treat process as a possible absolute presupposition is, however, also not enough. For absolute presuppositions are implicated in the existence of activities of thought and the activity of thought is itself a process. Absolute presuppositions are themselves embedded in a philosophy of process: they help us to understand what certain kinds of process involve, but they do not explain why process is important to philosophy. Alternatively, if absolute presuppositions are excised from that context they become eternal objects, much as Whitehead envisaged, separate from space-time. Collingwood's criticisms of Whitehead are relevant here — eternal objects are essences, the organisation of which we are unable to understand, and the existence of which renders us unable to understand the creativity of the world from which the essences stand apart.[37]

Process is not an arbitrary concept or a merely possible presupposition of contemporary thought. As we saw in the Introduction,

---

[37] R. G. Collingwood, *The Idea of Nature*. Clarendon Press, Oxford, 1945. pp. 172-173.

Ortega held that the unmediated datum of thought in the act of living is the act alone, and this is the radical reality. We are at a similar point in terms of Collingwood's philosophy. There is an important sense in which process is not merely absolute but, because absolute presuppositions are themselves embedded in an account of process, it is also necessary. In characterising reality as process, we are returning, therefore, to Collingwood's use of the ontological argument. On the ontological argument, the object of philosophy is categorical, not hypothetical; the object of philosophy exists. If philosophy is an activity of thought, then the activity of thought exists as its object. How the object of philosophy is characterized may change, but the point is that there is no choice but to provide such a characterization. Plato, Aristotle, Anselm, Descartes, Spinoza and Hegel each offered different characterisations of the object of philosophy but, on Collingwood's interpretation, they all subscribed to the ontological argument.[38] Collingwood himself offered a broad reading neither specifically focused on the existence of God, nor closed to new characterisations of the object of philosophy drawn from the features of contemporary thought.

A possible counter to Collingwood's use of the ontological argument is the idea that philosophy is all just a mistake — a trick that results from the use of language and leads us to believe that philosophy has an object because we are able to talk as if it has one. But there is no trick. If there were a trick, it could occur only through reflection. Reflection might be possible only through language, but the use of language is not itself the activity of reflection. If, as is argued in much contemporary thought, language is inherently inter-subjective, it is dependent on other processes. Sharing or, in Davidson's terms, 'triangulating' are such processes, but they are not reflection. We need to give an account of reflection before we can show the trick, but to give such an account simply is to reflect. In the case of reflection, we therefore face a process that exemplifies what it seeks to describe. Characterising this existent process is at the centre of philosophy. We might also see philosophy as needing to characterise sharing or 'triangulating' — which may turn philosophy of language into philosophy of history. In building a philosophy, however, we might take care not to detach language either from reflection or from the activities of sharing or 'triangulating'.

Alexander, Whitehead and Collingwood each attempted to characterise reality as process that creates new emergent forms. On this view, a process is more than a mere sequence or set of events or

---

[38] Collingwood, *An Essay on Philosophical Method.* pp. 123-127.

objects. Rather, it involves connection, relationship and order. As Collingwood noted in summarising Alexander's philosophy, 'quality depends on pattern'.[39] Collingwood attempted to avoid the difficulties he found in the thought of Alexander and Whitehead. He approached the task as a necessary attempt to specify the content of the existent object of philosophy, but saw that such specification could not end with the undifferentiated term 'process'. Process is going on, but it is necessary to make a distinction, within the world of process, between history and nature, or action and what is not action. Neither Alexander nor Whitehead adequately made this distinction. Collingwood, by contrast, found in mind or history the means to fully satisfy the ontological argument — we are both embedded in, and create, history by thinking of its object. In *The Idea of Nature*, he therefore argued that 'cosmological philosophy' or understanding of nature could advance beyond Alexander and Whitehead only by shifting focus from natural science to the concept of history.[40] For Collingwood, this also meant a shift in focus towards the concept of action, because history is the object created by action.

Earlier in this chapter, I suggested that a kind of realism is essential to second-order theories of history. We have since seen that, on Collingwood's use of the ontological argument, realism cannot simply be formal. Rather, the content of second-order realism in history is provided by the concept of action. The theory of action will show the possibilities and the boundaries of history. Because history is created through action, the boundaries of history are boundaries of what can be done and of what can be understood.

On Collingwood's rendering, the theory of the world as process has several consequences that will shape the issues discussed in later chapters. If the world that makes the objectification of thought possible is a world of process, there is still a need for a theory of thought and how it is objectified. Thought must also be seen as process, or there is a risk that we will fall back on a separate realm of eternal objects, much as Whitehead had done. In the next chapter, we will see that Collingwood attempted to develop an account of thought that places it squarely within the world of history and action.

---

[39]   Collingwood, *The Idea of Nature*. p. 159.
[40]   Ibid. pp. 175-177. There were three possible conclusions to *The Idea of Nature*; alternate versions were printed in Collingwood, *The Principles of History*. pp. 251-270. The status of each is discussed in Rex Martin, 'Collingwood's *Essay on Metaphysics* and the three conclusions to the *Idea of Nature*', *British Journal for the History of Philosophy*, Volume 7, No. 2, 1999, pp. 333-351.

CHAPTER 3

Thought and Logic

If the world that makes the objectification of thought possible is a world of process, there is still a need to provide a theory of thought and how it is objectified. Thought must be seen as process, and more specifically as action, or there is a risk that we will fall back on thought as a separate realm of eternal objects. In this chapter we will see that Collingwood's solution to this problem (following Hegel as much as Alexander and Whitehead) was to place thought within the overall context of consciousness, and to emphasise the development of consciousness from life. This overall approach led Collingwood to place logic within the same context. In this chapter I will examine how the philosophy of process and mind set conditions for logic. In the next chapter, I will show how his theory of question and answer met those requirements.

Collingwood gave his clearest account of mind in *The New Leviathan*, although he had developed the views stated there over the previous two decades. On his account, humanity as it is known by the sciences of mind is mind. Forms of consciousness, such as the consciousness of feeling, constitute mind. Knowledge is a late and specialised form of the development of consciousness. Knowledge depends not only on the existence of consciousness, but on reflection on consciousness. Collingwood called such reflection *'second-order consciousness.'* The role of second-order consciousness in the development of knowledge is to maintain our focus on an object, such as a consciousness of noise, while we conduct the processes that will lead to knowledge. There can only be knowledge if, firstly, 'certain specialized operations of thought' have been performed and, secondly, there is a second-order consciousness that the operations have been

performed. These 'specialized operations' include making suppositions, for example, fixing attention on a noise and supposing it to be
outside our heads. Once a supposition has been made, we must ask
questions logically connected to the supposition. The questions
might be about, for example, what it is outside our heads that is making a noise. Finally, we must answer our question; writing during
the Second World War, Collingwood answered that a Hurricane
fighter was making the noise outside his own head.[1]

The forms of consciousness develop from the simpler to the more
complex, and involve many stages of transition. None of the transitions is necessary; rather, it is contingent whether consciousness
develops from one level to another. When a transition occurs, however, it occurs in a particular way that depends on the nature of the
earlier stage of consciousness.

Feeling is the first level of consciousness, but it is, strictly speaking, merely preconscious until selective attention makes for a 'patch'
in the here and now and the feeling is named. Appetite develops out
of feeling when we compare one state of the 'here and now' with
another, and try to switch from one to the other. But this comparison
is possible only because of conceptual thinking. Collingwood
claimed that selective attention is already conceptual thinking, but
of a low kind, which progresses only on certain occasions, when the
mind has the requisite 'practical energy'.[2]

Every 'patch' of the here and now singled out by selective attention occurs within a context of evocative thinking, by which 'feelings
you do not find as "given' in yourself" are aroused. Such 'evoca-
tions' provide the context for selections and these elements together
form a 'concept', or perhaps several concepts. The relations between
the elements are logical, and are studied by logic, 'the science which
studies the structure of concepts'.[3] This definition of logic did not
limit logic to the structure of concepts, nor did it specify what that
structure might be. Collingwood had already given an account of
the structure of philosophical concepts in *An Essay on Philosophical
Method*. In that work, Collingwood argued that philosophical concepts were arranged in overlapping and hierarchical scales. But *An
Essay on Philosophical Method* left to one side the issue of how such
scales were developed, and so a logic of concepts, or of scales of

[1]   R. G. Collingwood, *The New Leviathan, or Man, Society, Civilization and Barbarism.*
      Revised edition, edited and introduced by David Boucher, with 'Goodness, Rightness,
      Utility' and 'What "Civilization" Means'. Clarendon Press, Oxford, 1992. paras.
      2.45, 4.18-4.3, 4.31-4.35. (Emphasis in original.)
[2]   Ibid. paras. 5.65, 6.28. 7.14, 7.21-7.29.
[3]   Ibid. paras. 7.32, 7.33, 7.39.

forms, would remain incomplete by neglecting the dynamic elements which formed them.

Appetite develops through passion into desire. Because desire involves alternatives, it also involves *'propositional thinking'*. For Collingwood, a proposition is principally 'an answer to a question'. Reflection on appetite tells us that we want something, but it does not tell us what it is that we want. Reflection on passion provides us with the idea of alternatives, of fear and anger as ways of reacting to what is not ourselves. Only at the level of desire is the question asked, 'which of the two alternatives do I want?' The distinction between truth and falsity also emerges first at this level, in the sense of *'true desires* and *false desires'*.[4] If logic is concerned with the structure of concepts, therefore, this cannot be limited solely to the level at which concepts first emerge. Rather, concepts appear in propositions and because propositions only occur in contexts that include questions, logic is necessarily concerned with questioning.

Since knowledge depends on asking questions, it involves the contemplation of alternatives. Knowledge, therefore, begins to emerge only at the level of desire, when a question is asked about real alternatives. Strictly speaking, propositional thinking is not yet knowledge, for it does not involve reflection on the process by which a proposition has been affirmed and, therefore, does not involve any 'conviction or assurance' that the affirmation 'is well and truly made.'[5]

Questioning takes two forms, practical and theoretical. Logic cannot, therefore, be limited simply to the development of knowledge, but encompasses knowledge alongside practical reason. For Collingwood, thought was primarily practical, and only theoretical in a secondary way. Thought is practical in that it leads us to decisions about whether to do a certain thing, or to ask a question about what has been done. Thought is theoretical when, for example, someone compares the temperature today with the temperature yesterday, examines the difference between hot and cold, or thinks about the cold.[6]

Thought becomes rational when a distinction is made, within the sphere of propositional thinking, 'between "the that" and "the why".' To think rationally is, said Collingwood, to think *x* because you think something else, *y*. Because thought is primarily practical, so is reason, as when we have a reason for doing something. Theoret-

[4]   Ibid. paras. 11.14-11.15, 11.22, 11.3. (Emphasis in original.)
[5]   Ibid. paras. 11.11-11.12, fn. 1 to para. 11.11, 14.22.
[6]   Ibid. paras. 1.63-1.66.

ical reason, or having reasons for believing that something is the case, is a modification of practical reason.[7] As we shall see in Chapter 5, Collingwood distinguished three forms of practical reason — utility, right and duty — as well as three corresponding forms of theoretical reason — teleology, natural law and history. The forms of reason are defined in terms of the kinds of answers that can be given to questions. Collingwood's account of questioning was, therefore, an account of thought in its development within consciousness. As will be seen in later chapters, by distinguishing between forms of practical and theoretical reason, Collingwood placed the theory of questioning behind his moral theory as much as his theory of history. Thought is objectified, then, in choices, where we give different kinds of reasons for actions. To give an account of such choices, reasons and actions, is to give an account of how thought has been objectified; thought is, therefore, objectified in history.

In Collingwood's theory of mind, as it had developed by the time he wrote *The New Leviathan*, the key level was desire. Our desires are many, and the propositions that may express them are therefore many. Our desires exist in a context of other desires, and propositions in a context of other propositions. But the very existence of multiple desires creates the dilemma of alternatives, and questioning as a way of resolving the dilemmas and making choices. The existence of many propositions in relation to each other creates the need for questions, but once questioning has emerged as an activity of mind, propositional thought exists in relation to this new context. Although, then, propositions exist and have some kind of meaning at a level of consciousness below that at which questioning emerges, it is only once questioning has emerged that our propositions can properly express our desires as choices. The process of questioning and answering makes our choices properly choices, and propositions properly propositions.[8] We have made choices, when we have made any statement whatsoever. Collingwood put this point emphatically in *An Essay on Metaphysics*, where he proposed that '*Every statement that anybody ever makes is made in answer to a question.*' By this proposition, Collingwood asserted principally the logical priority of questions, maintaining that the temporal priority of questioning occurred only in structured 'scientific' thought, rather than

[7]   Ibid. paras. 14.1-14.3.
[8]   This suggests that Donagan's criticism of Collingwood's view that propositions need contexts, and that these are supplied by question and answer complexes, as contrary to his own account of mind, is misplaced. See Alan Donagan, *The Later Philosophy of R. G. Collingwood*. Clarendon Press, Oxford, 1962. pp. 55-56.

in most unscientific thought — for which he gave an example of practical reason.[9]
Within Collingwood's theory of process, mind develops as a qualitatively new kind of process or existence, and rational thought is itself an emergent level in the development of mind. Collingwood's theory of logic was part of this account of mind and process. In this respect, it might appear that he had abandoned one of the major directions of logic in the late nineteenth and twentieth centuries — the separation of logic from psychology. During the past century, the dominant forms of logic have been based on a sharp distinction between logic and psychology. This distinction has been reflected in realism as well as idealism, and in formal and informal logic. Modern logic has been concerned, amongst other issues, with the formal validity of arguments, and implication has been one of its primary areas of focus. John Passmore has suggested that a crucial issue for logicians in the late nineteenth and early twentieth centuries was whether logic should be concerned with 'inference', and therefore with the 'human activity of inferring', or with 'implication', and therefore 'the formal relationship of implying'.[10] Among those who thought that logic must be concerned with inference were the British philosophers Bradley and Bosanquet, the German philosopher Lotze, and the Americans C. S. Peirce and John Dewey. The realist revolt against idealist metaphysics included the rejection by philosophers such as Moore, Russell and Whitehead, at Cambridge, and Cook Wilson at Oxford, of the term 'judgement' in favour of the term 'proposition', in order to drive away what they saw as remnants of psychology in idealist logic.[11]

[9]   R. G. Collingwood, *An Essay on Metaphysics. Revised Edition With The Nature of Metaphysical Study; Function of Metaphysics in Civilization; Notes for an Essay on Logic. Edited with an Introduction by Rex Martin.* Clarendon Press, Oxford, 1998. pp. 23-4. (Emphasis in original.)
[10]   John Passmore, *A Hundred Years of Philosophy. Second edition.* Penguin, Harmondsworth, 1980. p. 173.
[11]   James Patrick has suggested that to Edwardian idealists at Oxford, their 'emphasis upon unity of mind and experience was grounded in the conviction that logic and psychology were inseparable; that the truth of propositions enjoyed reality only as the content and function of some mind.' James Patrick, *The Magdalen Metaphysicals: Idealism and Orthodoxy at Oxford, 1901-1945.* Mercer University Press, Macon, 1985. p. 86. Patrick's views about the relationship between logic and psychology in the idealists may seem, at first, to be somewhat overstated. C. R. Morris pointed out that the discipline and techniques of logic were 'jealously distinguished from those of empirical psychology.' C. R. Morris, *Idealistic Logic: A Study of its Aim, Method and Achievement.* Macmillan, London, 1933. p. 1. Nevertheless, Patrick's study makes it clear that the need to distin-

Collingwood saw Bradley as a critic of nineteenth-century philosophers such as Hamilton and Mansel who had privileged psychology and raised it to a branch of metaphysics.[12] For Bradley himself, logic was never concerned with ideas as 'psychical events', but solely with 'an ideal content which is universal, and which assuredly is not the mental fact.'[13] Bradley also maintained that psychology and logic are different but one-sided studies of the same object.[14] Logic and psychology were, in this respect, like all other abstractions from concrete fact. Bernard Bosanquet, in turn, differentiated psychology from logic in that psychology dealt with 'the course of ideas and feelings' whereas logic concerned 'the mental construction of reality.'[15] The separation of logic and psychology could never be complete within such frameworks, because each was only an abstraction from a concrete unified whole. Only with the abandonment of such a conception could the separation become radical and complete, so it was only with the onset of realism in the early twentieth century that the distinction between psychology and logic became radical for much British philosophy.

The distinction between logic and psychology was followed into the definition of logic. For Bradley, Bosanquet and Joachim, logic could be concerned with the conditions of knowledge. In this case, logic could examine the nature of thinking in the sciences, the relationship of each type of thinking (and thereby each science) with each other, and their relationship to the activity of mind as a whole. In that way, logical analysis could lead to criticism of the adequacy of various sciences, showing the need for more reflection or of other kinds of reflection, such as metaphysics.[16] The demise of the various forms of idealism as significant movements in the English-speaking world meant the demise of their logic. Realism and the various movements that came in its wake rejected the idea of the concrete whole, and asserted a stronger distinction between psychology and logic. Consequently, for the greater part of the past century, logic has been developed on different foundations and with methods differ-

guish the two disciplines was intensified because idealistic logic had within it a strong empirical element.

[12] R. G. Collingwood, 'The Metaphysics of F. H. Bradley: An Essay on *Appearance and Reality*', December, 1933. [Unpublished manuscript formerly in the possession of Mrs Teresa Smith, subsequently placed with the Collingwood papers in the Bodleian Library, Oxford.] pp. 10-13.
[13] F. H. Bradley, *The Principles of Logic. Second edition.* Oxford University Press, Oxford, 1922. Vol. I, p. 14.
[14] Ibid. Vol. II, p. 613.
[15] Bernard Bosanquet, *The Essentials of Logic.* Macmillan, London, 1895. p. 4.
[16] Morris, *Idealistic Logic.* pp. 6-8.

ent from those of Bradley, Bosanquet or Joachim. The strong distinction between psychology and logic has barred logic from the consideration of any mental aspect of thought. To the extent that logic was defined as concerned with the validity of arguments, this involved a denial that there was anything mental which made for the validity of thoughts.

An important aspect of thought neglected when logic is fully separated from psychology is movement, passage or transition in thoughts, other than through deduction or a dialectic considered to be inherent in the concepts themselves. The modern distinction between logic and psychology has separated logic from thought. This leaves the ordinary activity called thought, of which logic is not the study, alongside formal validity — which is studied by logic but is not related to an ordinary activity of mind. A psychology that studied the mental aspects of our ordinary activities would not fill the gap. For such a study would leave out precisely those aspects of thought that Collingwood, in particular, held to be most important, the fact that thought involves knowledge and that our thinking is 'criteriological' — it operates with internal criteria of success.

An account of thought must consider its dynamic (or 'dialectical') elements; in this respect, it is unlike an account of validity in formal languages. But an account of movement in thought involves an account of the structure of thought, and this requires us to use logical concepts such as 'relation'. Similarly, to account for movement in thought is to discuss mind. In brief, an account of thought needs both logical (structural) elements and elements which relate to the nature of mind; it must be both broadly empirical and focused on universal or necessary elements within thought. But what are the elements that need to be joined in order to give an account of thought? To foreshadow the next chapter, the broad approach taken by Collingwood in his logic of question and answer was to join a specific account of logical structures with an historical conception of mind. If, then, all history is the history of thought, and logic is an account of thought, then logic accounts for historical processes.

What logic is, and what scope it has, is itself a philosophical issue. The claim that something is or is not logic is sufficiently problematic that Susan Haack has proposed the pragmatic criterion of resemblance to classical logic as a way to delimit the field.[17] Haack has noted that 'practically every non-standard "logic" has, at some time, been subject to criticism on the ground that it isn't really a logic at

---

[17] Susan Haack, *Philosophy of Logics*, Cambridge University Press, Cambridge, 1978. p. 4.

all'.[18] Such criteria suggest that what is primarily at stake in arguments about the definition of logic is a claim to inherit a mantle of authority over reasoning once held by the theory of Aristotle. Under the cover of that mantle have been a number of aspirations: to universality, to supply criteria of proof and disproof in the absence of a particular subject matter, or to develop a rigorous system which may describe or, alternatively, regulate intellectual practices. Collingwood sought the cover of this mantle by claiming that the theory of question and answer he developed was logic.

The field of logic can, however, be delimited in a different way, by determining its relationship and function within an overall approach to philosophy. In Collingwood's case, there was a need for a theory of thought within the framework of his theory of mind and process. In this respect, Collingwood sought to overcome the separation of eternal objects and processes that was present in different ways in Hegel, for whom the dialectic was a dialectic of concepts, and Whitehead, who distinguished eternal objects from processes. Whitehead, in particular, retained his logic of propositions at the same time as he developed a metaphysics and ontology of process. Yet Whitehead himself was critical of the influence of static, Aristotelian, accounts of logic that emphasised 'substantives and adjectives, to the neglect of prepositions and conjunctions.' As Whitehead also put this point, since what is actual is process there is no need for an 'antecedent static cabinet.'[19] By retaining a propositional logic, however, Whitehead had retained within his own philosophy a logic that was not expressive of process. Collingwood sought to overcome precisely this difficulty.

As with all the various logical reformers of the late nineteenth and early twentieth centuries, a crucial issue in Collingwood's approach to logic was the relationship between logic and psychology. How he came to his conclusions about the relationship was fundamental to what he took the relationship to be. In this respect then, tracing the evolution of Collingwood's thought is important to establishing the nature of his argument. Like the idealists, and unlike the realists, Collingwood's account of the world as process meant that there could be no absolute distinction between mental events and logical structures. Unlike the idealists, the issue of movement in thought was crucial to Collingwood because he conceived of the world as process, and human being as human acting. For Collingwood, there-

[18] Ibid. p. 7.
[19] A. N. Whitehead, *Adventures of Ideas*. (1933) Reprinted by Macmillan, New York, 1952. p. 356.

fore, there was also a unity between the psychological and the logical, though he was to take different views as to what form the unity would take. As his thought developed, he came to see the unity in a historicised form.

As early as 'Truth and Contradiction', Collingwood had emphasised the active character of thought and truth, though the fact that only one chapter has survived from this manuscript limits its use as a general statement of his position. Amongst Collingwood's unpublished manuscripts there is, however, one titled 'Draft of opening chapters of a *Prolegomena to Logic (or the like)'*, from 1920-1921.[20] The manuscript discussed 'the search for a concept of thought' and 'the search for a concept of Logic'. When taken as a criticism of certain conceptions in logic and psychology, the manuscript appears to be fairly complete; but it is incomplete in the sense that it did not include much in the way of a positive statement of Collingwood's own views.

Collingwood discussed the relationship between logic and psychology under the heading of 'the search for a concept of logic'. He argued for the identity of logic and psychology in a particular sense. Collingwood contrasted a conception of logic as the 'theory of thought as the unmoving contemplation of the unmoving reality', namely logic as a static study of thought, and the reality of process or 'mental change', commonly called 'thinking', and studied by psychology. He remarked that, although it might be expected that logic would deal with the process of thinking, 'the process of so-called thinking is quietly set aside by the logician', who undertakes to study something else, namely thought, 'a perfectly quiescent state of apprehension.'[21] The criticism of 'quiescent apprehension' was a standard part of Collingwood's critique of realism, though he did not make the point explicitly in this case.

Collingwood then raised the issue of the relationship between thought and thinking. The first alternative he considered was that thinking is a 'process preliminary to thought', a series of changes which are required in order to achieve knowledge. The important point to be made about this answer is that thinking is not knowledge, but it is action, and that this kind of action has value only as leading to knowledge. On this first account, psychology is a science of the

---

[20] R. G. Collingwood, 'Draft of opening chapters of a *Prolegomena to Logic (or the like)'*, (1920-1921). [Bodleian Library, Dep. 16.] (Emphasis in original.)
[21] Ibid. p. 41.

process, leading to knowledge, called thinking.[22] But Collingwood argued that there could not be such a science of thinking.

The plausibility of the distinction between thought and thinking comes from conceiving mind as at some point lacking contact with reality, and therefore needing to undergo a process in order to come into contact with reality or to achieve knowledge. This point had within it echoes of Henry Jones' argument that idealism did not need an epistemology because its ontology did not separate entirely from one another the knower and the known.[23] A similar criticism would apply to the argument that 'reality hides behind a veil' and that we have to pass through the veil in some way. Collingwood's own response to such an argument was, firstly, that to perceive the veil is also to perceive reality, and that the mind cannot be 'any more or less in contact with reality' at any one moment than at any other moment. Secondly, picking up a dilemma from Plato's *Meno*, Collingwood argued that unless mind already has some knowledge of 'the nature of reality, the process of thinking in order to acquire such knowledge cannot begin: if it *has* knowledge, the process is obviously not necessary.'[24]

Collingwood also rejected the idea that thinking might be a process moving in series with different states of thought. If that were so, a process of thinking would follow each thought; in turn, this would lead to a new thought, and so on. In brief, thought and will alternate. But, once a cognitive state has passed, to be replaced by action or volition, there is no reason why action should ever lead to another cognitive state. Collingwood argued that on the theory he criticised action could never produce thought.[25]

The conclusion to be drawn from these considerations was that there could be no science of thinking as distinct from thought. If action does not lead to thought, then only cognitive states join with cognitive states, and volitional states with volitional states; in that case, there is no reason to talk of any separate process of 'thinking' at all. Up until this point, Collingwood had investigated the distinction commonly made between two 'aspects of thought', studied by two sciences. The first, logic, was to be concerned with 'thought as true'. This involved abstracting thought from all process. The second science, psychology, was to study the process by which 'thought

[22]   Ibid. pp. 42-43.
[23]   Henry Jones, 'Idealism and Epistemology (I)', *Mind*. New Series. Vol. II, No. 7, July 1893, pp. 289-306.
[24]   Collingwood, 'Draft of opening chapters of a *Prolegomena to Logic (or the like)*.' p. 48. (Emphasis in original.)
[25]   Ibid. p. 54.

changes, alters, develops'. This involved abstracting thought from all questions of truth. The result of such attempts to distinguish logic and psychology was to show that, when logic and psychology are each treated as the 'absolute antithesis' of the other, the 'antithesis tends on closer inspection to disappear.' Collingwood used such arguments in the 'Libellus'; the same form of argument was now being applied specifically to logic. What, in fact, logic had treated abstractly 'as a special cross-section' of thought 'is really a temporal segment which takes time to traverse in thought.'[26]

Concluding his paper, Collingwood argued that psychology and logic could not, in practice, be separated, 'for the whole of logic is simply the psychology of scientific thought.' In addition, he argued that 'traditional formal logic is simply an attempt to describe what we do when we say that we are thinking.'[27] As such, logical formulations can be criticised in the light of existing empirical practices. In *An Autobiography*, Collingwood maintained that his archaeological work led him to the development of his views of logic.[28] This association was important, because if the case for a particular logic is principally that it has a role within an overall philosophical approach, to reject the premise of the overall theory is also to reject the logic. Relating logic to an existing practice provides, by contrast, independent grounds for criticism. As early as 1920 or 1921, Collingwood could have argued that the emergence of historical practice had led to a new logic; that he did not do so simply reflected the fact that his historical practices and his philosophy were both still developing. The fact that historical practice, in particular, served as the empirical touchstone for logic enabled Collingwood to continue to relate logic to his overall philosophical focus on process.

As his philosophy of mind developed, Collingwood drew stronger distinctions between the psyche, studied by psychology, and the realm of practical and theoretical reason. His 1920 and 1921 account of the unity of the psychological and the logical was not, therefore, complete. The psyche and rational thought are different levels of consciousness. One emerges out of the other, as a later stage in the development of consciousness. Psychology, for Collingwood, was principally a study of 'psyche' or 'immediacy', not 'reason' and 'mediation'. Thought, though, involves internal definitions of success and failure, which Collingwood described as the 'criteriological'

[26] Ibid. pp. 56-58.
[27] Ibid p. 59.
[28] R. G. Collingwood, *An Autobiography*. Oxford University Press, London, 1939. p. 30.

nature of thought. Psychology and logic cannot simply be joined together. What Collingwood's arguments did show was the necessity for the processive and dynamic character of thought to be conjoined with the structural elements. But, in his early writings, Collingwood wrongly identified the dynamic character of thought as a matter of psychology. Rather, his philosophy of mind posited that the dynamic character of mind is present in different forms at different levels of consciousness. Mind is dynamic in one way at the level of competing desires, but the rational thought which emerges as a way to solve the problem of competing desires must display a different kind of dynamic. Collingwood could not, therefore, maintain his position of 1920 and 1921.

Towards the end of his life, Collingwood suggested that history supplied the features of the science of thought he had previously attributed to psychology. In his brief 'Notes on Historiography', written while he was on board ship to and from the East Indies in late 1938 and early 1939, Collingwood wrote that logic, along with other philosophical sciences such as ethics, was an historical science. Collingwood remarked, in language similar to that in the earlier 'Prolegomena' that 'all that any logician has ever done, or tried to do, is to expound the principles of what in his own day passed for valid thought among those whom he regarded as reputable thinkers. This enterprise is strictly historical.' The major point he wished to attack was 'that validity in thought is at all times one and the same, no matter how people are at various times actually in the habit of thinking.'[29] The latter point represented a major divergence from his earlier views; there cannot be a science of thought, joining logic and psychology, if validity and process are considered timeless. To the extent that psychology professes to study mental processes as if they are natural or timeless, it must be replaced by an historical approach, and logic must be thoroughly historicised.

In light of Collingwood's later remarks about history and logic, it is now possible to redefine the significance of the nineteenth- and twentieth-century debates about the relationship between logic and psychology. We can now see these debates not simply as a question about the fate of psychology, but about the severing of logic from empirical considerations. Divorced from some relationship to empirical materials logic could not be anything other than a formal

---

[29] R. G. Collingwood, 'Notes on Historiography written on a voyage to the East Indies 1938-9', printed in R. G. Collingwood, *The Principles of History: and other writings in philosophy of history. Edited with an introduction by W. H. Dray and W. J. van der Dussen.* Oxford University Press, Oxford, 1999. p. 242.

study. It would be of no moment that there exist formal studies of propositions and their relationships if these did not claim the universal status of logic. As long as that claim is maintained, there are implications from the theory back into other areas of thought and action. Logic, therefore, does not stand apart from other areas of philosophy. Instead, it is important that logic be scrutinised in the light of how it relates to other theories and activities.

Distinguishing logic from psychology need not have led to the outright rejection of an empirical basis for logical studies. Rather, because of the traditional focus of logic on reason and argument, there were clear alternatives and precedents available within the tradition. As we shall see in the next chapter, both Collingwood and John Dewey took (different) empirical relationships up into their accounts of logic. Dewey and Collingwood each started from the idea that the conception of the world, and the concrete activities of mind, had developed since the time of Aristotle and that logic must change with them. For Dewey, scientific inquiry provided the lodestone, while for Collingwood it was archaeology and history. These differences do not, however, obscure the fact that each was offering a genuinely different account of the purpose of logic. In each case, the role of logic was not to be a technical study of formal elements of language and reason, but a theory of systemic activities of contemporary mind in action. Conceived in this way, logic is not of marginal relevance but a foundation for other theories and a tool for other practices. Logic developed on such lines must be tested against whether it enables the further development of the same systematic activities of mind it sets out to describe.

Whereas idealist logicians had proposed an unstable and incomplete distinction between psychology and logic, and realist logicians and their descendants maintained a radical distinction between the two, Collingwood strongly opposed each of these approaches. He had initially tried to argue for the identity of logic and psychology in a single science of thought, a view he later rejected. Collingwood subsequently sought to replace the unity of logic and psychology with a science of thought that should encompass processes as well as structures, and in which thought was seen as developing historically. Finally, Collingwood provided an empirical point of reference for logic in historical practice. In the light of Collingwood's concerns reviewed in this chapter, it seems likely that the inability of his many critics to understand the 'logic of question and answer' is based on deeper differences about the role and scope of logic. The most common criticism of Collingwood's theory of question and answer has been that it is not logic. Indeed, it would be more accurate to portray the theory as an attempt to redefine the role, scope and content of logic. How far Collingwood's theory met that goal will be considered in the next chapter.

CHAPTER 4

The Logic of Question and Answer

In this chapter, I will set out a theory that has had many critics and few supporters. Collingwood put forward his theory that logic is concerned with complexes of questions and their answers in a small number of publications and manuscripts. Nevertheless, he saw his theory as a major challenge to the logic of his time that took propositions as the fundamental unit of analysis. The theory has been widely criticised, particularly by those who have denied that it represents any form of logic. The paucity of defenders can be partly attributed to the fact that Collingwood left his logic of question and answer in an undeveloped form. There is also room to speculate whether Collingwood maintained the theory of question and answer until his death.

One of the strongest features of Collingwood's logic of question and answer is its relative simplicity. Collingwood set out most of what he had to say on question and answer in a few non-technical pages of *An Autobiography*, *An Essay on Metaphysics* and *The New Leviathan*. A second key feature of the theory is its empirical foundations, which Collingwood found in the practice of archaeology and history. The power of the theory would, however, be limited if it provided an account of a single kind of activity, and not of others; if there was no universal character to question and answer relationships the theory would lack relevance and insight. Conversely, the theory is most interesting when it is taken to have a universal character and is seen as logic. In particular, treated in this way, the logic of question and answer is the logic of historical reality, as much as it is the logic of historical practice.

The power of treating the theory of question and answer as logic is that the theory thereby explicates and deepens the general perspective of a world of process. It was, however, John Dewey who provided perhaps the most developed form of logic for a world of process. Dewey predicated his *Logic: The Theory of Inquiry* on a scientific world-view that emphasised process rather than static essences.[1] In this chapter I will explore how Dewey's and Collingwood's theories can each illuminate and reinforce the other, although there is no evidence of any direct influence by one on the other. I will set out some of the main points of Collingwood's writing on logic, together with some of the criticisms that have been made of it. I will then turn to consider Dewey's views on logic. If we approach Collingwood's theory with the example of Dewey in mind, we can see, in a way that Collingwood only sketched, that the theory of question and answer is deeply opposed to any idea that logic is a self-sufficient discipline. Rather, for Dewey and for Collingwood, logic requires other, more general, theories to provide it with purpose and meaning. In turn, logic must contribute to the broader aims of philosophy. After considering Dewey, I will restate Collingwood's logic of question and answer in such a way as to draw out more explicitly some of the elements sketched by Collingwood. This will bring to the fore the important philosophical role that is played by Collingwood's logic.

Collingwood wrote and published very little on logic, but attached great importance to the things he did write. He made a number of bold pronouncements, and suggested that his views on logic were central to other aspects of his philosophy. For example, in *An Autobiography*, Collingwood wrote that

> In logic I am a revolutionary; and like other revolutionaries I can thank God for the reactionaries. They clarify the issues.[2]

The 'revolution' that Collingwood thought he had achieved involved the replacement of a logic based upon propositions with the theory of questions and answers. Such claims for the importance of his own work have been distracting to critics and serve to hide Collingwood's reasoning.

---

[1] John Dewey, *Logic: The Theory of Inquiry.* John Dewey, The Later Works, 1925-1953. Volume 12: 1938. Southern Illinois University Press, Carbondale, 1991.

[2] R. G. Collingwood, *An Autobiography.* Oxford University Press, London, 1939. p. 52.

On Collingwood's theory, the proper unit of thought cannot be the proposition or statement, but is 'a complex consisting of questions and answers.'[3] He sought to replace the unit of logical analysis, but behind this lay an account of the purpose of logic. As we saw in the previous chapter, for Collingwood logic is a theory of thought. In Collingwood's account of mind, to ask a question is to undertake an activity where one of a set of alternatives is chosen; the chosen alternative answers the question. In particular, reflecting the idea that thought is primarily practical and only secondly theoretical, answers take form in human action initially as the choice of what is desired. Choice amongst alternatives involves proposition or assertion. Collingwood maintained that knowledge at its simplest level is the reaffirmation of a proposition resulting from reflection on the adequacy of the process through which the proposition was first made. It follows that knowledge depends on how questions are put and amongst what alternatives a choice is made. It follows also that there is no knowledge unless a genuine choice is made and this choice is tested in reflection.

Idealist logicians and philosophers, including Bradley and Bosanquet, had distinguished statements and their meaning from meaning in the eyes of those who utter the statement. For the idealists, the field of logic was the meaning of a statement or 'judgement' rather than that intended by the person. By contrast with the idealists, Collingwood argued that meaning, agreement, contradiction, and truth and falsity do not belong to propositions, statements or judgements.[4] His criticism of the idealistic logic was that it presented a confused mixture mainly consisting of propositional logic, but with elements of the logic of question and answer.[5] If the fundamental unit of thought was the question and answer complex, then it was inconsistent to treat judgements as the central unit of analysis.[6] Idealist logicians could not adopt a fully-fledged logic of question and answer because they lacked a theory of the systematic nature of

---

[3] Ibid. pp. 34, 37.
[4] Ibid. p. 33.
[5] Ibid. p. 52.
[6] This inconsistency is seen very clearly in C. R. Morris's summary of the idealist logic as it had developed by the early 1930s, particularly in the work of Bradley, Bosanquet and Joachim. Morris found in Kant the doctrine that the success of modern physics depended on 'putting nature to the question and extracting answers from her'. Morris even presaged Collingwood's language by asserting that '[e]very judgment is in truth an answer to a question'. Nevertheless, the idealistic logic he described remained a logic of 'judgements'. C. R. Morris, *Idealistic Logic: A Study of its Aim, Method and Achievement*. Macmillan, London, 1933. pp. 117, 157.

questioning.[7] A more recent perspective on the idealistic logic is that it was also incomplete. In particular, Graham McFee has argued that Bradley saw propositions as context dependent, in marked contrast to others such as Russell who saw propositions as independent of context and the sense and force of sentences as being clearly distinct. Bradley, however, did not provide an account of context dependence. McFee saw Collingwood's theory of question and answer as providing just such an account of context dependence, thereby challenging the idea that sense and force are distinct.[8]

There could not, on Collingwood's view, be any real distinction between 'utterer's meaning' and 'sentence meaning' because such a distinction presupposed the wrong unit of analysis. If the real unit of analysis is the question and answer complex, then any hard distinction between 'utterer's meaning' and 'question and answer complex meaning' becomes difficult to sustain. By focusing on complexes of questions and answers, Collingwood was drawn to emphasise 'what a man means', rather than the meaning of statements. It was at such points that Collingwood appeared most concerned with hermeneutics. From this perspective, it is not possible to ascertain 'what a man means by simply studying his spoken or written words'. Rather

> In order to find out his meaning you must also know what the question was (a question in his own mind and presumed by him to be in yours) to which the thing he has said or written was meant as an answer.[9]

Collingwood's account forces a claim about the meaning of a specific utterance to be supported by analysis of something beyond the language in which the utterance is made. The additional element needed to support a claim about what a statement means has to be discovered, but Collingwood thought that the form of that further element is described by the relationship between a question and an answer. The proper way to discover meaning is, on Collingwood's view in *An Autobiography*, by the use of 'historical methods.'[10] In this

---

[7]   Morris's discussion showed up other possible inconsistencies. He suggested that any particular question is insufficiently determined if seen only within the context of other questions. In order to determine which question we actually answer, Morris invoked 'the general laws of the mind and the particular mental context.' This approach opened up logic to psychology in a way that was quite inconsistent with the general aim of idealist logic. Ibid. p. 157.

[8]   Graham McFee, 'Bradley, Possibility and a Question-and-Answer Logic', in *Perspectives on the Logic and Metaphysics of F. H. Bradley*. (Edited by W. J. Mander). Thoemmes Press, Bristol, 1996. pp. 269-287. See pp. 277, 280-281.

[9]   Collingwood, *An Autobiography*. p. 31.

[10] Ibid. p. 39.

respect, the 'logic of question and answer' makes logical form analysable by assimilating it to the most appropriate science.

Collingwood's logic of question and answer was set firmly within his account of systematic, or scientific, thinking. In *An Essay on Metaphysics*, Collingwood clearly distinguished scientific thinking (including history) from unscientific thinking along the lines of the degree of conscious questioning that exists in each case and the relative orderliness of progression from one question to another question.[11] To the extent that we are thinking systematically, which question we ask and answer depends entirely upon which questions we asked and answered beforehand. Collingwood also made a distinction between a question 'verbally asked' and a question 'logically asked'; for to say that a scientist asks and answers particular questions does not mean that scientific thought depends on a particular verbal structure. Once distinguished from verbal form, the scope of the logic of question and answer can be more clearly seen. Collingwood argued, for example, that any 'problematic' statement involves questioning.[12] Psychology might well explain the occurrence of a verbal question, but this did not mean it had identified or explained the question being logically asked.

Some of the criticisms made of Collingwood's logic depend on ignoring his distinction between logical and verbal structure. A. J. Ayer remarked, for example, that it is 'plainly false' to maintain, as Collingwood did, that 'every statement ever made is made in answer to a question'. Ayer also rejected the idea that every question has a presupposition.[13] Such comments were echoed more recently by James Somerville, who observed that '[a]s a plain matter of fact, not all statements people make are made in answer to a question.'[14] This observation might be granted as long as questions are treated as verbal entities. But Collingwood himself had been careful to distinguish the issue of the verbal form of questions from the logical form of questions, and temporal priority from logical priority. To argue, with Ayer and Somerville, that some statements are made without answering a question is to pursue a linguistic issue but ignore the claim that there is a logical issue. To make the same point in terms of

[11] R. G. Collingwood, *An Essay on Metaphysics. Revised Edition With The Nature of Metaphysical Study; Function of Metaphysics in Civilization; Notes for an Essay on Logic.* Edited with an Introduction by Rex Martin. Clarendon Press, Oxford, 1998. pp. 23, 36-38.

[12] Ibid. pp. 274-275.

[13] A. J. Ayer, *Philosophy in the Twentieth Century.* Unwin, London, 1984. p. 198.

[14] James Somerville, 'Collingwood's Logic of Question and Answer', *The Monist.* Vol. 72, No. 4, October 1989, pp. 526-541. See p. 537.

Collingwood's broader philosophy of mind, we would have to argue that people do not choose amongst alternatives when they desire something, and this seems a more difficult point to sustain. Indeed, as we shall see later in this chapter, the current tendency to treat questions as sets of their possible answers has some affinities to Collingwood's focus on choice amongst alternatives.

Somerville also claimed that Collingwood 'failed to distinguish a question from a problem.' In Somerville's view, problems can be expressed through questions, but 'not all questions pose problems.'[15] This criticism might appear to hold for questions as verbal structures, in the sense that I may utter some words in such a way that it sounds as though I have asked a question when I am just uttering words in a certain format. In this case, there seems to be no problem needing to be resolved. To use Collingwood's terminology, no question has arisen in this case, and so my words are not expressing a question at all. If we accept, as Collingwood did, a distinction between the verbal form of questions and their logical form, then there is no difficulty in the relationship between questions and problems. Rather, questions arise only when there is a problem needing attention. We could argue, against Somerville, that even the simplest forms of question, those involving 'yes' or 'no' answers, or less complex 'wh' questions such as 'which' or 'what', present a problem of choice.

Questioning can be done in a desultory manner or systematically. In Collingwood's terms, as the process of questioning and answering becomes more rigorous, it becomes scientific.[16] To be scientific is to pay particular attention to the relationship between the question and the adequacy of the answer. This requires the question to be well formed and the answer to be precisely related to the question. Further, the process of assurance must be undertaken with equivalent rigour, leading more truly to knowledge. The activity of question and answer is nevertheless constant in all thought that involves alternatives. In so far as it involves propositions or assertions, every statement involves a choice and arises from a question. Reflecting the differences inherent between scientific thinking and everyday forms of thought, there are also degrees of consciousness about the specific question being asked and as to whether a question is being asked at all.[17]

---

[15] Ibid. p. 538.
[16] Collingwood, *An Essay on Metaphysics*. pp. 22-23.
[17] Ibid. pp. 23-24.

There are limitations to how far the question and answer complex can be decomposed into other units. Collingwood was not consistent in identifying the components of the complex. In *An Autobiography*, he wrote as if there were only two terms — questions and answers.[18] In *An Essay on Metaphysics*, he maintained that each question has a presupposition, which stands in a logical relationship to that question and causes it to arise.[19] Some presuppositions are themselves questions, but others, which he there called 'absolute presuppositions' are neither questions nor answers. A short set of notes on logic which Collingwood wrote in 1938-1939 similarly recognised questions, propositions which answer those questions, and suppositions which can give rise to questions and may be related to other suppositions.[20] The theory propounded in *The New Leviathan* recognised alternatives, but only the chosen or desired alternative (and the objects of aversion) is properly an answer or proposition.

While it would be possible to see the different accounts of the unit of logic that Collingwood had given as evidence of the unfinished nature of his theory, this would miss a key point, for each of the elements of the theory situated the logic of question and answer in a different context. Collingwood's logic was linked into a broader theory of mind by the place of question and answer in desire and aversion. Likewise, the theory of presuppositions is an element in the relationship between complexes of questions and answers and, through the theory of absolute presuppositions, was related to Collingwood's metaphysics. The correlative nature of questions and answers, and the relations between complexes, reveal an historical character, which itself means that Collingwood's metaphysics is necessarily historical.

Collingwood envisaged that it would be possible to reinterpret traditional logical concerns such as the nature of truth and contradiction and the categories of quality, quantity, relation and modality in light of the proposed new unit of analysis.[21] Propositions cannot themselves be true — only the question and answer complexes in which they are involved can be true. The logic of question and

---

[18] Collingwood, *An Autobiography*. pp. 29-43.

[19] Collingwood, *An Essay on Metaphysics*. pp. 21-22, 25-27.

[20] R. G. Collingwood, 'Notes for an Essay on Logic', in Collingwood, *An Essay on Metaphysics*, pp. 422-427.

[21] For Collingwood's explicit treatment of truth and contradiction, see Chapter 1 of this study and Collingwood's *An Autobiography*, pp. 33-39; 'Truth and Contradiction: Chapter 2', (1917), [Bodleian Library, Dep. B16]; and 'Notes for an Essay on Logic', in Collingwood, *An Essay on Metaphysics. Revised Edition*, p. 426.

answer, therefore, involved the rejection of both main theories of truth current in Collingwood's time. The correspondence theory of truth must be rejected because question and answer complexes cannot merely correspond to facts. The coherence theory of truth must be rejected because it is a theory of the relationship between propositions alone. On Collingwood's account, only complexes of questions and answers can be true.[22] In his historical practice, which he took to be indicative of the proper meaning of truth, Collingwood emphasised truth in history as conclusive argument, based on exhaustive interpretation of evidence, to answer a specific question. The concept of truth applies to historical claims about absolute presuppositions, but not to the presuppositions themselves.

Collingwood's claim to be a revolutionary in logic has generated criticism but not genuine controversy. The responses to Collingwood's claims have tended to fall into a number of camps — 'this simply isn't logic', 'this isn't logic, but it might be something else' or 'this isn't logic, but some elements might be relevant to logic'. While these responses are in no way variations on a single theme, they do share some important similarities. Firstly, each starts out from an idea of what logic is. Most commonly, the assumption is that logic is a study concerned with propositions, truth and proof. Alan Donagan, for example, described Collingwood's account of the logic of question and answer in *An Autobiography* as 'an embarrassment'.[23] For the most part, Donagan dealt with Collingwood's claims to have developed a 'revolutionary logic' by restating key elements of modern propositional logic. Donagan singled out Collingwood's claim that, to propositional logicians, every indicative sentence in a well-constructed language expresses only one proposition, which is true or false. Against that claim, Donagan argued that propositional logicians have no necessary commitment to an ideal language, and that some indicative sentences may express no proposition at all, while the same proposition may be expressed by several indicative sentences.[24]

More recently, Rex Martin has claimed that Collingwood's late manuscript 'Notes on Logic', although it addresses questions and answers, contains 'no *logic* of question and answer'. The reason for

---

[22] We have previously seen that in 'Truth and Contradiction: Chapter 2' Collingwood developed a holism about truth as an activity of comprehending views that start outside each other — a view that implies the existence of complexes similar to those articulated in the theory of question and answer.

[23] Alan Donagan, *The Later Philosophy of R. G. Collingwood*. Clarendon Press, Oxford, 1962. p. 56.

[24] Ibid. pp. 58-59.

this is that the notes do not contain the 'claim that either the meaning or the truth of an assertion is logically dependent on the question it is said to be answering.'[25] Martin, therefore, identified the existence of a universal claim about meaning or truth, similar to that made in *An Autobiography*, as a criterion for logic.

A second way to interpret Collingwood's theory has been to say that it is hermeneutics, rather than logic. Louis Mink, in particular, was careful to dampen Collingwood's claim to be a revolutionary in the field of logic. Mink's main point was that the 'logic of question and answer' was not logic at all but 'reflection on logic' or a 'theory of the process of inquiry'.[26] For Mink, the logic of question and answer should not be assimilated to logic but to hermeneutics, the theory of interpretation.[27] Mink was right to point out that Collingwood's theory relates to inquiry, but this is not itself enough to reject the idea that it remains a system of logic. Mink's reason for disregarding the claims of the logic of question and answer was that the theory is not concerned with proof but with discovery.[28] This seems to miss the general point of Collingwood's criticism, that what counts as proof is specific to the activity.

A third and potentially fruitful way to interpret Collingwood's claim to be a revolutionary in logic is as simply one amongst many attempts in the twentieth century to define an alternative logic with three truth-values (in this case, true, false and absolutely presupposed).[29] Interpreted in this way, his theory is a precursor to other theories, although not necessarily much of a challenge to the major logical theories of the twentieth century.

Since the 1950s, sophisticated accounts of question and answer have been developed within an overall logic concerned with statements and propositions. Collingwood's account of question and answer, then, might be seen as a precursor to this more recent and fulsome work. A number of writers, including Belnap, Hamblin and

---

[25] Rex Martin, 'Introduction' to Collingwood, *An Essay on Metaphysics*. p. lxxxi. (Emphasis in original.)

[26] Louis O. Mink, *Mind, History, and Dialectic: The Philosophy of R. G. Collingwood*. Indiana University Press, Bloomington, 1969. [Reprinted by Wesleyan University Press, Middletown, 1987.] p. 123.

[27] Ibid. p. 131.

[28] Ibid. p. 124.

[29] This interpretation appears, for example, in R. A. Young, 'Collingwood's Logic of Questions and Answers', *Bradley Studies*. Vol. 3, No. 2, Autumn 1997. pp. 151-175. See p. 157.

Hintikka have contributed to this field.[30] The logic of questions has also been applied in analytical philosophy of science by writers such as Bas van Fraassen, while the influence of Karl Popper led Joseph Agassi to emphasise questioning in science, and so to revisit Collingwood's logic.[31] To varying degrees, these writers recognised affinities or debts to Collingwood's work on the subject.

There are important differences between this more recent work and Collingwood's theories, and these need to be emphasised. Analytical philosophers such as Hintikka, Aggassi and van Fraassen have discussed the theory of questions most commonly as part of a theory of method or inquiry. Collingwood's theory necessarily included such concerns but, in my view, his aim in characterising his theory as logic went beyond those of inquiry. Collingwood's theory of questions is thus a more general theory than the majority of discussions in the analytical tradition, as well as those in the hermeneutical tradition.

A second major difference between analytical theories of questions and answers and those of Collingwood is the priority they give to propositions. In the analytical view, questions are interrogative sentences, just as propositions are expressed in declarative sentences.[32] Bas van Fraassen put the point directly, echoing Belnap: '[a] theory of questions must needs be based on a theory of propositions'.[33] Collingwood would agree that propositions are part of a theory of question and answer. He would, however, have disagreed with the implicit conclusion that the logic of questions is a corner of propositional logic that deals with a certain type of linguistic expression. The debate over questions, answers or propositions, is not simply about these units, but about what qualifies as logic, and priority amongst the concepts that form part of it.

Belnap and Steel have defined the meaning of questions as 'the range of answers that the question permits', explicitly distinguish-

[30] See, for example, Jaakko Hintikka, 'Questioning as a Philosophical Method', in *Principles of Philosophical Reasoning*. (Edited by J. H. Fetzer). Rowman and Allenheld, Totowa, 1984. pp. 25-43.

[31] Bas van Fraassen, *The Scientific Image*. Clarendon Press, Oxford, 1980; Joseph Agassi, 'Questions of Science and Metaphysics', *The Philosophical Forum*. New Series, Vol. 5, 1974. pp. 529-556. Popper's views on some theories of Collingwood can be found in Karl Popper, 'On the Theory of the Objective Mind', *Objective Mind: An Evolutionary Approach*. Revised edition. Clarendon Press, Oxford, 1979. pp. 153-190.

[32] C. L. Hamblin, for example, discussed whether all questions are imperatives, and the nature of imperative questions. C. L. Hamblin, *Imperatives*. Basil Blackwell, Oxford, 1987. pp. 27, 78-80, 201.

[33] van Fraassen, *The Scientific Image*. p. 137.

ing this approach from the idea that the meaning of a question is a process or programme.[34] On this view, answers select alternatives from a set.[35] Belnap and Steel aimed to formalise elementary questions such as 'whether' and 'which' that involve requests for information, and did not seek to formalise 'problem-solving situations' or 'requests to be freed of vague puzzlements'.[36] This approach assigns to 'whether' and 'which' questions the role of delimiting and retrieving information through true answers. The limits set by Belnap and Steel are important to the resulting theory. It is not clear, for example, that 'what', 'when', 'who' or 'why' questions, particularly if asked in an historical context, involve delimitation or retrieval of information. In such cases, the role of the question seems to be as much about formulating possible sets of answers as it is with limiting the set of possible answers, and has as much to do with the process of selecting an answer as with the answer selected. That is, at least in the case of historical thought, questioning involves the development and application of criteria of answerability, and so a question is not reducible to the set of statements that may meet those criteria.

More recently, analysis by Wisniewski has broadened the range of question-types to be considered, and in the process restored some of the concerns that are so evident in Collingwood's approach. Wisniewski sees questions as conclusions in inferential processes of thought, or as premises that lead to other questions.[37] Questions therefore arise in processes of questioning and answering, where we can pass by inference from a declarative sentence to a question, or from a question (with or without declarative sentences) to a further question.[38] For Wisniewski, there are three broad types of question. Firstly, there are those with '*finite sets of direct answers*', such as many 'yes' or 'no' questions.[39] Secondly, there are those with infinite sets of direct answers.[40] Thirdly, there are questions specifying in detail 'the number of entities called for'.[41] Wisniewski sought to formalize the notion that 'big questions' can be answered by asking 'smaller

[34] Nuel D. Belnap, Jr. and Thomas B. Steel, Jr., *The Logic of Questions and Answers*. Yale University Press, New Haven, 1976. p. 2.
[35] Ibid. pp. 34-35.
[36] Ibid. pp. 4-5, 11.
[37] Andrzej Wisniewski, *The Posing of Questions: Logical Foundations of Erotetic Inferences*. Kluwer Academic Publishers, Dordrecht, 1995. (Synthese Library, Volume 252.) p. xi.
[38] Ibid. pp. 2-4.
[39] Ibid. p. 74. (Emphasis in original.)
[40] Ibid. p. 75.
[41] Ibid. p. 80.

questions' arising from it in a series.[42] When an initial question is sound relative to 'previously accepted premises', and the 'smaller questions' implied by a 'big question' and other declarative premises are 'yes' or 'no' questions, the search for a correct answer takes place through the smaller questions.[43] Wisniewski also recognised that, even where direct answers are possible, questions need not seek for direct answers. Rather, what may be sought is the reasoning for a conclusion.[44] Wisniewski's work on questions therefore points back to broader issues of the role of logic within philosophy.

If we simply rejected Collingwood's account of question and answer, we would have avoided, rather than dealt with, his attempt to redefine the scope of logic. His broader project emphasised the relationship between logic and human activity, the place of logic as a part of philosophy, and the relevance of logic in illuminating other practices. On each point, Collingwood's approach was significantly broader than the traditional accounts of logic as concerning rules of argument. His theory differed from recent conceptions of logic that are built upon the analysis of certain features of language. His account of questions also differs significantly from recent analytical approaches to questions because of the emphasis it places on the activity of questioning. Collingwood's theory has affinities with that of John Dewey, who sought to provide empirical foundations for a broad reform of logic. Before re-assessing Collingwood's theory of question and answer, it is therefore useful to first consider Dewey's theory.

Dewey was inspired by the contemporary confusion in debates around logic to introduce a distinction between the 'ultimate' subject matter of logic, and its 'proximate' subject matter.[45] Dewey's distinction was between the ultimate how and why of logic as a study and the proximate units or means of logical analysis, such as propositions, affirmation and negation; the ultimate subject matter must account for the proximate subject matter. The criteria for what is to count as logic exist prior to the full development of a system of logic. In turn, the criteria for logic embody elements of a real practice, which exists prior to the theory. For Dewey, 'logic is a naturalistic theory' and 'a social discipline'.[46] In these terms, we can see that

---

[42]   Ibid. p. 189.
[43]   Ibid. pp. 191, 195.
[44]   Ibid. p. 90.
[45]   Dewey, *Logic: The Theory of Inquiry*. p. 9.
[46]   Ibid. p. 26.

Collingwood sought to offer an account of the ultimate subject of matter of logic that would lead to a new proximate subject matter. Neither Dewey nor Collingwood accepted the notion that distinguishing logic from psychology meant separating logic from empirical considerations. Rather, it meant seeking other ways to characterise the empirical foundations of logic. In each case, the role of logic was not that of a technical study of formal elements of language and reason, but that of a theory of systemic activities of contemporary mind in action. Conceived in this way, logic is not of marginal relevance but a foundation for other theories and a tool for other practices. Logic developed on such lines must be tested in terms of whether it enables the further development of the systematic activities of mind that it describes.

If we follow the idea that logic is naturalistic, we need, however, to identify the activities or experiences that form the basis for theory. These include the experience of rigorous thought and the identification and resolution of problems. They include also the development of our own ideas and practices, and the reality of the shared inheritance and development of ideas and practices amongst groups of people. If logic is naturalistic, it must give form to such experiences. The way in which it can do so is by showing the characteristics of the most developed examples of such activities — for Dewey this was natural science. For Collingwood, history was the most developed example of systematic thought that enables conclusions to be drawn from evidence, where the object of knowledge is past and so cannot be the subject of immediate apprehension.

Dewey's theory involved a concept of inquiry as activity; he explicitly rejected any notion of immediacy, and instead placed a strong emphasis on the existential origins and import of inquiry. In Dewey's theory, firstly, a real situation is problematic for a being. This is expressed as unease, leading to a need for resolution, and given conscious statement as a question. Secondly, there follows a process of exploring resolutions to the problem. This is an activity of conscious being and takes form as systematic inquiry, in which alternatives are rejected or accepted. Third, a resolution is found which may be more or less complete. The resolution is not simply a matter of theory, but of practice. The conscious expression of this resolution is as an affirmation. Finally, a new situation exists, in which the initial resolution is a constituent element and the process of resolution has changed the being that experienced unease.[47]

Dewey's theory might appear to allow psychological elements back into logic, but the same view can be presented without any such allusions. H. S. Leonard, for example, a key figure in the more recent development of the logic of questions, distinguished between practical and theoretical problems, and saw thought as one way in which problems can be approached (the others being trial and error and imitation). Logic is therefore a group of principles for using the method of thought in order to resolve problems.[48] On Leonard's view, thought begins by recognising a problem, moves through efforts to solve it, and leads to the adoption of beliefs that solve the problem. Analysing a problem begins 'by formulating it in a question.' A question, however, can be more or less adequate to the problem, and problems that are more complex can be seen as a series of connected questions.[49]

For Leonard, all questions, including 'yes or no', 'which' or 'what' questions, have presuppositions that serve as their necessary context. Unlike Collingwood, Leonard maintained that presuppositions, whether factual or formal, must be true in order for a question to be valid.[50] In Leonard's view, largely reflected in subsequent literature, the account of a question is framed around the kind of propositions that make the question decidable or enable an answer to it to be true. The account of problems, thought and questions therefore develops into an account of propositions. The requirement that presuppositions be true makes it difficult, however, to see how thought about what is distant, past, theoretical or postulated could also be rigorous on Leonard's terms. In addition, the requirement of truth makes it difficult to see how a complex problem that must be decomposed into a series of questions could ever be satisfactorily answered.

Dewey's theory gave a strong statement of the experiential origins of inquiry; the primary meaning of inquiry is practical, and the original situation, exploration, resolution and new situation are to be

[47] Ibid. pp. 108-120. Compare Dewey's view with Ortega's: 'To live, then, means always finding oneself immersed in specific circumstances and having to do something to keep one's head above water.' What man does in response to the confused circumstances he finds himself in, is construct a life-programme. Jose Ortega y Gasset, *Historical Reason*. (Translated by Philip W. Silver.) W. W. Norton, New York, 1984. p. 66.
[48] H. S. Leonard, *Principles of Reasoning. An Introduction to Logic, Methodology, and the Theory of Signs*. Dover, New York, 1967. pp. 4-7, 11.
[49] Ibid. pp. 22-24.
[50] Ibid. pp. 33-35, 37.

understood as real. The intention of the theory was to account for all activities, not just a narrow range.[51] In particular, Dewey portrayed inquiry as the controlled transformation of indeterminate situations into situations that are determinate and which convert the elements of the original situation into a unified whole.[52] In this respect, Dewey's account of inquiry was also focused on the complexes that arise from the activity of inquiry; Collingwood's theory of question and answer had a similar real basis in the activity of mind. Dewey's theory proposed that such complexes of activity take one central form. Although there is a close alignment between Dewey's theory of inquiry and the account of inquiry given by the theory of question and answer, one advantage of Collingwood's theory is that it does not require all activity to be defined as inquiry.

Because Collingwood's own work contains the elements of a theory of logic, but not the worked out theory itself, it is necessary to restate it. With one eye towards the example of Dewey, it is now possible to suggest some ways to fill in some of the gaps in the theory.

Questions and answers are not primarily linguistic entities. Rather, they are elements of activity that may take a linguistic form. Questions and answers will take primary form as practical choices and decisions. In this sense, question and answer are coterminous with rigorous thought. The linguistic form of questions and answers serve to make more precise, and render public, the process by which choices are put and decisions made. In their most rigorous and precise form, questioning and answering are constitutive of scientific thought.

Questions and answers are related to each other, and this relationship is central to the theory. A well-formed question may have a precise answer, which resolves the specific dilemma or choice that has been posed. A precise answer will resolve a clearly expressed question; there is, however, no prior basis for assuming that it resolves other questions. A precise answer is, therefore, effective only in relation to one specific question. For that reason, an answer can be understood only in relation to that specific question.

A question may be put in a number of ways, and over a significant period. On Collingwood's theory, which in this respect is fundamentally different to later accounts of the logic of questions, the fact that a question can be expressed does not mean that it will have an answer at any given point in time. Rather, if the question has genu-

[51] Tom Burke, *Dewey's New Logic: A Reply to Russell.* University of Chicago Press, Chicago, 1994. pp. 112-114.
[52] Dewey, *Logic: The Theory of Inquiry.* pp. 108-109.

inely been put, that is, if it represents an actual dilemma, there will be a process of trying to answer the question. A question may be the same question even if it is expressed in different language, and at different times. The answer at any one point in time may be different to the answer that would be given at a different time. For these reasons, a given question and answer must be located in a specific context before either can be understood. This requirement is not a function of the type of question asked, for example historical or practical rather than scientific and theoretical. Instead, it is a function of questions in so far as they are well formulated, and answers in so far as they are precise.

Question and answer are to be conceived as processes or activities rather than static entities. A question will arise through the articulation of choice. As activities, questions have an historic dimension and specificity and this opens them up to criticism. Questions can be the subject of criticism, as being well formed or ill formed. Answers can be criticised as being more or less adequate to a specific question, but only a fully adequate and well formed answer can be said to resolve a question. The theory of question and answer is built on the relationship between the two, and the primary concept in this relationship is adequacy, which can here be interpreted broadly to include appropriateness and satisfaction.

The concepts of supposition and presupposition stand outside the main body of the theory. Each concept helps to develop an account of how questions may arise, and of how complexes of questions and answers may succeed each other in related series. Supposition is a contingent concept: a supposition may be made or not made, and may be changed from question to question. In each case, the function of the supposition is to establish the conditions where choices require to be made, that is, in which questions may arise. Presuppositions, on the other hand, may change but are contingent in a different sense. A presupposition limits (to the point of determining) the questions which may subsequently be asked, because it restricts the further choices which are available. Typically, a presupposition to a further question will be an answer to a previous question.

The theory of question and answer is necessarily concerned with relationships within complexes. Collingwood's theory is also necessarily concerned with relationships between complexes of questions and answers. Although Collingwood did not himself draw many conclusions about relationships between complexes, when viewed in this way the theory has the potential to open up analysis of many concepts such as inquiry, tradition, authority and development.

Each of these concepts can be seen to involve specific forms taken by processes of questions and answers, without the introduction of additional psychological elements.

Since Collingwood did not draw out the point, the question must be asked why the theory of question and answer does not simply end with single complexes. There are two main reasons why it should go further. Firstly, the theory is focused on activity. It is a function of activity that new questions may arise (new choices may be required) because other questions have been answered. Two dimensions of relationships that emerge for this reason are subordination and sequence. Secondly, a question formed in one way may not be answerable because the alternatives are not clear, distinct or complete. To the extent that a choice is still required, there will of necessity be a process of reformulating the earlier question. A key dimension that emerges for this reason is development. Neither of the two reasons for attending to relationships between complexes of questions and answers is psychological; rather they refer to the nature of questioning, particularly its emphasis on adequacy. It is possible, even highly likely, that both reasons will be instantiated in any particular case of questioning. It follows that each of the three dimensions outlined may similarly be instantiated in any particular case.

If subordination, sequence and development are relationships between complexes of questions and answers, they serve also to bring other key concepts into the foreground. One way in which the logic of question and answer could be further developed would be to formalise a number of key concepts in the question and answer logic. Such formalisation might proceed along the lines sketched briefly below. For example, 'inquiry' is one important standard form for relationships between complexes. In inquiry a question and answer complex is followed by one or more other complexes in which the original answer (A) delimits the terms of the following question (Q_1). The subsequent answer (A_1) is related to the original question (Q) but will not typically be substitutable for A. In turn A_1 may delimit further choices for Q_2, and so on. In the series, A_n will always be relatable to Q, and the nature of that relationship may be characterised variously as one of subordination and development, but will not be knowable without reference to the sequence Q to Q_n. In that sense, inquiry is not determined *a priori*.

There is scope to apply the same approach to other concepts. In a narrow reading of 'tradition', the original complex Q-A is not followed by Q_1-A_1, but may be restated at different times as Q^{T1}-A^{T1}, to

Q^{Tn}-A^{Tn}. In this case, any Q and any A are sufficiently similar that they may be substituted for one another without losing the relationship within any single question and answer complex. Traditions may cease to be effective in generating complexes of questions and answers; a question can be asked following any A in the series that cannot be substituted in other complexes of the series. Traditions are not therefore constraints on questioning, but serve to define terms in a series of question and answer complexes.

'Authority' can be seen as a relationship between question and answer complexes in which the emphasis is placed on the substitutability of any of $A...A_n$ for any other $A...A_n$. This may occur in a number of ways. Firstly, alternatives to A may be excluded in framing the choice. Secondly, the original question or choice may be suppressed and replaced with a question for which A is the appropriate answer (such as through the 'corruption of consciousness'). As an example, someone who accepts the authority of Newton may frame a question as if the circumstances were similar to those of Newton's original question and the same choice of alternatives were available. Alternatively, Newton's original dilemma about a particular issue may be suppressed in favour of one which gives the answer that it is Newton's view which is to be preferred. In either case, authority represents a disengagement from the original dilemma or choice and is therefore a major counter-point to inquiry.

It is not answers that develop but questions. 'Development', then could be seen to involve restating Q as $Q...Q_n$ in terms of the answers $A...A_n$; Q_n will be related to Q in that it does substitute or replace Q. Development is also temporal, as $Q...Q_n$ and $A...A_n$ may be stated at times $t...t_n$, but there is no simple one to one correlation between either Q_n-A_n or t_n. In that sense, questions posed at very different times may represent the one line of development. There is, therefore, a fundamental difference between the dialectical character of question and answer and the dialectic of Hegel.

Hegel had located dialectic within concepts themselves, and this move had led to the bifurcation of his theory of history into the development of the concept and the deeds of human beings. In *An Essay on Philosophical Method*, Collingwood sought to show that some concepts, as they develop, form scales which exhibit the relationships Hegel had identified in his dialectic. Yet Collingwood's account of 'philosophical concepts' was not an account of all concepts, nor did it purport to show the dialectical process by which the development of concepts occurs. Against this background, the logic of question and answer is dialectical in two senses. Firstly, it is dialectical in showing movement in thought, from question to answer, and how one question and answer complex follows from or leads to another complex. Secondly, it is dialectical in showing the process by which concepts may develop into a scale of forms. Hegel's dialectic of concepts, therefore, is encompassed and made explicable by the logic of question and answer set within the context of human agency. For Collingwood, agents pose questions and answer them; the dialectic of concepts is subsumed within the theory of agency.

There is an important sense, however, in which Collingwood did not fully draw out the dialectical character of the logic of question and answer. A question is posed logically when an agent has different desires amongst which they must choose. Once the question is posed, there is an attempt to answer the question and resolve the dilemma. Every question and answer complex is a necessary whole involving movement and duration. Two core notions of the logic of question and answer are, therefore, the concepts of the adequacy or inadequacy of an answer to a question, or a complex of question and answer to a series, and how a question can arise or fail to arise, singly or in a series. Collingwood considered the issue of arising more fully than that of adequacy, but the two are closely related.

For Collingwood, as well as for Dewey, there are questions because situations are problematic to a being. In Collingwood's account of mind, there are choices to be made. The context of new questions, however, also includes particular previous answers. There is an issue, therefore, as to how new questions arise against this background. Collingwood put this point in terms of how the right question arises in a sequence. In his short 'Note for an Essay on Logic' written on his trip to the East Indies in 1938-1939 Collingwood noted only that an assertion gives rise to another question in so far as the assertion is itself a supposition.[53] Collingwood's account of logic placed great emphasis on the difference between questions that do arise and those that do not arise. A question that does not arise in a certain sequence cannot be part of that sequence. To foreshadow issues that will be discussed in later chapters, when we are reconstructing an historical process, our reconstruction of some sequence as the one process depends on our capacity to differentiate the questions that did arise from all others which did not arise in an agent's situation. But the difference between questions that do and do not arise presupposes some account of how they may arise and a detailed account of this seems to be lacking in Collingwood's writ-

---

[53] Collingwood, 'Notes for an Essay on Logic', in Collingwood, *An Essay on Metaphysics*. pp. 422-427.

ings. We can, however, see the outlines of a fuller theory of arising that builds on the notions of adequacy and inadequacy.

The notion of adequacy in the theory of question and answer is related to Dewey's concept of a real resolution of a problem and to the concept of truth. Dewey characterised propositions as providing a provisional resolution of a problem that is fully resolved existentially. This characterisation also can be applied to the theory of question and answer. On this theory, a proposition can be true only if it adequately answers the question or problem it is intended to address — a proposition cannot be true unless it is also the right answer to a specific question. It is not sufficient that a proposition could be offered as a solution to some question or other, for unless it has been offered as a real solution to some specific question it is simply an untested alternative amongst others. In issues of theory, the true answer is one that fully resolves the problem — one that does not leave unresolved issues outside itself. The practical corollary of theoretical truth is efficacy in resolving the particular problem at issue. In moral matters, the truthful answer is the one that most completely addresses the question we have asked ourselves about our present situation and future action, and will generally be so by virtue of the rigour with which a complex issue has been pursued.

The mere truth of something is less important than the capacity to judge that a particular answer is true, for this allows the answer to be used or relied upon in particular ways. An answer cannot be judged to provide knowledge or truth unless it is explicable as fully adequate to a specific well formed question. The fact that a particular answer is fully adequate will suggest that it may provide knowledge, but the judgement that it does so depends upon criticism. On the other hand, an answer may be judged inadequate, and yet remain the right answer — the answer had to be given at a particular point in time, under specific circumstances. Rightness is not equal to truth, but this does not diminish its importance in any sense.

Adequacy is defined primarily in terms of a particular complex. In so far as an answer is adequate, the question has been resolved and there is no necessary reason for the answer to give rise to other questions. One way in which the logic of question and answer accounts for movement from a previous answer to a new question is, therefore, by treating the answer as in some senses inadequate. To say that a new question arises from a certain answer is, in one important way, to imply that it is inadequate, and therefore not an answer at all. As a point of fact, it may be that most human beings provide inadequate answers to the questions they pose, and so 'inadequacy' may be a powerful analytical tool and concept. A similar analysis would apply to the inadequately posed question.[54]

Taken together, the inadequacy of our questioning and the inadequacy of our answers would provide a potent basis for historical analysis and criticism. Collingwood's later work, with its focus on the crisis of contemporary civilisation, is based upon the two poles of adequacy and inadequacy. His arguments about the corruption of consciousness in *The Principles of Art* and other later writings on civilisation are important because they show how failure to express emotion distorts action and self-knowledge. If questions arise to enable us to deal with the dilemmas we face, the corruption of consciousness leads to our failure to fully pose the right questions in our situation. Collingwood's central remedy was the restoration of our capacity to know our emotions and desires, and hence to pose the right questions adequately. To extend our capacity to know ourselves is to enable us to provide adequate answers to our questions. Collingwood's concern with religion, emotion, art and metaphysics were central to the first task; his concern with history and reasoned action were central to the second.

The logic of question and answer requires a theory of how adequate questions follow from adequate answers. In light of Collingwood's broader philosophy, to pose a question adequately is to have expressed one's emotions fully and without reservation, to know what one desires, and to know the alternatives between which one must choose. To have answered the question adequately is to have chosen one of the alternatives in the most reasoned way possible. As we shall see in the next chapter, Collingwood argued that to answer a question adequately is to act from 'duty'.

There are two broad approaches to the problem of questions following from adequate answers. Both approaches are necessary in a full account of movement in thought. The first way in which a question arises from an adequate answer is that the answer simply creates a new situation in which we face new dilemmas and pose new questions. Our question, therefore, has an historical pedigree but is not simply the original question posed in a different way. In this

---

[54]   If the first answer is inadequate, what may appear to be a new question may therefore be the same question posed anew. But the same question is also a genuinely new question, because it occurs in a new situation, against the background transformed by our earlier efforts. This provides an historical rendering of the realist idea of 'eternal questions', which Collingwood criticised.

sense, the dialectic of thought comes from the movement of mind in general, which leads us to desire competing things.[55]

Wisniewski has drawn attention to questions as the conclusions of inferences, and formalized the way in which lower level questions can answer higher level questions. In terms of the logic of question and answer, the second way in which a question arises from an adequate answer is if a particular series of questions is embedded within (and comprises) the process of answering a higher level question. For example, Collingwood's question (in *An Autobiography*) of why his car would not start is not, as he implied, a poorly formed question that cannot be answered as it stands.[56] Rather, it is a question of a different order to questions, that Collingwood did answer, about whether there might have been something wrong with the spark plugs or some other specific part.

To use Collingwood's example, answering questions about spark plugs is part of the process by which we answer our question about why the car does not start. Indeed, this is the only way in which our unanswerable question becomes answerable. Nevertheless, if the spark plug is not working we have, at the end of the process, an answer to more than a question about spark plugs. In this example, we also have a clear, adequate and complete answer to the question of why the car did not start. The number, nature and sequence of our questions about particular parts of the car's engine are entirely dependent on our previous conception of how a car works. Our conception of how cars work is, therefore, the presupposition for all our more specific questions. The second way for thought to move from an adequate answer to a new question can, therefore, be restated in terms of how a presupposition of each question in the series requires that we think in a certain sequence.

[55]   P. F. Strawson's remark that questions may fail to arise because the conditions for their arising do not obtain sits neatly with this view. See P. F. Strawson, *Introduction to Logical Theory*. Methuen, London, 1964. p. 18. For Strawson, calling into doubt the assumptions that support a question prevents the consideration of the truth and falsity of the statement made in answer. Belnap, by contrast, has argued that questions can fail to arise for logical as well as circumstantial reasons. For example, a question may be irrelevant to a set of questions, which for him means that the answers to the question are not relevant to answers to other questions in a set, where relevance involves implication. Secondly, a question may fail to arise because the answer is known, such as when a question is rhetorical or trivial. Third, the question may fail to arise because it is 'foolish', as when there is no true answer, and it is known that there is no such answer. See Nuel D. Belnap, Jr., 'Questions: Their Presuppositions, and How They Can Fail to Arise', in *The Logical Way of Doing Things*. (Edited by K. Lambert.) Yale University Press, New Haven, 1969. pp. 23-37. See esp. pp. 35-36.

[56]   Collingwood, *An Autobiography*. p. 32.

We are now in a position to summarise the considerations of this and the previous chapter, in three broad areas. Firstly, we have seen that Collingwood gave, at best, a sketch of the relationship between questions and answers. A fuller statement of the theory can be given by relating Collingwood's theory to that of Dewey. Other theories of questions and answers, such as those of Belnap and Wisniewski, differ from Collingwood's in that they are framed as theories of propositions or language. Leonard's view, however, was akin to that of Dewey in terms of a higher level theory, but was translated into a theory of propositions and language. Both Collingwood and Dewey saw propositions and assertions as necessary elements of logic. Their views differ from those of later writers because they aim to set propositions within an overall context.

Both Collingwood and Dewey have been criticised for offering as logic a theory that is not logic. Their theories do not fit within most current definitions of logic. Nevertheless, each sought to redefine the purpose of logic, and not just the 'proximate units' with which it works. This approach can be justified on philosophical grounds. We may assume, in particular, that those theories of logic are preferable in which there is a clear sense of the ultimate subject matter of logic, and where there is a clear link between the ultimate subject matter and the proximate concepts that comprise the body of a logical theory. For each writer, logic was a study of real activities that have changed since the time of Aristotle and are pervasive in contemporary cultures. These activities are real and constitutive of the world, and not simply methods for understanding it. In each theory, the activities studied by logic, and in which it finds universal and necessary elements, now reflect a world in process, with no fixed point of reference or essence. To generalise the point made by Dewey and Collingwood, logic deserves its claims to be dealing with universal and necessary elements of activity only to the extent that it reflects these general conceptions.

The break between logic and psychology in the nineteenth century could have led in two different directions. The dominant interpretation has been that logic must become a formal or technical study. Dewey and Collingwood took an alternative view, claiming that logic can have an empirical element that is not psychological. This approach has the advantage that it preserves a focus on logic serving the broader needs of philosophy. In turn, Dewey and Collingwood held a conception of the world and of mind that was in need of logic in order to draw out the structure of thought. The principal reason for treating seriously the claim that the theory of question and answer is logic is, therefore, that it is grounded in a reconsideration of the role of logic and a requirement for a broader consistency between logic and philosophy.

If we regard the theory of question and answer as logic, we gain tools with which to examine the universal and necessary elements of activity. Logic is then seen as a piece of philosophy, rather than apart from it. In turn, logic must demonstrate its relevance to other areas of thought. In this chapter, I have intimated some ways in which the logic of question and answer could help us to build historical analysis. The logic of question and answer also illuminates moral practice, because it shows the existential importance of systematic identification and resolution of problems. In the next chapter, we will see how problems are, in turn, fundamental to Collingwood's account of self-creation. So conceived, moral practice is the subject matter of history, and the theory of thought is the logic of history.

CHAPTER 5

Moral Philosophy and History

The previous chapters have shown the importance that Collingwood placed on a number of related concepts, including action and
history. For Collingwood, philosophy became increasingly concerned with the development and application of such concepts.
Within this context, his theory of mind focused on an account of
rational choice. If the theory of mind showed the necessity of choice,
logic showed how choices are made. In this chapter, we will see that
Collingwood's moral philosophy focused on reasons for choices.

Collingwood's distinctive account of moral philosophy emerged
as an account of the concept of action. In his view, action was a key
element of the world of process, and a pre-eminent example of those
philosophical concepts he characterised as developing in a scale of
forms. By tracing the concept of action in his moral philosophy, we
will see how Collingwood came to align moral philosophy and philosophy of history, or the capacity for rational choice with the understanding of situations that give rise to choices, and within which
choices are made.[1] The analysis of Collingwood's moral philosophy
in this chapter prepares the ground across which we can move in
later chapters to consider the character of history and historical
knowledge that emerged from his concepts of action and history.

Unlike his views on logic, however, Collingwood's moral philosophy was worked out explicitly, in numerous publications and
manuscripts, over more than two decades. It is therefore possible to

---

[1] There is a full account of Collingwood's moral thought, and its bearing on social
and political philosophy, in David Boucher's, *The Social and Political Thought of
R. G. Collingwood.* Cambridge University Press, Cambridge, 1989. See esp.
Chapters 3 and 4. My account in this chapter is broadly consistent with
Boucher's.

see, in a way that is difficult to do for his logic, how his later, and more developed, views on moral philosophy emerged by a process of reasoning that sought to clarify distinctions and better reveal linkages between concepts. Understanding what Collingwood had to say in moral philosophy is, significantly, a case of understanding how he came to say it.

David Boucher has rightly characterised Collingwood as seeking a moral criterion that would overcome perceived deficiencies in objectivist, universal, rule-based, moral theories and in subjectivist moral theories that focus on desire and utility. In this respect, Collingwood continued a tradition beginning with Rousseau's attempt to unite desire with will, objectivism with subjectivism, through the 'general will' and continued in Kant's search for a way to overcome the dualism of desire and reason, down to Bradley, Bosanquet and Croce in more recent times.[2] In Collingwood's philosophy of mind, desire gives rise to reason, because competing desires require choices to be made between alternatives. In his moral philosophy, reason comes to replace capricious choice, and the kinds of reason that we may have for choosing to act in a certain way also reflect the degree of rationality we achieve. Articulating a moral criterion beyond utility and rules involves, therefore, specifying a kind of reason for choice that is not encapsulated in either, and that is more fully rational than both. Collingwood reached his conclusions on what such a reason would involve only slowly.

In his 1921 'Lectures on Moral Philosophy', Collingwood defined moral philosophy as a 'study of conduct'. Collingwood was careful to distinguish conduct from behaviour, and moral philosophy from behaviouristic psychology. Behaviourism failed to distinguish machine movements from the involuntary reflexes of living organisms or from the 'deliberate choice of a rational being.' Moral philosophy, on the other hand, could not abstract the 'outward and visible' elements of conduct from the consciousness of an act, whether it concern 'desire, motive, duty' or some other form of consciousness. In Collingwood's view, an 'outward act is rendered intelligible by its inward or conscious aspect.'[3] Intelligibility comes only when the 'outward' aspects of our action are not abstracted from its conscious aspects.

---

[2]   Boucher, *The Social and Political Thought of R. G. Collingwood.* p. 79.
[3]   R. G. Collingwood, 'Lectures on Moral Philosophy for M[ichaelmas]-T[erm]-1921: written at various times, May — October, 1921.' [Bodleian Library, Dep. 4.]. p. 1.

If moral philosophy deals with conduct, ethics deals with choice. Choice is a form of action that selects one out of a range of possible options. How are such actions possible?[4] Ancient ethics focused on the criteria for choice. Modern ethics was, in Collingwood's view, focused on the faculty of choice. Yet, inevitably, the attempt to address one problem must reflect upon all of the other related problems. A history of ethics would try to show how ethical thought had treated 'one single central problem (what is action?)' by restating it, from time to time. At one time, the problem was to establish by what criteria we choose. At another time, the problem was to establish the nature of the faculty of choice. But a history of ethics would show 'these subordinate ethical concepts as transformations of a single concept of action.'[5]

In 1921, Collingwood did not offer his students a fully developed ethical theory. Rather, he offered them an argument for the need to exercise care and reason in ethical issues. He advocated a searching, thorough and careful conscience, which would seek out good without falling prey to enthusiasms built upon abstract caricatures of good and evil. Those who adopted Collingwood's approach would have exercised a 'perpetual reservation' in ethical issues. But their reservation would not imply any 'weakness or hesitation in action'. Reservation meant 'merely the refusal to lose one's balance in acting', and the determination to search out the 'whole fact' as distinct from 'the superficial and the obvious.' It was particularly important to Collingwood's argument that reflection leads us to make up our minds about a course of action. There can be no war between thought and action, for to think is to act and action is impossible without thought.[6]

In later years, Collingwood was to rewrite his moral philosophy lectures extensively and frequently. His later lectures attempted, in many respects, to elaborate and correct points he had made in 1921. Initially, he struggled to specify more clearly the moral approach he was trying to advocate. Subsequently, there was a transition in his work from trying to clarify a moral approach towards clarifying his ideas about history. By 1940, the links between Collingwood's account of the world as process, his theory of moral action and his view of history had become very close. In that year, Collingwood was able to follow his lectures on moral philosophy with his lectures on 'The Idea of History', much as he had already done in his work

---

[4]   Ibid. p. 2.
[5]   Ibid. pp. 5-6.
[6]   Ibid. pp. 119-120.

towards *The Idea of Nature*. At that stage, Collingwood's moral philosophy was completed by his account of history. In the first stages, however, his moral philosophy developed in a more self-contained manner, an approach that he was to break down only later.

Collingwood's 1921 account of moral philosophy was incomplete in several respects. Firstly, 'perpetual reservation' is neither a type of consciousness nor an activity. Rather, it is a characteristic attitude towards certain activities. But, for Collingwood, moral philosophy was an account of self-conscious action and conduct. The question that arises is 'what action is qualified by our perpetual reservation'? In his 1921 lectures, Collingwood used historical practice as an example of such action, though primarily as an analogy. A fuller description of self-conscious action was needed.

Collingwood's initial account of moral philosophy was incomplete in another important sense. In particular, many aspects of social or political action could simply not be dealt with by his early ethical theory. Although we may exercise 'perpetual reservation' when we wish to pass moral judgement on others, these are not the only kinds of judgement relevant to our relations with other people. Collingwood's theory needed to accommodate all kinds of action without compromising his account of the reservation needed in moral judgement. In his later work, Collingwood went on to make a number of distinctions that would address the need for a clearer moral theory. For example, he clearly distinguished between moral judgements and political judgements, such as punishment. On his later view, political action, and political judgement, are manifestations of action according to rules. Punishment is, therefore, primarily a political or social act, rather than a consequence of moral condemnation.

In the 1920s, Collingwood made more explicit his equation of moral philosophy with the theory of action. His 1923 lectures were entitled 'Action: Lectures on Moral Philosophy'. Collingwood now distinguished between mechanical, teleological and moral actions. The characteristic feature of moral action, and therefore the characteristic feature of moral issues, was choice. There was no distinction to be made between choice and right choice. Not to choose 'what is ultimately worth having', was to avoid altogether the work of creating oneself. If we turn out wrong, it is not because we made the wrong choice but because we did not really make a choice at all.[7] He

---

[7]   R. G. Collingwood, 'Action: Lectures on Moral Philosophy. 1923. (16 Lectures, written Sept 1923 for Mich[aelmas]. term 1923. Rewritten and expanded in Mich[aelmas] term 1926).' [Bodleian Library, Dep. 16.] p. 2.

cited, in this connection, the maxim 'only make up your mind and you will make it up rightly.' Nothing outside the will can dictate to it how to act well. We must, therefore, achieve a full consciousness of our actions and choices.[8]

Collingwood's 1923 moral philosophy lectures were intended to contribute to his students' developing consciousness of action and choice. He argued that our character is not static, but is formed by our reflective actions.[9] It is not easy to make up our minds, but difficult. If we desire virtue, for example, we imply that the opposite, wickedness, exists in us and must be overcome. Our desires are themselves conflicting, so that a mind that desires is a mind divided against itself.[10] But the fact that we are divided does not mean that we should look to will to deliver us from our desires. Desire and will are not distinct faculties of the mind, but moments in the one process. In the same way that a question 'looks forward' to an answer, so 'desire is action as it were taking aim.'[11]

Since our desires are competing and incompatible, we must bring discipline to them in order that we can act at all. Collingwood described this process as analogous to the way two disputants in a discussion each work out that they 'really mean' to say the same thing. In fact, each of the theses is modified or altered by the process. Disciplining our desires is, then, like discovering the truth. Choice is hard work because of the dialectical nature of the process. To make up our minds about incompatible desires is never an automatic process, and victory does not go merely to the desires we feel most strongly.[12]

The dialectical nature of choice, which transforms our desires, transforms therefore our self or mind. Through exercising choice, we create a new self and a new situation. In each new situation, we have different emotions and desires, and therefore new choices to make.[13] We create ourselves by our choices, but we also come to know ourselves the same way. In turn, we create our minds by striving to know ourselves.[14] On Collingwood's view

> To create oneself and to know oneself are the same thing; knowledge is altogether action and action is altogether knowledge, and the opposite

---

[8]   Ibid. p. 6.
[9]   Ibid. p. 22.
[10] Ibid. pp. 27-28.
[11] Ibid. p. 29.
[12] Ibid. p. 29-30.
[13] Ibid. p. 31.
[14] Ibid. p. 33.

of knowledge, namely doubt or questioning, is identical with the opposite of action, namely desire...[15]

There is only one activity though it has two aspects, the cognitive
and creative.[16] But self-creation or freedom is not always and everywhere the same. The actions of ants and human beings or of crimi-
nals and Saints may each be free, but different types of action differ
in the extent to which they overcome the obstacles to perfect self-
creation, perfect freedom and, therefore, perfect action.[17]

'Action' is, in Collingwood's terms, a philosophical concept, and
so it is structured as a 'scale of forms'. The scale of forms for the concept 'action' is driven by progressively greater self-knowledge.[18]
Collingwood's account of the scale began with space and time series,
and progressed through motion, chemical arrangement, the life of
organic matter and reflex action. At a higher level, instinct is conscious, but not reflective, action. Instinctive agents have the freedom
to obey their own appetites. They are also, however, slaves to their
appetites. There is choice only where there is reflection. Reason
emerges first as memory, then imagination and finally as thought.
Will, reason and choice are the same in that they involve the existence and consciousness of alternatives.[19]

Choice is either capricious choice or choice for some reason.
Capricious choice is a lower form of choice. It is in relation to the reasons for choice that moral philosophy becomes most fully developed, and it was in this area that Collingwood's continued revision
of his views bore most fruit. Early in the 1920s, he was content to distinguish only two kinds of reason for choice. Firstly, we may choose
one alternative over another not for its own sake but as a means to
some end. Collingwood called this choice for the sake of 'utility'.[20]
Secondly, we may choose something as itself of value, without
regard for the utility of our choice. Collingwood's term for this form
of choice was 'duty'.[21] This analysis was consistent with that of
Croce, who distinguished between utilitarian and economic, or
moral and ethical, forms of the 'practical spirit'.[22]

[15]   Ibid. p. 35.
[16]   Ibid.
[17]   Ibid. p. 38.
[18]   Ibid. p. 42.
[19]   Ibid. pp. 77-78.
[20]   Ibid. p. 82.
[21]   Ibid. pp. 83-84.
[22]   Benedetto Croce, *Philosophy of the Practical, Economic and Ethic.* (Translated by
       Douglas Ainslie.) Macmillan, London, 1913. p. 310.

The culminating issue in the whole of Collingwood's moral philosophy was the precise nature of reasoned choice. The highest form of reasoned choice must be the highest in the scale of action. The highest form of reasoned choice is consequently the most fully developed form of will, freedom, self-knowledge and self-creation. Because, for Collingwood, the mind is whole, there cannot be two faculties of reason, so the same point is also the highest form of theoretical reason. In his later years, Collingwood was to identify history as the highest form of theoretical reason.

Our ends and means form a complex whole. When we choose an act in order to achieve something else, we will the means and the ends simultaneously. We do not first will the means and then will the end; nor do we first will the end and then will the means to achieve it. To posit an end without also willing the means is fantasy rather than will.

We can understand an act in terms of its utility, but this form of explanation must always remain deficient. Our desires may specify a particular kind of action, but our choices are always particular and specific. We may satisfy hunger in many different ways. Understanding why we choose to do so in one way rather than another requires more than an understanding of the utility of the means to the end. In Collingwood's view, choice for the sake of utility cannot explain the particular nature of the choices we make, but only 'the organisation of parts' within the complex we do choose. To approach a choice through its utility, therefore, is to leave a significant element of caprice.[23]

The utilitarian form of practical reason, therefore, cannot provide an explanation for why an agent chooses a particular course. To say that one end is only the means to another is not to resolve the problem but merely to postpone it. At some point, we must choose something as good in itself. According to Collingwood's view during the early 1920s, to choose the good simply because it is good is to act in accordance with duty. Our subjective sense of duty is called our 'conscience'.[24]

To act in the consciousness of your duty is, on Collingwood's account, to know that your actions will have deep consequences for yourself for all time. Your choices are 'in some sense crucial for your entire fate.' At this point of his argument, Collingwood moved beyond his earlier moral ideal of 'perpetual reservation' to give a more positive statement to his views. When we recognise 'the infi-

---

[23]   Collingwood, 'Action: Lectures on Moral Philosophy. 1923.' pp. 82-83.
[24]   Ibid. p. 66. [pre-1927 version.]

nite gravity and momentousness of any given act', we are taking 'the conscientious attitude towards that act.' Although we can never know all of the consequences of our action, 'it is necessary to realise vividly that it will have infinite consequences.' To choose out of duty is to be conscientious about the consequences of our actions. Conscience is, however, merely subjective. A moral theory must also deal with issues such as our relationships with other persons. It therefore appears that it is possible to live a life of duty only if we will universally.[25] This key doctrine from the philosophy of Kant, and the problems it raised, was to be a fulcrum around which Collingwood's moral thought developed.

To will universally is to legislate. But, in practice, when we confront a situation for which we have legislated, we find that the law is not enough to determine our actions. For in any particular case we may 'take a conscientious view of the situation' which renders legislation either 'unnecessary' or even 'vicious'. Law, therefore, fails to overcome the defects of 'utility' and 'conscience'. To complete the theory, then, another element would be needed. In 1923, Collingwood posited that beyond conscience and law lay 'absolute action'. Finding that legislation was unnecessary and conscientiousness was possible in any particular situation, Collingwood suggested that we call on our 'a priori certainty' that our acts, and those of other people, will be conscientious.[26] Collingwood's theory of rational choice was completed by an element for which we have no reason.

In 1929, when he rewrote his moral philosophy lectures, Collingwood revised his theory of choice to make it more fully rational. In particular, he was dissatisfied with the distinctions he had made between caprice, utility and duty. From 1929 onwards, Collingwood distinguished between three kinds of reasons for choice, namely utility, right and duty. He saw these reasons as 'moments which imply each other in such a way that any rational act exhibits all three.'[27] Collingwood gave the same analysis over a decade later in *The New Leviathan*.

Collingwood's moral theory is significantly different from others now current in analytical philosophy, and the differences are instructive. For contemporary analytical philosophers such as, for example, Philip Pettit, the 'good' relates to 'universal properties' which 'make one state of the world better than another', while the

[25]   Ibid. pp. 67-68, reverse. [pre-1927 version.]
[26]   Ibid. p. 76. [1923 text.]
[27]   R. G. Collingwood, 'Moral Philosophy Lectures, 1929.' (Revised in 1930.) [Bodleian Library, Dep. 10.] p. 95.

'right' relates to 'what makes one option right and another wrong' when we face a genuine choice.[28] In Collingwood's own day, similar views were particularly associated with the philosopher W. D. Ross.[29] For Collingwood, by contrast, the 'good' meant the 'chosen' and, if we chose at all, we chose that act as being good.[30]

To choose what is right is to choose what is good, but this is only one form of good. To choose something because it is useful is another form of good. On one approach, the right and the good are first distinguished from one another, and then linked again in particular theories such as utilitarianism; moral theories may be rivals in the sense of excluding each other. Collingwood tried to preserve the insights of utilitarianism at the same time as he tried to use the insights of Kant. Moreover, he justified his approach by arguing that each form of choice represents a kind of reasoning. As Collingwood's pupil, T. M. Knox, was later to write, '[c]hoice and good are correlatives; and different sorts of choice are correlative to different sorts of good; and these different sorts of good correspond to different levels of moral experience.'[31]

It might be objected that Collingwood confused the process of deciding on a course of action with the means for evaluating possible choices. His approach, however, implied that evaluation exists solely for the sake of decision. A means of evaluation is just a means to enable us to decide. The real issue is not, therefore, to find reasons for preferring, for example, Kantianism over utilitarianism, but to elucidate the forms of practical reason in order to show how and in what ways such theories relate to each other on the same scale of forms.

Some contemporary philosophers do, however, make distinctions between utility, right and duty. Ronald Dworkin, for example, has distinguished political theories as 'goal-based', 'right-based' or

---

[28] Philip Pettit, 'The contribution of analytical philosophy', in *A Companion to Contemporary Political Philosophy*. (Edited by Robert E. Goodin and Philip Pettit.) Basil Blackwell, Oxford, 1993. pp. 7-38. See p. 22.

[29] W. D. Ross, *The Right and the Good*. Clarendon Press, Oxford, 1930.

[30] R. G. Collingwood, 'Goodness, Rightness, Utility: Lectures delivered in H[ilary]T[erm] 1940 and written as delivered. Forming a continuation of those on Feeling, Appetite, Desire and Will; delivered in the previous term. Written Dec. 1939 — Feb. 1940', now printed in R. G. Collingwood, *The New Leviathan, or Man, Society, Civilization and Barbarism. Revised edition, edited and introduced by David Boucher, with 'Goodness, Rightness, Utility' and 'What "Civilization" Means'.* Clarendon Press, Oxford, 1992. pp. 391-479. See esp. pp. 420-421.

[31] T. M. Knox, *Action*. George Allen & Unwin, London, 1968. p. 80.

'duty-based'.[32] Utilitarianism is clearly 'goal-based', and Tom Paine's theory of the 'rights of man' is 'right-based'. Like Collingwood, Dworkin associated the 'duty-based' theory with Kant.[33] Unlike Collingwood, however, Dworkin took Kant's account to exemplify a 'duty-based' theory. For Collingwood, as we shall see, Kant's theory of the categorical imperative was not a satisfactory theory of duty. Rather, in Collingwood's view, the categorical imperative remained a theory of rules governing action. Only by criticising Kant, and seeking to do anew that which Kant tried but failed to do, did Collingwood arrive at his own theory of duty.

As his views matured, Collingwood saw that the distinction between means and ends must be 'a universal and necessary characteristic of action'. In every action, we can distinguish between 'that which we have reason for doing' and 'the reason which we have for doing it'. This form of analysis makes utilitarian moral philosophy possible. As a moral philosophy, utilitarianism focuses on the relationship of means to ends.[34] Economics, as a study of 'exchange value' is principally a study of utility, and therefore represents the theoretical form of reasoning from means to ends.[35] In 1933, Collingwood expressed the view that economics, for example, utilises concepts such as 'exchange', 'production', 'wealth', 'labour' or 'money', the importance of which goes so far beyond economic facts or behaviour as to be 'co-extensive with rational action in general.' In that sense, there is a philosophical science of economics, alongside the empirical study of exchange, which studies a certain 'universal characteristic of rational action', namely the 'concept of expediency.'[36]

Just as there is a philosophical science of economics, so there is a philosophical science of politics. In his earlier moral philosophy lectures, Collingwood had equated duty with the choice of the good in itself. In 1929, Collingwood argued that the goodness which 'belongs to an act that is an end in itself, is called rightness.'[37] Legislation and planning are elements of rightness that, following F. H. Bradley and examples of common usage, Collingwood took to mean

[32] Ronald Dworkin, *Taking Rights Seriously. New impression with a Reply to Critics.* Duckworth, London, 1978. p. 171.
[33] Ibid. p. 172.
[34] Collingwood, 'Moral Philosophy Lectures, 1929.' pp. 96-97.
[35] Ibid. p. 99. See also R. G. Collingwood, 'Economics as a Philosophical Science' (1925), reprinted in R. G. Collingwood, *Essays in Political Philosophy. Edited with an introduction by David Boucher.* Clarendon Press, Oxford, 1989. pp. 58-77.
[36] R. G. Collingwood, 'Lectures on Moral Philosophy, 1933.' [Bodleian Library, Dep. 8.] p. 89.
[37] Collingwood, 'Moral Philosophy Lectures, 1929.' p. 103.

'following the right rule'. To deal with 'similar situations by similar measures is called a rule: and therefore a plan may be expressed as a rule or system of rules.'[38] For Collingwood, 'unity' and 'plurality' were transcendental universals, or universals of which 'everything is an instance.'[39] Since unity and plurality are 'logical moments' in the concept of action, 'every act must be a plan and every plan an act'. Because each action is a complex of other acts, 'the establishment of the Principate by Augustus' may count as 'one act' with many parts. The philosophical origin of politics lies in organised action.[40] The State is not the only organiser of action. Politics, therefore, is 'bound to overflow the limits of the state and to appear wherever there is action of any kind.' Like utilitarian action, political action is a transcendental aspect of each and every reasoned choice.[41]

An action is right if it conforms to rules; the rule itself may be right in relation to deeper rules. But can we determine whether these rules, in turn, are right? To say that one rule is right in terms of a deeper rule merely postpones the question. Collingwood thought that the question '[w]hether the ultimate and most fundamental rules are right' is a question with no meaning. If we are to understand the 'binding force' of ultimate and fundamental rules, we must seek it not in the idea of rightness, but somewhere else. For Collingwood, the clue, but not the solution, to what lies beyond rightness was to be found in Kant's idea of the categorical imperative. Kant's categorical imperative commands obedience to the form of law. Collingwood argued that in every instance where we apply a rule, we obey the rule of 'obeying the rule which is appropriate in the circumstances'. Collingwood proposed to call the rational activity which has the 'task of making and unmaking all rules except the one formal rule that rules must exist' by the name 'duty'. In any concrete situation, we not only obey some rule but also choose which rule we will obey. 'Rightness' explains only our choice to obey a certain rule. Duty applies to our decisions about which rule we shall obey. Our concern with the goodness of ends and rules gives our action their moral character.[42]

---

[38] Ibid. p. 105.
[39] Ibid. p. 7.
[40] Ibid. pp. 106-107. Compare Collingwood's account of the 'establishment of the Principate' as a single act that is also a plan and a complex of acts with Davidson's argument that 'If an event is an action, then under some description(s) it is primitive, and under some description(s) it is intentional.' Donald Davidson, *Essays on Actions and Events*. Clarendon Press, Oxford, 1980. p. 61.
[41] Collingwood, 'Moral Philosophy Lectures, 1929'. p. 108.
[42] Ibid. pp. 131-136.

When we act morally, we ask ourselves whether our ends are good and if we are following a good rule. We can do so only because we are in 'complete command of the situation' and of ourselves. We cannot have such command of ourselves if our mind is divided against itself, as it is in the case of desire. Purchasers and vendors are logically distinct, as are rulers and subjects, but there can be no such divisions in the case of duty.[43] Duty, or morality, 'means making yourself responsible for your own actions.' Duty involves being responsible to ourselves for the decisions we take as rational beings. The rationality of others is essential to our own rationality, and so our duty involves respect for others.[44]

Collingwood's approach to duty was quite different to that of most other British philosophers of the late nineteenth and early twentieth centuries. F. H. Bradley, for example, saw duty as the obverse of right. For Bradley, while the concept of right related a universal to a particular, duty was simply the relationship of the particular to the universal; duty was will realizing the universal.[45] For Bradley, the good will was the realization of 'my station and its duties' and of a further personal ideal morality. Yet Bradley's theory was permeated by an opposition between what ought to be and what is. The contradiction was never overcome in the sphere of morality, but only in religion.[46] For Collingwood, by contrast, duty was that sphere of morality in which our will is fully concrete, and there is no gap between what we in fact do and what we ought to do. Much later than Bradley, W. D. Ross saw right and duty as synonyms, to be distinguished from 'morally good'. Since the 'right act' refers to one or more of a set of acts, duty applied to doing ' "one or other" ' act.[47] For Collingwood, by contrast, duty and right were distinct, and duty could refer only to one specific act.

For Collingwood, our actions are true actions only if we take responsibility in the form that he envisaged. If we who are capable of rational action are truly to act at all, we must act morally.[48] Collingwood acknowledged, however, that the word 'duty' also has some connotations — such as 'blind obedience' to traditional rules — that make it a 'bad name' for what he had in mind. Nevertheless, he argued that the 'wealth of meaning and the depth of moral

[43]   Ibid. pp. 140-141.
[44]   Ibid. p. 146.
[45]   F. H. Bradley, *Ethical Studies. Second edition.* Clarendon Press, Oxford, 1927. p. 208.
[46]   Ibid. pp. 313-314.
[47]   Ross, *The Right and the Good.* pp. 3-6.
[48]   Collingwood, 'Moral Philosophy Lectures, 1929.' p. 142.

experience' which could be found in Kant's treatment of duty, or Spinoza's treatment of morality, showed that no other term was adequate to the task.[49]

Articulating the concept of duty, and the experience that could justify its theoretical prominence, was the major challenge for Collingwood's moral philosophy. As he refined his concept throughout the 1930s, Collingwood came to equate duty with history. A key role for the philosophy of history, then, is to show that historical thought provides us with knowledge of our duty.

In 1932, Collingwood returned to the different meanings of the word 'duty'. One meaning relates to 'putting our will into a certain state'. A second meaning involves our 'acting in certain ways, doing certain things, as a result of having our will so disposed.' This second meaning was connected, in Collingwood's view, with 'what it is right to do.' The second meaning is not distinct from 'rightness'. For Collingwood, duty proper concerns only 'victory in the moral struggle', rather than doing the right thing.[50]

Collingwood differentiated rightness from duty more comprehensively by arguing that the 'moral consciousness' had always to 'override' rules; it was not enough to override any one particular rule but, rather, 'the spirit of rule in general.' On the surface, Collingwood's new formulation of duty seems to contradict the 'one formal rule that rules must exist'. But, since utility, rightness and duty are moments of every action, moral actions are also regularian actions. The distinctive characteristic of duty, therefore, is that moral action 'creates a new law out of the ashes of the old, affirms new ends more desirable than those it renounces, and so sets right and expediency alike on a firmer basis than ever.'[51]

Our acts are always concrete or particular. We always perform *this* act, and not just one act of a certain kind. Collingwood argued that the idea of duty is an idea of concrete action. That is, it is our duty to perform a particular act in a particular situation.[52] It might be objected that it is our duty merely to try to do a certain act, since we cannot be sure that we can, in fact, do it, and 'ought implies can'.[53] Collingwood regarded this view as, from the practical perspective, a form of defeatism. Philosophically, he regarded this view as mistaken because it treats will in abstraction from what it does. On this

[49] Ibid. p. 149.
[50] R. G. Collingwood, 'Moral Philosophy Lectures. New Ms., 1932.' [Bodleian Library, Dep. 7.] p. 92.
[51] Ibid. pp. 107-108.
[52] Ibid. p. 107.
[53] Ibid. p. 117.

view, then, doing our duty would mean 'bringing about in ourselves the psychological state of trying'. We say someone is 'trying' when they demonstrate effort. But trying is most apparent when people do not succeed in their aims. The objection amounts to recommending to a person that they demonstrate maximum effort, but ensure that they do not succeed.[54]

In Collingwood's view the will is definite; that is, we will to do a certain act, not another which simply resembles that act. If there is no act, there is no will. Although the idea of duty involves bringing about a state of will, Collingwood argued that we have brought about that state only when we have done something. In particular, we must have done that which is our duty.[55] There can be 'no intentions' in the 'world of duty'. For, 'if we really intended to do our duty, no less than if we really tried to do it, we should already have done it.'[56] If history is related to duty, then it cannot deal with intentions abstracted from actions; intention inheres in actions. This argument is critical to our understanding of many of Collingwood's other doctrines, particularly his claim that historians re-enact past thoughts. Collingwood's argument undermines any interpretation of re-enactment which places the sole emphasis on historical agents' intentions separately from the acts they in fact performed.

In order to convey to his students the concrete individuality of duty, Collingwood pointed to occasions when people feel that they are in some kind of 'moral crisis'. On such occasions, we tend to break the 'rules of human conduct' and to sacrifice our interests. We have to deal with a particular urgent issue, and find that we have no option but to do one specific thing. Where we have no choice, we say that 'being the kind of man I am, I could not have done otherwise than as I did'. Saint Paul, Saint Augustine and Martin Luther all talked of their actions in this way. In a time of moral crisis, we also have 'an intense consciousness of freedom.'[57] For our actions on such occasions clearly determine who we are. To act in consciousness of our duty is to take full conscious responsibility for what we will be in the future. Such action is fully free. My general duty is, by acting in accordance with duty, to 'determine myself as will'. As Collingwood put the point, '[t]o decide is to be a will, and to be a will

---

[54] Ibid. pp. 119-120.
[55] Ibid. p. 120.
[56] Ibid. p. 99.
[57] Collingwood, 'Lectures on Moral Philosophy, 1933.' pp. 112-114.

is to decide; the decision to be a will is therefore the essence of will itself.'⁵⁸

In *An Autobiography*, Collingwood returned to the theme of duty, without using the term, and linked it to history. Collingwood observed that we act without rules in two kinds of circumstances, each of which is both more common than his earlier comments about religious figures might suggest and requires that we have a strong sense of our situation. In the first group of cases we have no choice but to act, but have no rule on which to base our acts. Such cases include new situations, or the actions of those who are inexperienced or ignorant. A second kind of situation occurs when we believe that acting according to the available rules would be inadequate. On Collingwood's view, this second group of actions without rules involves situations we take very carefully, rejecting desire, self-interest and rules to deal with them appropriately. In such circumstances, rules would serve only 'the low-grade morality of custom and precept'. Rule following, then, keeps 'action at a low potential' by failing to deal adequately with situations in which we find ourselves. A higher level of action is possible, therefore, only if we see our situation more clearly. History can give us the necessary trained eye for situations — it may give insight, where science can offer only rules. History, therefore, is key to the diagnosis of moral or political problems. If history informs us about the present, it is both vital and practical.⁵⁹

In his 1940 lectures on moral philosophy, Collingwood returned to themes he had first addressed in the 1920s and early 1930s, in language clearly related to that of *The Idea of History*. For example, he continued to argue that there 'is no such thing as an absolutely simple and indivisible action.' Rather, every action is 'a complex of actions.' The distinction between means and ends, which is characteristic of the utilitarian consciousness, is made when we reflect on the complex structure of our actions.⁶⁰ Similarly, when we are conscious of doing something as a means we are also 'conscious of choosing it for the sake of' the end it serves.⁶¹ The analysis is intrinsic to the act. In moral philosophy and in history, 'what matters is to find out what analysis the agent applies to [his act] in his own conscious-

[58]   Ibid. pp. 116-117.
[59]   R. G. Collingwood, *An Autobiography*. Oxford University Press, London, 1939. pp. 100-106.
[60]   Collingwood, 'Goodness, Rightness, Utility'. p. 437.
[61]   Ibid. p. 452.

ness of doing it, or having done it, or being about to do it.'[62] What were the agent's ends, and what were their means? Just as 'utility' involves the distinction between means and ends, right also involves analysing and choosing parts of the one action. Specifically, we choose the universal or rule and we choose an individual act which falls under it; thereby we choose to obey that particular rule.[63] We consciously obey, disobey and make rules. Our capacity to make and unmake rules is a 'revolutionary idea', and represents our discovery, in political terms, of 'self-government'.[64]

There are many ways to satisfy the one rule. There may be, for example, a rule that I should return to their rightful owners all the books that I have borrowed; Ross had used this example in order to show that it is my duty to ensure that my friend has the book. For Ross, duty and right were synonyms, and the rightness of my act is derivative of its producing the state of 'my friend having the book.'[65] Collingwood and Ross each recognised that there are many different ways to return a book. Collingwood argued, from this point, that the rule may be satisfied by many specific acts. When I choose one of these ways, I exclude the possibility of returning the book in another way. Literally, any of the alternatives would suffice, for each is right. If I exclude some of the options, I thereby exclude myself from doing many right actions. In terms of a rule, this does not matter. But it matters greatly if I fail to do something that is my duty. In this case, to fail to perform one specific act is 'always a dereliction of duty', which cannot be remedied by some other act. Collingwood argued that, without this condition, 'it would not be true that "ought implies can".'[66] In the end, 'ought implies can' means that when we are conscious that we ought to do something specific then we are also conscious that we can do it, and conscious that we cannot do anything else.[67] Since one can discharge a rule in multiple ways, every rule is a 'disjunctive imperative'. Kant, though, talked of a 'categorical imperative', and meant by it a specific rule. On Collingwood's analysis, all rules are disjunctive imperatives. His concept of duty was his own way to express the truth contained in the idea of the categorical

[62] Ibid. p. 461.
[63] Ibid. p. 453.
[64] Ibid. p. 457.
[65] Ross, *The Right and the Good*. pp. 42-47.
[66] Collingwood, 'Goodness, Rightness, Utility', p. 466.
[67] Ibid. p. 479.

imperative, while rejecting Kant's idea that the categorical imperative must be a rule.[68]

For Collingwood, we act as we do, out of duty, because we have no option. Utilitarian and regularian explanations of an action assume a difference between what is to be explained and that by which it is explained. In that sense, the idea of duty cannot explain our actions because our actions and our obligations are 'identical'. To say that 'I did this because I had to do it' is not to give an explanation but to utter a tautology. But a person who expresses this tautology shows that they have had a certain kind of self-conscious experience. They are calling attention to the fact that they are aware of themselves performing an individual action, and simultaneously aware that they are 'acting in an individual situation.' Such action is a response to a specific situation, and not to another merely like it; both the action and the situation that has given rise to it are completely individualised.[69]

It would appear that Collingwood, whose moral theory began with choices between alternatives, in the end abandoned the idea that there are alternatives. Such a conclusion would, however, significantly misunderstand the concept of duty and of a scale of forms. An action does not cease to be a means to an end because we can see it as having been done out of duty. Existing rules for action do not cease to apply when we choose to act without them. In the analysis of actions performed by other persons, or in our own process of choosing, utility and right continue to be reasons for choice. But such explanations and reasons will be incomplete, because they will not address the specific situation in which choices have been, or will be, made. The concept of action or choice out of duty does not leave us without options because it is impossible to conjecture alternatives, but because the choice represents the compulsive conclusion to a particular chain of reasoning. The only option we can undertake is the one to which our reason compels us with a full understanding of our situation and ourselves. Understanding the situation in which the agent found themselves and the compulsive reason for their choice completes the analysis of their action.

Moral practice, then, requires a form of thought that permits us to understand our situation and to deal adequately with its individuality. Moral philosophy, in turn, requires a theory of thought that enables the individuality of situations to be understood and compulsive conclusions to be reached.

---

[68]   Ibid. p. 466-467.
[69]   Ibid. pp. 473-475.

Collingwood argued that history is the form of theoretical thinking which deals with the individuality of actions. When we study, for example, the French Revolution, we are studying individual actions in an individual situation. Our study is itself individual. Every historian reconstructs the French Revolution in their mind in a way that is possible only at that time, with the documents or other evidence available then, and with methods of interpretation as they have developed up until that time. Historians are conscious not only of the individuality of the past, but of their own situation and present actions. The French Revolution was a complex of actions in which 'every detail had to be what it was', because the 'whole was what it was.' Our consciousness of history, therefore, is a 'consciousness of a necessity which cannot be stated analytically in terms of reasons and consequences.' The agents whose acts comprised the French Revolution found means to their ends, and obeyed the rules they chose to obey. Therefore, they 'did not act capriciously.' But of their choice of ends, and their choice of just those rules they did obey, we can say only that they did pursue those ends, and did follow those rules.[70]

For Collingwood, the analysis that identifies duty is a relatively new feature of moral philosophy, but the analysis itself follows the emergence of the fact of choice according to duty. Our consciousness of history and our consciousness of duty are the same thing. Our consciousness of history has developed over a long time, but Collingwood argued that it had not yet fully developed. Therefore, the consciousness of duty had not become fully developed.

Collingwood thought that, in his own time, people continued to analyse actions in utilitarian or regularian ways, at the expense of their individuality. It is only possible to fully understand past acts as individual when we see our own acts as fully individual.[71] It is not that understanding the individuality of an action precludes any utilitarian or regularian analysis. Rather, the historical understanding of individuality completes those analyses, for it shows that the end was chosen because it had to be chosen. We come to see the means as having been chosen because they had to be. Similarly, the element of caprice in regularian analysis is eliminated when we answer the historical question of 'how it came about that a certain agent on a certain occasion chose to obey that rule and not a different rule, and to obey it in that way rather than another.' In brief, the agent had no choice but to recognise the rule and no choice but to obey it in the way they

---

[70] Ibid. pp. 475-476.
[71] Ibid. pp. 477-478.

did. The historical task is, for example, to show how Gladstone, being the man he was, in the situation in which he saw himself, came to support Irish Home Rule in the way he did.[72]

An historian with the attitude that Collingwood described would not pass moral judgement upon Gladstone. Our own moral victories would be gained not by condemning him, but by our own struggle to understand our situation and our duty. We can only achieve that understanding by understanding the past actions that have created our situation and our selves. Writing during the era of Fascism and Stalinism, Benedetto Croce wrote that all of history is created by human liberty, and that liberty alone is the subject of history.[73] We can add that because it is the story of liberty, history is the story of moral struggles.

On Collingwood's argument, an historian must try to show the necessity of the actions he is studying. If criticism reveals that what he first took to be necessary to a certain agent in a certain situation was not in fact necessary his task would not yet have been done. In other words, there are rational and objective (in the sense of belonging to the object) bases of criticism of historical works. Collingwood's account also implied that the defects in an historical account may result from the historian's poor understanding of action. Therefore, rational and objective external criticism of historical work is possible from the point of view of moral philosophy.

Can we ever hope to understand the individuality of an action in the way that Collingwood suggested? Is it possible that there is another level of rational choice? Can we be sure that the moral conception of action, culminating in the idea of duty, is the full conception of action? Collingwood's theory of the scale of forms posited no upper limit to the development of the one concept. The theory of action is a prime example of such a scale. History is linked to the upper point in the scale, the idea of duty. If moral action moves beyond the sphere of 'duty', then 'history' too would be left behind. Historical thinking would no longer help us to fully understand actions.

Collingwood's theory, however, was a logical theory, and not one about the precise characteristics of individual actions. It may be that we should distinguish other ways to analyse action besides the utili-

[72] Ibid. pp. 478-479.
[73] Benedetto Croce, *History as the Story of Liberty*. (Translated by Sylvia Sprigge.) George Allen and Unwin, London, 1941. p. 59.

tarian or the regularian.[74] We would need to show that the new form of analysis is not reducible to any other form, that it is a way in which people analyse their own actions, and that it applies universally to all actions. To some extent, it is irrelevant to Collingwood's moral theory how many forms of analysis there are, or what we choose to call them. Rather, what is important is that some forms of rational choice retain an element of capriciousness. The only way to remove this capriciousness is to treat the act as fully individual. Collingwood identified duty and history as the practical and theoretical orientations of individualised action. To argue that other perspectives provide an alternative view of individuality is, in the end, to argue only about the scope of duty and history as they now exist. If our moral consciousness were to somehow move beyond its current sphere, such a development would merely enrich the individuality of actions. What we mean by 'history' can change, and our ideas of 'duty' may continue to develop. But, in Collingwood's terms, we cannot get beyond the logical concept of individuality, and because history and duty focus on this individuality, we may change them, but cannot get beyond them. To put the same point in other terms, Davidson has pointed out that our language of action is a language of concrete individuals, which he has also called 'unrepeatable particulars'. The truth of a sentence that involves this language requires 'dated, particular events'.[75] Collingwood's accounts of duty and history can, then, be seen as pointing out that our moral analysis, or analysis of reasons for actions, is incomplete unless it deals with such concrete individuals.

How, though, can we understand our situation, the choices we must make, and our own acts, in order to act more rationally? That is, how are history, the understanding of history and moral philosophy brought together by the individuality of actions? In the next chapter, I will examine in closer detail Collingwood's treatment of individuality in duty and history.

---

[74] At least one of Collingwood's critics has attempted to partly revise Collingwood's forms: see A. J. M. Milne, 'Collingwood's Ethics and Political Theory', in Michael Krausz, ed., *Critical Essays on the Philosophy of R. G. Collingwood*. Clarendon Press, Oxford, 1972. pp. 296-326, which distinguishes personal well-being from utility and social morality, and places regularian thinking below the level of practical reason. See also Milne's earlier book, *The Social Philosophy of English Idealism*, George Allen and Unwin, London, 1962.

[75] Davidson held open the possibility that the grammar of such sentences can be deceptive, but was also sceptical of attempts to develop alternatives. Donald Davidson, *Essays on Actions and Events*. pp. 181-187.

CHAPTER 6

Duty and Individuality

Collingwood worked within a philosophical tradition that stretched from Vico to Croce, and which emphasised that thought is objectified in history. The tradition recognised both subjectivity and objectivity, and sought to unite them in a theory of concrete, immanent, will. Collingwood developed the theory to show that human action was the source of reason in history, and reason was expressed as choice in individual acts. The previous chapter showed that, for Collingwood, moral philosophy became progressively aligned with philosophy of history as well as with history. The moral concept of duty was related to the philosophical concept of history, and each concept was objectified in the process of history.

In *The New Leviathan*, Collingwood clearly expressed the mutually reinforcing relationship he saw between the three areas of thought:

> **18.51.** For history is to duty what modern science is to right, and what Greco-Medieval science was to utility: a picture of the outer world, painted in colours that the painter has already learned to use for his self-portrait.

> **18.52.** The consciousness of duty means thinking of myself as an individual or unique agent, in an individual or unique situation, doing the individual or unique action which I have to do because it is the only one I can. To think historically is to explore a world consisting of things other than myself, each of them an individual or unique agent, in an individual or unique situation, doing an individual or unique action which he has to do because, charactered and circumstanced as he is, he can do no other.[1]

[1] R. G. Collingwood, *The New Leviathan, or Man, Society, Civilization and Barbarism. Revised edition, edited and introduced by David Boucher, with 'Goodness, Rightness,*

For Collingwood, the consciousness of duty is self-consciousness, determining action. The theory of duty asserts the existence of a form of thought that is both free and necessitated. The existence of this form of thought can be attested in our own experience, in so far as the experience can be described separately from utility and right. The ideas set out in the passages of *The New Leviathan* just quoted can be approached in a number of ways — from the perspective of philosophy of history; as elements in a broader history of ideas; and from the perspective of moral philosophy. Each idea has experiential and logical dimensions, and both metaphysics and a theory of knowledge are embedded within them.

Viewed from the perspective of the philosophy of history, the problem of action is how to understand acts as compelled individual choices in individual situations. To explore this problem we need to give an account of the particular process or object that history is — the subject of Chapter Seven. History is also knowledge, and Chapter Eight will show how compelling conclusions are possible in history because the object of history and the process of investigating history share a common logic of question and answer.

For Collingwood, the emergence of duty and history is the story of a self-conception that elevates the human potential to solve human problems, and provides a foundation for a new historical civilisation and morality. In Chapters Nine and Ten, we will examine in more detail the broader history to which the emergence of these two concepts belong.

Viewed from the perspective of moral philosophy, the problem of action is how to choose. As we saw in the previous chapter, because each act is individual, it cannot, in the end, be chosen for the sake of rules or utility. Rather, it is chosen in relation to a situation as we understand it, and the choice is ultimately compulsive. How, though, can an individual choice be obligated in an individual situation? The current chapter will explore this question, beginning with Collingwood's treatment of individuality.

Duty has a strong logical dimension: it is that which fully explains an act, or constitutes its individuality. Without this logical dimension, duty would be important only in so far as people used the language of duty to explain their actions. Because Collingwood interpreted duty logically, he saw duty as an element of all choices or actions. The logical dimension of duty was less apparent in many of Collingwood's earlier discussions, but became prominent in his

---

Utility' and 'What "Civilization" Means'. Clarendon Press, Oxford, 1992. paras. 18.51 and 18.52.

later work. By contrast, his account of individuality was more explicit in his earlier writings, and presumed in his later work.

As we saw in the previous chapter, Collingwood's account of duty developed as a response to the inadequacy of utility and right as complete explanations of actions. In turn, the reason why this was an issue for Collingwood was that he shared the traditional idea that the subject of history and philosophy is the individual.

In much contemporary philosophy, an individual is one of a sort: 'individual' is a concept related to the concept of classes. By contrast, in the tradition to which Collingwood belonged, individuality char- acterises reality. History was the traditional focal point of the theory of the logical individual, because history has been seen to be con- cerned with something other than generalised concepts. Colling- wood adopted this view, but also came to recognise that concern with the logical individual is not simply confined to history. Rather, on Collingwood's view all knowledge is in some sense concerned with the individual because it is concerned with fact. Nevertheless, scientific thought treats unique facts as instances rather than as con- crete historical events.

Croce assimilated science to the activity of generalisation, and his- tory to that of individualisation. For Collingwood, this was a false distinction. A scientist generalises, but so does an historian. For example, an historian might generalise about certain classes of manuscript. If there is a difference between the scientist and the his- torian, it is not that the one generalises and the other does not. On Collingwood's early view, the difference between each activity lies, instead, in the different objects thought about.[2] As his thought devel- oped, Collingwood also rejected that basis for the distinction.

Collingwood took issue with the tradition, dating from ancient Greece, which held that science is the knowledge of what is univer- sal, and that history is knowledge of the particular. This dualistic view led to one tendency amongst the Greeks, and a different ten- dency amongst modern Europeans, and Collingwood considered each to be flawed. The Greeks exalted knowledge of the universal; the same tendency was evident in nineteenth-century attempts to turn history away from collecting facts towards the development of laws. By contrast, Collingwood thought that recent Western philoso- phers, for example Mach, Bergson, James and Croce, viewed 'reality as process, movement, change or becoming' and epistemology as

[2] R. G. Collingwood, 'Croce's Philosophy of History', (1921), reprinted in *Essays in the Philosophy of History: R. G. Collingwood*. (Edited by W. Debbins.) McGraw-Hill, New York, 1966. pp. 3-22. See pp. 18-19.

having history at its centre. The status of science as a universalising mode of thought was now in question, for true knowledge was held to be knowledge of the particular. In that respect, modern philosophy followed Berkeley.[3] Much later, in *The Idea of History*, Collingwood wrote that Locke, Berkeley and Hume had reorientated philosophy towards history.[4]

For Collingwood, universal concepts and particularity are abstractions from individuality. There is no knowledge of either the abstract particular or the abstract universal. Rather, there is knowledge only of 'the individual'. Through science, we come to know 'the individual interpreted fact'; sense data and concepts, or particular and universal, are simply abstractions from the individual fact. There can be no inductive logic, because there are no pure particulars with which induction can begin. Concepts cannot be 'induced'; rather, to be induced they must be presupposed. A geologist, for example, does not spend time making inferences from facts to general truths, but applies the concepts of geology to interpreting what they have seen. A geologist sees a country geologically, and understands it in those terms. To be a chemist is to interpret various changes through certain general formulae. In the same way, the science of mechanics interprets motions through a particular set of concepts. Collingwood argued that mathematics is not a body of equations and formulae but the application of equations and formulae 'to the interpretation of our own mathematical operations.'[5] Each fully developed science presupposes a more commonplace form of activity. History and science generalise, but give knowledge only of the individual. To the extent that earlier philosophers aligned history with the particular, and science with the universal, this pointed to a difference in how they had reflected upon each form of knowledge — contrasting science as an activity with history as a product.[6] For Collingwood, the issue was to see history as an activity alongside science as an activity, but without falling for the inductive fallacy or treating universal and particular as really existing.

[3]   R. G. Collingwood, 'Are History and Science Different Kinds of Knowledge?', (1922), reprinted in *Essays in the Philosophy of History: R. G. Collingwood*. pp. 23-33. See pp. 24-26.

[4]   R. G. Collingwood, *The Idea of History. Revised edition, with Lectures 1926-1928, edited with an introduction by Jan van der Dussen*. Clarendon Press, Oxford, 1993. p. 73.

[5]   Collingwood, 'Are History and Science Different Kinds of Knowledge?'. pp. 26-30.

[6]   Ibid. pp. 31-33.

In *Speculum Mentis*, Collingwood asserted that the historical consciousness sees the world as a world of fact.[7] By definition, a fact is concrete; if we understand a fact at all, we understand it in all its actual features and relations. Because a logical individual unites both universal and particular, it is possible to see a fact as instantiating a law or rule. But, if an historian wants to understand why something happened he should turn not to laws, but to other facts. If he wants to understand the cause of something, he may find it in the actual relationships of one fact with some other fact. For history, fact is the 'absolute object.'[8] Within the world of fact each part is representative of the whole, for each fact includes its relations.[9] In a subsequent article on 'The Nature and Aims of a Philosophy of History', Collingwood argued that there is an important sense in which historical facts are connected to each other and, when we construct a coherent history, we show the relations of necessity that bind one event to another.[10] To construct such a history is, though, to go beyond treating a fact as an instance.[11] Rather, it is to treat it as individual or unique. Against this background, utility and right are incomplete accounts of reasons for action because they are inadequate to their object — the individual, unique, action, related as one fact to other facts.

Earlier philosophies of thought objectified in history broke down, at some point, into a distinction between the logical and the actual. Collingwood's moral philosophy presents a key point at which such a breakdown could occur in his own thought. In particular, Collingwood saw duty as a logical, universal moment in each action. However, his account of the experience of acting according to duty tended to emphasise the exceptional character of choosing from duty (as in the case of major religious figures) and the emergence of the theory of duty in relatively recent times.

In Collingwood's philosophy, duty played multiple roles. Duty was central to defining what it meant to know the human past. Knowing our duty was also central to knowing how to act. Each of these roles of duty itself emerged over time. Since, for Collingwood, practical reason took primacy over theoretical reason, we should

---

[7] R. G. Collingwood, *Speculum Mentis, or The Map of Knowledge*. Clarendon Press, Oxford, 1924. p. 211.

[8] Ibid. pp. 217-218.

[9] Ibid. p. 220.

[10] R. G. Collingwood, 'The Nature and Aims of a Philosophy of History', (1924-1925), reprinted in *Essays in the Philosophy of History: R. G. Collingwood*. pp. 34-56. See p. 37.

[11] Ibid. pp. 40-41.

expect that the practical origins of action according to duty were considerably older than the theoretical understanding of the concept. In *The New Leviathan*, Collingwood claimed that the practical origins of duty could be found around the time of Hammurabi (circa 2100 BC). Under the Romans there had been some refinement, but a long period of relative confusion followed where duty was consistently entangled with right and utility.[12]

In the lectures from which *The New Leviathan* was drawn, the historical consciousness aligned with duty was said by Collingwood to have emerged only in the time of Kant. This was also the time at which the idea of duty began to re-emerge more clearly.[13] The conditions for further progress in history were laid in the time when the idea of duty also developed anew, and the progress of each concept was inextricably intertwined with that of the other.[14] In a brief passage in *The Idea of History*, Collingwood suggested that, with history only beginning to come out of its 'scissors and paste' period, the seventeenth century had enough of a grasp of human freedom to argue the merits of free-will and determinism. In Collingwood's time, though, the methods of scientific history were the domain of even ordinary writers of history and detective fiction.[15]

On Collingwood's moral philosophy, to choose rationally is to choose for a reason. To choose in a fully rational manner we must know for what reason we have chosen. There must have been a time, then, before Hammurabi, when no one could choose an act because it was his or her duty. There must also have been a time when people could choose to act only intermittently or incompletely from duty, the element of utility or right predominating. Being unable to choose for a certain reason means that we simply do not have the option of choosing to do *x* for reason *y*. The actual course of history is therefore very different to what it would have been if people had always been able to choose from duty.

What does it mean to say that people could choose to act from duty only intermittently or incompletely? Between, say, Hammurabi and Kant, people must have been only occasionally aware that they could determine their actions concretely through reason. On most

[12] Collingwood, *The New Leviathan.* para. 18.5.
[13] R. G. Collingwood, 'Goodness, Rightness, Utility', in Collingwood, *The New Leviathan.* See pp. 477-478.
[14] Such a characterisation seems very neat; in *The Idea of History*, Kant was said to belong to the 'Threshold of Scientific History' rather than to the period of scientific history itself. The discrepancy is not, however, material. Collingwood, *The Idea of History. Revised edition.* pp. 93-104.
[15] Ibid. pp. 319-320.

occasions, choices were expressed in the general terms of rules or utility. Collingwood himself said that '[t]he evidence is that the word duty, in a very large number of well established usages, means nothing more nor less than conformity with rules.'[16] It would seem, in this context, that only a major crisis would force people to abandon their habit of assimilating duty to rule. Indeed, as we saw in the previous chapter, from a relatively early stage in his own development of the concept of duty, Collingwood held that the best way to understand duty was in terms of moral crisis.[17] He pointed to the exceptional character of choice according to duty at the same time as he asserted that duty 'is not one way in which mind may act, it is the only way in which mind can act if it is to be mind at all.'[18]

Collingwood's 1940 moral philosophy lectures explored the theoretical dimensions of duty without considering in any detailed sense the experience of acting according to duty. *The New Leviathan* simply stated the doctrine of duty in a summary form. Did Collingwood simply leave out the experiential dimensions of duty? If so, should we take his earlier statements as representing well-considered views he saw no need to retract? Alternatively, do the omissions indicate a more fundamental problem — the inability to fully reconcile the logical and the actual?

On Collingwood's account, the practical concept of duty has emerged at a definite time. For centuries after its emergence, to act from duty was exceptional; Collingwood conveyed this through his examples of moral crisis. Only at a recent stage in its development, since the late eighteenth century, has action from duty become consistently possible. In what sense, then, is duty a universal element of all action?

Furthermore, if history is correlated with duty, the modern historian must see each historical act in terms of duty. Since reason has developed historically, however, not all acts could have involved agents acting out of duty. It seems, therefore, that the modern historian must inevitably, and systematically, distort the past. One way for this distortion to occur would be for each historian to see every act as a crisis. Another way is for historical agents to be seen as having duties and obligations they could not in fact have.

---

[16] Collingwood, 'Goodness, Rightness, Utility'. p. 463.
[17] For example, Collingwood, 'Action: Lectures on Moral Philosophy. 1923. (16 Lectures, written Sept 1923 for Mich. term 1923. Rewritten and expanded in Mich. term 1926).' [Bodleian Library, Dep. 3.] pre-1927 conclusion, pp. 67, 69; 'Lectures on Moral Philosophy, 1933.' [Bodleian Library, Dep. 8.] pp. 112, 113.
[18] R. G. Collingwood, 'Moral Philosophy Lectures, 1929. [revised in 1930].' [Bodleian Library, Dep. 10.] pp. 95, 141.

It is important to recognise that a problem of distortion arises for only two of the three main stages in the development of the concept of duty. There is a problem for histories of the period before Hammurabi, when duty did not exist at all as a practical or theoretical concept. There is also a problem for the period between Hammurabi and Kant, when only some acts were done in the consciousness of duty. In the most recent stage, the problem does not arise. In the current stage, the view of the historian would coincide with the self-conception of historical agents.

We could claim, then, that Collingwood presented an adequate view of the relationship between historical agents and historians for the whole of the last two centuries. Historians would, therefore, only systematically falsify the past for periods before Kant. As Collingwood was himself an historian of Roman Britain, and he claimed that his reflections on history arose from his own experience as an historian, it seems impossible that he would have meant to be understood in this way. A philosophical conception of history must be a conception of the whole of history, not just of some specific era.

There are two broad approaches to solving the problems raised by the logic and experience of duty. The first approach is to view duty within the overall scale of forms for the concept of action. The second is to focus on the key role played by consciousness of duty.

The difficulties in Collingwood's theory of duty emerge when his theory is examined through the lens of a traditional, classificatory, theory of universal concepts. Such theories set boundaries between related universals in such a way that if x is one thing it is not also the other. On the other hand, Collingwood's own theory of universals, which showed them as arranged in a scale of forms, took emergent universals as typical of philosophical concepts. Collingwood worked out this theory in the course of his moral philosophy lectures. Moral concepts, such as the 'good' were taken as primary examples of philosophical concepts in *An Essay on Philosophical Method*. As late as *The New Leviathan*, the forms of reason were presented in the same ascending scale of forms Collingwood had propounded since the late 1920s. This theory provides a means to interpret duty in such a way as to avoid the apparent difficulties with Collingwood's theory.

On the scale of forms for the concept action, all rational action has attempted to be fully rational; that is, all action has attempted to be action determined by duty. Action has only emerged and become rational over time. In the modern era, the concept of duty has become both practically and theoretically independent of rules and utility. This development was the culmination of a process in which the human capacity for rational action had been progressively realised. The sense of crisis is one part of the experience of acting in a fully rational manner. The theory of duty is an account of the significance and gravity of human actions. Because people have become capable of choice that determines their actions fully, the act of choosing has become more significant. More so than in earlier periods, our choices now self-consciously determine what kind of people we will be. The significance that could in the past be captured only through a sense of moral crisis is now apparent in all actions.

Historians have been groping to achieve a modern viewpoint at the same time as other thinkers have attempted to develop a modern moral philosophy. We should say, therefore, that it is legitimate and necessary for historians to view the past in terms of duty because that was how people had been trying to act all along. Such a view seems to coincide very closely with the key conceptions of *The Idea of History*, the 1940 'Lectures on Moral Philosophy' and *The New Leviathan*, but it does not fully resolve the problem. For it still amounts to saying that we should write histories of the period before Kant as if they were modern history.

To avoid the problems I have been discussing, it is necessary to reconsider the experience of duty in the light of its logical status, and therefore to place Collingwood's emphasis on moral crisis in the context of his logical point. To achieve a coherent view, we should see the experience of duty as our consciousness of the necessary individuality of our actions. Duty is action in the consciousness that 'here I stand; I can do no other', where the experience is justified by the logical individuality of each action. We are only sometimes aware of ourselves as performing an individual act. At other times, we are relatively passive, and so do not act at all. Sometimes, too, we choose only capriciously — this is not fully action either. When we are acting, and not merely passive, we will be conscious of the individuality of our actions.

Collingwood made such points in his 1940 lectures on moral philosophy: '[t]he fact of duty…is the fact that an agent is sometimes aware of himself as doing an action which is an individual action…the fact that an agent is aware of his action or his situation as unique'. Our acts are always individual acts, and sometimes we are fully conscious of this fact. This point is used to justify the equation of duty with history: '[e]very situation which the historian studies is an individual situation; every action is an individual action.' The French Revolution is not merely an instance of a revolution, it is 'the

French Revolution.' The people who made this unique act were acting out of duty. That meant that their actions were not capricious,
though they were utilitarian and were in accordance with rules.
Nevertheless, the people whose actions constituted the French Revolution went beyond utility and rules because their ends and the
rules they obeyed were just those they recognised, and not otherwise; the means and ends they adopted, and the rules they obeyed,
were individual and not merely general.[19]

The experience of moral crisis that accompanies some actions
should be seen as a heightened consciousness of the individuality of
actions, together with the consciousness of the gravity of every act.
Each choice determines the kind of person one is. Every historical
agent has performed individual acts in individual situations, and so
every historical act is rightly understood as an act of duty. Our
capacity to act and our capacity to choose are, however, part of the
history of self-consciousness. The concept of duty is relatively modern, so people have not always understood that they were acting
from duty. To use the broad history that Collingwood proposed,
before Kant people did not understand their choices as fully as is
possible today. Since Kant, people can understand their acts in all of
their individuality. Consequently, we can now choose more self-
creatively. The historian of the period before Kant does not falsify
the past by seeing each act as performed out of duty. Rather, they
reveal a period in which the human capacity to choose was less than
it has since become.

The theory of duty asserts that there is a form of thought which is
free, because it is rational, and necessitated.[20] The element of com-

---

[19]   Collingwood, 'Goodness, Rightness, Utility'. pp. 475-477.
[20]   This is a Kantian theme and, as early as 1948, Gerd Buchdal noted an analogy be-
        tween Collingwood's philosophy of history and Kantian ethics. Buchdal, how-
        ever, thought that it was re-enactment, rather than duty, that brought these
        themes together. Adopting Kantian language, Buchdal suggested that re-
        enactment was Collingwood's answer to the question 'How can autonomous
        construction be compulsive?' Buchdal argued that the relationship between one
        reconstruction and another involves necessity only if what the historian recon-
        structs is thought. Only through re-enactment do we come to know a past
        whose facts can be related necessarily to each other. Whatever the merits of
        Buchdal's theory as an account of re-enactment, his analysis is germane to the
        concept of duty. In particular, he drew attention to a potential rift between the
        freedom of reason, manifest in his interpretation as the autonomy of the histo-
        rian in reconstructing the past, and the power of evidence to compel conclu-
        sions. G. Buchdal, 'Logic and History. An Assessment of R.G. Collingwood's
        Idea of History', *The Australasian Journal of Philosophy*. Vol. 26, 1948. pp. 94-113.
        See pp. 96, 105. Alan Donagan replied to Buchdal, amongst others, in 'The Veri-
        fication of Historical Theses', *The Philosophical Quarterly*. Vol. 6, No. 24, July

pulsion in choices made for reasons of duty originates in self-consciousness. How, though, is it possible for an agent to come under the obligation to perform a specific act? The moral dimension of this problem is how we can understand our situation, the choices we must make and our own acts, in order to act more rationally. The epistemological dimension to this question is how an agent comes to know his obligation. The metaphysical issue is that the agent must belong to an object with distinctive characteristics in order for the obligation to arise.

By linking moral issues to those of history, Collingwood stood in stark contrast to a second and contemporaneous approach to the issue of obligation. The Oxford realist H. A. Prichard, writing in 1932, thought that there were only two possibilities for how obligations could arise. Either there is something in the objective situation that establishes our obligations, or there is something in our subjective thought that makes the obligations arise. Each alternative faces seemingly insuperable difficulties, and it is not possible simply to eliminate the objective view, yet Prichard thought that some form of the subjective view must be true.[21] What Prichard did not consider was that his original distinction might be false, and that the subjective and the objective might be united in an historical situation created by thought. Collingwood, then, offered an alternative to an existing dilemma in moral theory.

For Collingwood, thought was primarily practical. The purpose of moral philosophy was to enable people to act better, and this meant making choices more rationally. Collingwood argued that we realise ourselves as free rational agents when we choose to act from duty. He believed that our self-knowledge and a true understanding of the situation in which we find ourselves could determine our actions. The idea of duty means that when we have such knowledge, we know that there is only one act possible for us, being who we are, in our situation. Collingwood believed that thought is collective, rather than private, and therefore the same analysis applies to collective action.

W. H. Dray has raised doubts as to whether history and moral philosophy can be relevant to each other in the way that Collingwood envisaged. Dray noted that Collingwood saw historical thinking as a

1956, pp. 193-208. Buchdal responded, in turn, with 'Has Collingwood been unfortunate in his critics?', *The Australasian Journal of Philosophy*. Vol. 36, No. 2, August 1958. pp. 95-108. See p. 104.

[21] H. A. Prichard, 'Duty and Ignorance of Fact' (1932), reprinted in his *Moral Obligation, and Duty and Interest: Essays and Lectures*. Oxford University Press, London, 1968. pp. 18-39.

way of clarifying a situation, and that he had turned to history as the way to resolve practical social and political problems. How, then, if history does not predict the future, can it be that 'knowing the facts of one's situation...enables one to decide what to do'? What we do must also depend on what other people decide to do.[22] Dray's query shows the need for a fuller statement of Collingwood's own, incomplete, account of moral obligation. We have, however, by now seen what the elements of such a statement might be. It ought, therefore, to be possible to restate the theory, just as we restated the theory of question and answer in Chapter Four.

On Collingwood's theory, my self-knowledge is at the same time knowledge of others. Knowing how to act means knowing oneself in one's own situation. Since other agents are part of such situations, to know those situations truly is to know, as well as one can, what other agents have tried to do. Historical thought does not involve prediction, but the fully individual act must take account of other people's means and ends, together with the rules they may choose to follow. The only way to know what other people have done is through the methods of history. Since, for Collingwood, an act may be regarded as a complex of actions, and the organisation of actions over time is a plan, only historical knowledge gives us knowledge of other people's plans.

To place duty in the broader context of Collingwood's philosophy, the emergence of mind in a world of matter is more than an epiphenomenon; it transforms the world by bringing into it something with novel powers. Similarly, the emergence of rational consciousness from the psyche transforms the world in a radical way. Rational mind brings into existence new kinds of processes that differ dramatically from natural processes because they are reasoned and capable of self-generating progress. This is the historical world, and it is a world we create by living as rational consciousness, and can understand only as concrete reason or history. For Collingwood, the development of human potential requires the self-critical exercise of reason. Changing consciousness has transformed the choices that can be made, and the rise of history as a form of thought that parallels duty in practical reason has transformed the way in which acts can be understood.

---

[22] W. H. Dray, 'Comment', in *Objectivity, Method and Point of View: Essays in the Philosophy of History*. (Edited by W. J. van der Dussen and Lionel Rubinoff.) E. J. Brill, Leiden, 1991. pp. 170-190. See p. 187.

Reason is based upon the expression of desire, and choices between desires create a process where reason is objectified in history. Mind as action creates history, and therefore the proper way to examine a life is through the methods of history. The unusual step in Collingwood's thought was to apply the methods of history, which are most commonly applied to understanding others, to understanding oneself. Because knowledge of self is also knowledge of others, Collingwood closed off any peculiar and privileged role for personal intuition in self-knowledge — all self-knowledge requires reason. In the same way, he sought to close the gap between self and others through a common way of understanding each. Indeed, one becomes other by acting, and so we can only understand ourselves through the means by which we understand others.[23] Collingwood also denied that there is any immutable human nature, and so no fixed science of human nature. What people have become is, therefore, what they are. The only knowledge of human beings as mind is historical knowledge.

Action is oriented towards the future and so it seems paradoxical that the way in which we are to determine future action is to examine past actions. In many ways, the project of social sciences that assume fixed elements in human nature or social life has been to find ways of predicting the future, or at least to increase our knowledge of probable future developments. Because the focus on the future is therefore made explicit, it seems that the social sciences, rather than history, would be of greater relevance to determining future actions. Against that view, on Collingwood's approach the problem of prediction is particularly pronounced in human affairs because mind transforms itself through its actions, and the outcomes of such transformations cannot be known in advance.

On Collingwood's account, rules and generalisations have a useful but preliminary role in concrete knowledge or decision-making. The primary value of generalisation, therefore, is in helping to know the past better by drawing attention to particular relationships or classes of activity. Prediction and the establishment of probable future developments have a role in orienting our future actions, yet because they involve generalisations such methods can never result in concrete reasoned actions. To the extent that generalisations are relied upon, they distort the problem of choice, which is always to perform an individual act in an individual situation.

---

[23] As we shall see in Chapter 8, for Collingwood, historical thinking involves inferences from evidence to what has been done.

The choices we face, the options we have, and the situations in which we choose, all form part of what Collingwood took to be history. Knowing what options we have available to us requires knowing what we are capable of, and we know this not in terms of any general considerations, but simply in relation to what we have already made of ourselves. A key element in each situation is the action of others, and we can think through the likely actions of others by considering their previous actions and establishing what it is they are trying to do. We can think in this way irrespective of the content of other people's intentions; it does not matter whether other people are malevolent or supportive. Rather than make predictions of others, what is required is to infer the concrete choices that other people have to make. They may make quite different choices than those we anticipate, but understanding those choices is itself part of understanding them better. The strength of history in making future choices is that only history provides knowledge in each of the areas required for action to be chosen — our situation, our options, and the choices that others face.

To lead a life according to duty would be to emphasise self-creative action. That is, the life of duty is a life where we reason concretely to all our actions, so that each and every action is determined by reason and the element of caprice is eliminated. Such reason is not restricted to particular kinds of actions alone, nor to particular occasions. Rather, duty is a moment or element of every action and choice, and so every action may be done from concrete reason or duty.

For Collingwood, concrete obligations may arise from a process of reason. On his view, historical thinking provides the compelling arguments we need in order to make determinate choices. In Chapter 8, we will see to what extent Collingwood was able to articulate a conception of historical thought that could meet the requirements of his moral philosophy. Now, though, assuming that there may be compelling historical arguments, we need to consider what is morally compelling about them. Why would our thought about the past compel a certain action in the present that will determine our future? Collingwood's own writings do not, in this respect, adequately show how historical understanding compels determinate actions. His general approach would mean that, provided our consciousness had reached a certain level of development, we would know what our duty was. If we find that we do not know our duty, it is because our consciousness has not developed to the appropriate level. But this is a restatement of the idea of duty, not an elucidation of how it functions.

If we understand our situation and ourselves, we may well see that there is only one course open to us, and so we may choose it. But much more is required by Collingwood's concept of duty than the fact that we choose some action and have narrowed down the range to just one. As we have seen, the obligating factor cannot simply be the concurrence of certain rules, or the fact that several analyses of likely benefit may point us in the one direction. Such factors can only narrow the field, and do not compel us to act. Even in his most fully developed lectures and notes on moral philosophy, there is little discussion of this question. Rather, at the end of such documents as his 1940 'Lectures on Moral Philosophy', Collingwood was content to assert that if we do understand our situation and ourselves we will know what we must do.[24]

Nevertheless, Collingwood's philosophy permits the omission to be rectified. Obligation is a logical relationship. In the realm of moral action, we come to know ourselves by drawing conclusions in arguments based on evidence. Similarly, to understand a situation is to reach a conclusion based on evidence. Collingwood thought that duty is reason, obligating action. Our actions, therefore, are conclusions to our arguments. The question we ask ourselves at any given time is which amongst our competing desires will we pursue. We eliminate various options because they suit our interests less, or go against principles we follow. Beyond such considerations, one act is necessitated by our conception of our situation and ourselves. This is what we choose.

There are two sources of compulsion in our choice. One kind of compulsion arises because our choice is the conclusion to a process of reasoning, and not because of some inherent characteristic of the act itself. That is, we choose to do the only thing we can do at the risk of no longer acting rationally. We are compelled to accept the conclusion of our own argument, at the risk of no longer reasoning at all, and so being blown in many different directions by our competing emotions and desires. The second element of compulsion arises because our choice relates to self-knowledge. We have to choose the only thing we can do at the risk of no longer being the person we have become. To do otherwise would be the most vicious form of insincerity. Our actions would not be self-creative but only destructive, and so not truly actions; as Rudolf Bultmann put a similar point,

---

[24] Collingwood, 'Goodness, Rightness, Utility'. pp. 474-479.

our acts of self-knowledge are decisions.[25] Bultmann argued that we aim at genuineness in our actions but that this is also demanded of us: '[our] genuine willing is at the same time [our] being obliged. The realisation of [our] genuine life stands before [us] as obligation as well as intention.'[26] For Collingwood, the elements that make our arguments compelling could not exist apart from one another, for our self-creative decisions occur in a context of constructive reason.

In concrete practical reasoning from duty, therefore, we regard ourselves as characters in particular histories. Along with all historical agents, we come with motives and pasts that serve to define our situations. We know certain things about our situations and we may try to discover other things we did not already know. This is particularly so in relation to the motives or intentions of other actors. Considerations of utility and right or principle limit and define our options in broad terms. Our knowledge of our own intentions, powers and convictions serves to further specify and render concrete our reasoning. The conclusions to our reasoned narratives are expressed as actions.

Duty, then, refers to a way in which life is carried on, rather than a set of prescriptions about the choices that should be made. This seems to rank all choices alongside each other, as of equal significance and deserving of similar attention. When every choice is said to have potentially limitless consequences, no account will be paid to the range of consequences that may flow from different kinds of decisions. Similarly, if every choice is thought to be equally grave, no attention will be paid to the particular gravity of various alternatives. Yet it seems hardly plausible that all kinds of choice either merit or require the same level of attention. The theory of duty, therefore, seems to lack discrimination, precisely because it involves a way of choosing, and not a theory of what are the best choices to make. If this is so, then the root of the problem is Collingwood's equation of good with what is chosen.

Collingwood's moral philosophy, however, asserts that history and moral thought are mutually important for each other. We cannot, therefore, know the gravity of any actions simply by their subject matter. The only way in which we can know their significance is by knowing in what processes the decisions have their place, and what place they take in each process. The idea of duty, then, does not trivialise any decision, but locates the significance of each decision in

[25] Rudolf Bultmann, *History and Eschatology, the Gifford Lectures 1955*. Edinburgh University Press, Edinburgh, 1957. p. 136.
[25] Ibid. p. 140.

its individual context. For the same reason, the theory of duty gives a prominence to particular decisions that accord with the character of the agent's life. By contrast, the theory of intrinsically important choices is a remnant of the theory of eternal truths.

Collingwood's moral philosophy enjoins us to live rationally, in the light of duty. But what reasons can we offer for living in this way? On the arguments we have considered above, it is rational to live explicitly in the light of duty because this is how we have been trying to live when we have been rational at all. That is, until our actions are fully determined by reason, they are not yet rational, and to fully determine our actions is to make reason concrete. Furthermore, this way of life has been made possible by the history of which we are the latest creations, and is the fullest expression of that history in so far as it concerns the way we choose. By living in such a way, we may create ourselves most fully, determining our actions by our reason.

In this chapter, we have seen that duty carried a heavy burden in Collingwood's thought, shaped by the alignment he maintained between moral philosophy, history and the philosophy of history. Collingwood's theory presented the life of duty as the life with the greatest awareness of ourselves in our contexts; he held that we enjoy the greatest scope for action only with such self-knowledge. It has become clear that behind the concept of duty there are strong ideas about the object of history and the possibility of compelling historical knowledge. Without these ideas, it is not possible to account for how situations arise, and how we can gain the knowledge needed for acting in accordance with duty. The next two chapters will revisit the concept of history that sits behind the concept of duty. Then, in the final two chapters, we will see how the life of duty opens up, as Collingwood held, the possibilities of human affairs, and how a life of duty, when lived explicitly and openly, can be the basis for a civilisation of understanding.

CHAPTER 7

The Historical Object

History is an object and a subject, a creation and a study. For Collingwood, the philosophy of history covered both historical knowledge and the object of history, but without separating them. History is an attempt to know an object, and to investigate the activity of history it is necessary to concern oneself with what the historian is trying to know, and how.[1]

In earlier chapters, I have suggested that Collingwood saw thought as objectified in history and the object of history as created by action. This view of the object of history implies that history is constituted by reason. In this chapter, we shall return to some features of this view to enable us to better see what follows from it. We shall also see, therefore, what history is not. In particular, history is not nature; reason must be distinguished from what is not reason. How the distinction between history and nature is drawn is a key issue in determining what history can include; that is, what can those, whose reason constitutes history, make?

Alongside the distinction between history and nature, there is a distinction between natural scientific and historical thinking, whereby neither is reducible to the other. (Collingwood's distinction between law and duty was itself a reflection of the irreducibility of history to natural science.) Historical thinking is an activity of reason that reflects the characteristics of its object; as an activity of reason, it forms part of its object at the same time as it provides knowledge of its object. Since history objectifies the activity of mind, we shall see that history, as object and as subject, is the self-knowledge of mind.

[1]   R. G. Collingwood, *The Idea of History. Revised edition, with Lectures 1926-1928, ed-ited with an introduction by Jan van der Dussen.* Clarendon Press, Oxford, 1993. pp. 1-3.

Historical thinking, therefore, is a key element in determining what the makers of history can make.

But if history is reason, what are we to make of emotions? I will conclude this chapter by considering whether emotions belong to history, or simply to nature; can they be known historically, or only through natural science? Collingwood's account of reason begins with desire, and so his account of choice and reason would unravel unless emotions are part of history.

I have earlier maintained that Collingwood held that actions are the objectification of thought in history; these actions and thoughts constitute the object of history. Hegel had seen history as the 'emptying of Spirit into Time'. Collingwood, by contrast, united logic with human acts, and made time-fulness an inherent element of his theory. By 1928, he had come to conceive of history as 'a logical sequence of reactions to situations'. If this is so, then there can not be materialist or naturalistic histories.[2] As a logical sequence, history must be a genuine development, and the role of the historian is therefore to 'see the inner structure of his subject as a development.' The unity of history, or of a period, is a 'unity of thought'.[3] In another early paper, Collingwood identified the 'business of the historian' as being the discovery of 'problems [that] confronted men in the past, and how they solved them.'[4] In 'The Nature and Aims of a Philosophy of History', he sympathised with the view that, although there is a plan in history, the plan 'does not pre-exist to its own revelation'. Where Kant held that 'history has a natural plan for creatures who have no plan of their own', Collingwood's view, by contrast, was that history 'is a drama' that is 'co-operatively extemporised by its own performers.'[5]

To say that history is constituted by actions is not to say all that there is to say about the object of history. Rather, because action constitutes history, history is an object constituted by the contingencies of thought, choice and reason. Collingwood, therefore, conceived of history as free from any presumed, pre-existing, philosophical conception of 'man'. He criticised the idea of spiritual substance and

---

[2]   R. G. Collingwood, 'Outlines of a Philosophy of History', printed in *The Idea of History. Revised editioni*. pp. 426-496. See p. 476.

[3]   Ibid. pp. 478-479.

[4]   R. G. Collingwood, 'The Theory of Historical Cycles', (1927), reprinted in *Essays in the Philosophy of History: R. G. Collingwood*. (Edited by W. Debbins.) McGraw-Hill, New York, 1966. pp. 76-89. See p. 85.

[5]   R. G. Collingwood, 'The Nature and Aims of a Philosophy of History', (1924-1925), reprinted in *Essays in the Philosophy of History: R. G. Collingwood*. pp. 34-56. See p. 36.

those, such as Hume, who were simultaneously critics of such ideas but nevertheless maintained substantialistic accounts of human nature within their broader philosophies. On Collingwood's interpretation, Hume dispensed with the idea of spiritual substance and, therefore, implied that 'mind is what it does', and 'a mind's nature is nothing but the ways in which it thinks and acts.' In that sense, 'mental substance' became 'mental process'. For Hume, however, the 'laws of mental process are ready made and unchanging from the beginning.' He did not, therefore, fully realise the significance of his own critique of spiritual substance.[6]

For Collingwood, by contrast, since mind is what it does, 'human nature' is simply a name for 'human activities' and a change in the abilities of people is, therefore, a change in their human nature.[7] Human activities, however, needed to be understood in terms of a distinction between mental process and historical process. It was also necessary to emphasise the need of mind to create the rules it obeys. Indeed, in Collingwood's view, the two distinctions became one — 'all [mental] process is not historical process. A process is historical only when it creates its own laws'.[8] Collingwood's emphasis on the need of thought to make its own rules or laws reflected his view that thought is criteriological and was expressed most clearly in the concept of duty. In moral action, the need to create the rules that we obey drives the moral consciousness from action according to rule towards the idea of an individual act in individual circumstances. For Collingwood, in solving problems, raising new ones, creating new rules, or moving beyond them altogether, the activity of mind changes human abilities; 'human nature', therefore, develops through human history.

Historical thinking is one of the human abilities that develop in history; it leads to the development of historical knowledge. Historical knowledge is mind reflecting on its own actions and development, and thereby coming to know itself (to know its abilities), by knowing what the human mind has been capable of in the past. History, then, provides the self-knowledge of action as reason, determining human nature. This self-knowledge of history as reason must, in turn, become creative of history and human nature. Historical thought, by bringing to light history as the story of self-creation, brings about the power of self-creation. For thought to judge its own acts against its own criteria requires self-reflective consciousness.

---

[6] Collingwood, *The Idea of History. Revised edition.* pp. 76, 83.
[7] Ibid. p. 226.
[8] Ibid. p. 83.

The self-reflective character of thought leads to an attempt to make the process of thought, and therefore the process of history, more satisfactory to its own developing standards. Cats may have the rudiments of an historical life, but historical processes become more historical to the extent that thought becomes more rational. Collingwood provided his clearest argument that the process of history leads to the self-creation of human nature in *The Idea of History*. In that book, he maintained that, through historical knowledge, our understanding of past actions, 'man creates for himself this or that kind of human nature'.[9] The rationality of thought depends on a self-conscious recognition of the characteristics of thought. Collingwood argued therefore, that

> it is only in so far as this process ['the historical process, the process of thoughts'] is known for a process of thoughts that it is one. The self-knowledge of reason is not an accident; it belongs to its essence.[10]

History as an object, then, is the self-knowledge of mind, where mind, like language is conceived as existing only through interactions with others and with the world. At the same time, history is the self-creation of mind; in history, self-knowledge and self-creation are the same thing.

Collingwood's point about self-knowledge and self-creation has also appeared in earlier chapters, but must be incomprehensible to those who think about history as simply one field of knowledge amongst others. It would be similarly incomprehensible to anyone who treated thought or language as solitary or private activities. In either case, the development of historical knowledge has no broader philosophical significance. In Collingwood's case, however, thought is inherently public:

> whatever subjective idealism may pretend, thought is always and everywhere *de jure* common property, and is *de facto* common property wherever people at large have the intelligence to think in common.[11]

Where thought is common property, the development of historical thinking represents the emergence of ability held in common. Similarly, if history is not a corner of mind, but a universal element of all action, the emergence of this ability held in common must affect all action. Collingwood's claims about the role of history in the self-cre-

---

[9]   Ibid. p. 226.
[10] Ibid. p. 227.
[11] Collingwood, 'Outlines of a Philosophy of History', in Collingwood, *The Idea of History. Revised edition.* p. 450.

ation of human nature presuppose these broader concerns and extend their application.

The theme of self-knowledge appeared early in Collingwood's work. In *Speculum Mentis*, Collingwood held that history is whole and coherent because the object of history is 'the knowing mind' itself. The object of history is not simply individual. Rather, it is mind in its concrete, individual, development.[12] In *Speculum Mentis*, however, history was said to fall short of knowing its object, and was therefore supplanted by philosophy as the final level of thought, which provides the self-knowledge of mind sought by history.

In his later work, Collingwood assigned the self-knowledge of mind to history, and drew from it the conclusion that history was also self-creation. For many commentators, this shift in the position of history appeared to involve the replacement of philosophy by history. As T. M. Knox was first to assert, in the original edition of *The Idea of History*, Collingwood appeared to have become a historicist. An alternative way of reading the change from Collingwood's earlier to later accounts of history and self-knowledge is, however, to approach it not as a re-evaluation of history, but as a re-evaluation of the activity of mind. In short, and consistent with the view that thought is objectified in history through action, Collingwood came to more completely identify the activity of mind as constituting the object of history. On Collingwood's later view, historical processes and the process of thought could not be separated from each other. Thought can only exist in the process known as history. Thought is not, therefore, the presupposition of historical process. Neither is the existence of an historical process 'the presupposition of historical knowledge.'[13] The two exist only together, as a system. History, then, did not replace philosophy, but philosophy that takes the activity of mind as its subject must become what Collingwood called 'a complete philosophy conceived from an historical point of view.'[14]

In *The Idea of History*, Collingwood ventured the idea 'that history is "for" human self-knowledge.' To know yourself is to know what you are capable of. We can only know what we can do because we know what we have done. It follows that the 'value of history…is

[12] R. G. Collingwood, *Speculum Mentis, or The Map of Knowledge*. Clarendon Press, Oxford, 1924. pp. 238, 241.
[13] Collingwood, *The Idea of History. Revised edition*. pp. 226-227.
[14] Ibid. p. 7. I will return to the question of the relationship between history and philosophy in Chapter 10.

that it teaches us what man has done and thus what man is.'[15] Our powers to do particular things are discovered by us through our historical knowledge, and so we may develop those capacities. We have, therefore, in Collingwood's view, a 'duty' to develop our historical knowledge for the sake of 'reason itself.'[16]

In a brief section from *The Principles of History* published in *The Idea of History*, Collingwood maintained that 'our knowledge that human activity is free has been attained only through our discovery of history.' This is the parallel view of the development of the concept of duty, but seen from the perspective of history rather than moral philosophy. As humanity has discovered and developed the idea of history, it has, simultaneously, discovered and developed the idea that human action is free. That is, the compulsion existing in history is 'imposed upon the activity of human reason' not by something external to it, 'but by itself.' In that sense, the freedom of reason from external compulsion is the idea that the process of thought involves logical and temporal relations that are independent of process or relations in the natural world.[17]

The actual development of freedom, then, has been conditional on the development of forms of understanding. The story of the emergence of history as a form of self-knowledge is a story of progress, but all progress remains conditional. In Collingwood's view, progress is possible, but not for all forms of thought. There is progress only when thought, having solved problems in a first phase, faces other problems which arise from that solution. Even then, the second set of problems must be solved while holding on to the first set of problems and solutions — there must be 'gain without any corresponding loss'.[18]

Where there is no thought, there is no historical process, and no progress. There is development in art, but not progress, because, for Collingwood, art develops out of immediate experience, and immediate experience is not part of the historical process. Nor can there be

---

[15] Ibid. p. 10. Compare Collingwood's view on this issue with that of Manning Clark: 'The historian of Australia should tell his story of our past so that we might know who we are and what we are likely to be.' Manning Clark, *Speaking Out of Turn: Lectures and Speeches, 1940-1991*. Melbourne University Press, Melbourne, 1997. p. 126. For example, one might say that, in Australia, the European culture is at a point of pursuing reconciliation with the land and its original inhabitants. One might add that this is a single reconciliation, achieved through self-knowledge of the consequences of past actions for each, such knowledge shaping the capacity of that European culture to continue to live as it has.

[16] Collingwood, *The Idea of History. Revised edition.* pp. 226, 228.

[17] Ibid. pp. 315, 317.

[18] Ibid. p. 329.

progress in feelings such as 'happiness or comfort or satisfaction'. If morality arises solely 'out of unreflective experience', then it arises out of the 'process of nature', rather than that of history. But if 'our social institutions' are historical, and give 'expression' to 'moral ideals' then, to the extent that our moral life consists in dealing with these institutions, there may be progress in moral life. Collingwood found a similar 'double aspect' in the spheres of 'economic life', 'politics and law'. In the fields of 'science, philosophy, and religion', however, the double aspect of a partly non-historical dimension and a partly historical dimension does not exist, because each is historical. Progress is fully possible, therefore, in each of these areas of thought.[19]

In Collingwood's conception of history, progress must mean the coming to be of new, specific, types of action, thoughts or situations, that are considered improvements. For a participant to judge something an improvement, he must compare a past state with a present state. This means that a revolutionary will be able to see a revolution as progressive to the extent that he is also an historian. In turn, an historian can only make comparisons by engaging with the same development − in the next chapter, we will see that this implies re-enacting the change and its consequences. Since it is not possible to know the whole range of consequences of change, it is not possible to pronounce whole periods and ways of life as good or bad. Nevertheless, most accounts of progress towards the present, and of cycles of greatness and decadence, purport to judge whole periods.[20]

Passing judgement on whole periods creates peculiar philosophical problems that give rise to similarly peculiar solutions. In his recent rehabilitation of the concept of progress, for example, Gordon Graham posited an 'impartial observer' as the judge of progress across the whole of a period. Graham's theory is, however, necessarily that of a participant rather than an impartial observer. He posited the concept of progress as the strongest of the 'shapes' the past may take, on the rational grounds that it can include other 'shapes' such as decline and collapse, and also meet the desire for an intelligible past or a 'sacred history'.[21] If it is possible to judge one theory superior in this sense there is, then, no need for the verdict of an 'impartial observer' before we can judge progress. Graham's rehabilitation of progress, therefore, is credible to the extent that it meets

[19] Ibid. pp. 330-331.
[20] Ibid. pp. 324-328.
[21] Gordon Graham, *The Shape of the Past: A Philosophical Approach to History*. Oxford University Press, Oxford, 1997. See pp. 62-67, 77-78.

Collingwood's criterion that progress involves holding on to past solutions while offering up others.

We can judge progress only if we have historical knowledge. But there can be progress only if historical knowledge retains in our thought the earlier achievement to pass into the next achievement. As Collingwood pointed out, a great deal of historical change may occur, without progress. In his terms, if we do not know what problems were solved by capitalism or by war, we will not see what problems now need to be solved. We may change either capitalism or war without historical knowledge, but then 'we shall have lost our hold on one group of problems in our anxiety to solve the next.'[22] The achievement of historical knowledge, then, is a pre-condition for the further development of a reasoned historical process. To the extent that we do achieve a more reasoned historical process, we will, of necessity, have a greater historical knowledge, and our change will be not blind change but progress.

If the object of history is the self-knowledge of mind as action, history is, therefore, not other things. Because history is a particular kind of process, historical process must be distinguished from processes of other kinds. This distinction can be made in terms of whether a process involves action or reason. For Collingwood, history should be distinguished from nature, because one involves reason and the other does not. This distinction must, in turn, be reflected in an account of how history and nature are known. History is not, for example, geology because the process of history is a process of thought and that of geology is not. The language in which we understand the world differs between historical studies and natural studies. The distinction is not, however, simple to make, because Collingwood was committed to an account of the world as process, in which different forms of thought have developed by analogy with each other, at different periods.

In the lectures that he gave in the 1930s, posthumously published as *The Idea of Nature*, Collingwood identified three broad views of nature, each of which could be understood at least partly in terms of the relationship between nature and mind. Firstly, the Greek view of nature, according to Collingwood, was that of a 'world of bodies in motion', a world 'saturated or permeated by mind.' The permeation of nature by mind was the source of 'regularity or orderliness in the natural world', and therefore 'made a science of nature possible.' Secondly, Renaissance scientists and philosophers, such as Galileo, Descartes and Newton, denied that the world of nature was 'an

---

[22] Collingwood, *The Idea of History. Revised edition.* p. 334.

organism', and asserted that nature as studied by physical science 'is devoid of intelligence and of life.' Movement in this physical world came from outside, for the natural world was as a machine, only 'set going for a definite purpose by an intelligent mind outside itself.' In philosophy, this conception set the problem of how mind can be related to mechanical, non-mental nature. Since the nineteenth century, however, a third, modern, view of nature had begun to emerge. Collingwood considered that this new movement was still experimental or formative in relation to the state of its cosmology. The fundamental feature of the modern view of nature, though, was an 'analogy between the processes of the natural world as studied by natural scientists and the vicissitudes of human affairs as studied by historians.'[23]

Collingwood, then, posited the emergence of modern ideas of nature and history that broadly paralleled the emergence of duty from right. The modern idea of history was emerging out of an idea that wrongly aligned history with the procedures of natural science, and influenced, in turn, a new idea of nature. The idea of duty as a form of moral consciousness was emerging from the idea of right, or law. Action according to rule was, in turn, closely aligned with the idea of natural law. The development of each of these conceptions affected others, such as the concept of civilisation.[24] If the idea of nature is developing by analogy with human affairs, it is nevertheless important to show that the concepts remain distinct. Collingwood approached this problem in both *The Idea of Nature* and *The Idea of History*.

The conception of history that influenced the idea of nature included, as its fundamental categories, the ideas of process, change and development. The major achievement of history as a science was to show that it was possible to develop 'solidly and demonstratively based' knowledge of an object which was 'constantly changing'.[25] Under the influence of modern history, the idea of progress in the field of history became the idea of evolution in natural science. The impact can be seen in a comparison of modern ideas with those of Hegel. Where Hegel had seen only logical transitions between nature and mind, modern cosmology emphasised time and an evo-

[23] R. G. Collingwood, *The Idea of Nature*. (Edited by T. M. Knox.) Clarendon Press, Oxford, 1945. pp. 2-9.

[24] R. G. Collingwood, 'What "Civilization" Means', printed in Collingwood, *The New Leviathan, or Man, Society, Civilization and Barbarism. Revised edition, edited and introduced by David Boucher, with 'Goodness, Rightness, Utility' and 'What "Civilization" Means'*. Clarendon Press, Oxford, 1992. pp. 480-511. See p. 487.

[25] Collingwood, *The Idea of Nature*. pp. 10, 13.

lutionary view of nature.[26] In *The Idea of History*, Collingwood stated that an account of nature as a process was not, however, equivalent to the idea of natural evolution, since nature included cyclical processes.[27]

Since Hegel, the idea of evolution had been at first an idea in biology, and then in cosmology. The importance of the biological idea of evolution was that it broke down the dualism of matter and mind by introducing a third term, 'life'. Within the physical sciences, the concept of activity — for example, the activity of electrons — as being fundamental to matter meant that the concept of matter also came to resemble that of life. In particular, for Collingwood, 'what matter is' meant 'the same thing as it doing what it does.'[28] There was an obvious parallel here with his view that mind is what it does, and therefore there was an analogy between mind and nature. In turn, such a view presupposed a unitary account of the world as process — a presupposition standing equally behind the language of mind and the language of matter.

In the 1930s, then, Collingwood was trying to find a more sophisticated concept than 'becoming' in order to treat mind and matter as activity. But his later theory left at least one unresolved problem. How is it that there is a way of acting called mind, and another way of acting called matter? It is that which has transpired which leads matter and mind to be what they are. So, the differentiation of mind from matter, or kinds of minds and matter from other kinds, could only be accounted for by giving a narrative of their development.[29]

In *The Idea of History*, Collingwood showed that the relationship between nature and man was a key concern of thinkers such as Herder, Kant and Hegel. From Herder, subsequent philosophy inherited the task of distinguishing between nature, which is process ruled absolutely by law, and man, who is conceived as a process 'governed (as Kant was to put it) not by law simply but by consciousness of law.' The problem was to show 'that the life of man is an historical life because it is a mental or spiritual life.' In Kant,

[26] Ibid. pp. 121-122, 131.
[27] Collingwood, *The Idea of History. Revised edition.* p. 321.
[28] Collingwood, *The Idea of Nature.* pp. 134, 148.
[29] Such a narrative must be both temporal and logical at the same time. Implicit in such a narrative was the evolutionary cosmology of Alexander and Whitehead. In Collingwood's view, the weakness of these two great philosophers was that they carried with them a relic of the positivist philosophy of the nineteenth century. In particular, they viewed cosmological philosophy as reflection on what the natural sciences had to say about nature, without considering that other forms of thought, such as history, were also relevant to the idea of nature. Collingwood, *The Idea of Nature.* p. 176.

Collingwood found an assimilation of history to nature, in the sense that Kant had treated history as a spectacle or a phenomenon under scrutiny. Yet, Kant's view of mind as self-legislating, and therefore free, led to the view that the human race becomes rational in the course of its development.[30]

Hegel distinguished natural processes and historical processes, because he allowed evolution in history while denying evolution in nature. The truth in this view was, according to Collingwood, that human history is 'the life of thinking beings.' To prefigure a debate I will discuss more fully in the next chapter, since historians re-enact thoughts of historical agents, history as a succession of events can only include acts that can be re-enacted. History, as the object of historical knowledge, is the 'history of thought.' Since history consists of actions, and actions involve thought that can only be known through re-enactment, 'reason' must be the 'mainspring of the historical process'. Finally, Hegel saw that, if all history is the history of thought, and reason is the mainspring of the historical process, then 'the historical process is at bottom a logical process.'[31] Logical concepts are necessary to history because to describe thought is to use logical terms.

Collingwood further articulated the key distinction between history and nature in his discussion of the theory of Georg Simmel. Collingwood claimed that Simmel confused natural processes, where the past dies, with historical processes, where the past lives because it is re-enacted in the mind of the historian.[32] The object that historians can know is thought, and thought involves logical relations. By contrast, nature involves not logical relations but relations of natural law, in which the universal law stands outside the particulars of nature. In history, the universal is involved in the process and develops through it; human nature comes into existence through the historical process itself. In a 1934 version of what became *The Idea of Nature*, Collingwood argued that history is a process of self-creation that consists of human activity. Historical acts pass in and out of 'existence', but not out of 'being'. Rather, historical acts can be studied again and again. They are, therefore, 'concrete eternal objects'.[33]

---

[30] Collingwood, *The Idea of History. Revised edition.* pp. 92-93, 97, 101, 103.

[31] Ibid. pp. 115-117.

[32] Ibid. p. 171.

[33] R. G. Collingwood, 'Conclusions to Lectures on Nature and Mind', printed in *The Principles of History: and other writings in philosophy of history.* Edited with an introduction by W. H. Dray and W. J. van der Dussen. Oxford University Press, Oxford, 1999. pp. 250-270. See pp. 263-264.

What the characteristics of a process of thought might be had been a crucial issue in the philosophical tradition of thought about history. In the late 1920s, Collingwood argued that thought is a form of non-causal determination. To be a thinking agent is to be 'free and intelligent'. We are put into a certain situation, and in this situation we act as freely and intelligently as we can. Every event that expresses thought 'is a conscious reaction to a situation, not the effect of a cause.' It is true that a certain situation may lead to a certain action on the part of an agent, but that is only because 'the agent is guided by certain principles', such as the rules of chess when we play that game.[34] The determining elements in an historical process are, therefore, the situation to which an agent reacts and the principles that they follow. In the late 1920s, Collingwood had not developed his full account of moral action and therefore he emphasised rightness rather than duty.

In the late 1920s, Collingwood was concerned to clearly distinguish what he called the 'conditioning' inherent in a process of thought from any idea of causality. He argued, for example, that '[a] thought can never be either an effect or a cause', only part of 'a sequence of conditioned and conditioning elements.' The major difference between the principles we follow in conscious action and causal laws in natural science is that principles operate consciously. Indeed, we cannot follow a principle except when we think it; to cease to think of a principle is for the principle to 'cease to operate'. For that reason, we cannot discover these principles except by historical study, for they are 'historical phenomena' coming in and out of existence, developing and being replaced.[35]

There were considerable similarities between the discussion of conscious principles in the late 1920s and Collingwood's later discussion of presuppositions in *An Essay on Metaphysics*. There was also, however, an important difference. In the later work, Collingwood identified three senses of the word 'cause'. The first sense was an 'historical sense'. The second was associated with 'practical sciences of nature' and the third with 'theoretical sciences of nature'. The 'historical sense' of the word 'cause', which Collingwood took to be the primary sense, was almost identical to the earlier idea of non-causal determination of thought. In the historical sense, 'that which is "caused" is the free and deliberate act of a conscious and responsible agent, and "causing" him to do it means affording him a

---

[34] Collingwood, 'Outlines of a Philosophy of History.' p. 475.
[35] Ibid. pp. 474-475.

motive for doing it.'[36] While Collingwood clearly changed his views on the use of the word 'cause', the central element of his view remained the same in 1940 as it was in the late 1920s. There are forms of written history utilising constant causal laws rather than principles. To write history in this way is, in Collingwood's view, to turn history into nature, forgetting that 'nature has no history.' Indeed, by setting up constant causal laws, historical materialism rejects the 'diversity of the principles on which men act'. It is this diversity which, on Collingwood's view, 'individualises historical periods'. Yet, it cannot be wholly false to suggest that some laws hold across the diversity of principles. A common core of principles of rationality develops historically and across periods. It follows, therefore, since history is a process of thought, that there must be a common core of historical processes.[37]

History is a particular kind of process, in a world of process. Law-governed or causal processes comprise the field of nature. Will-governed and, in that sense, free processes constitute history as a law-creating and not simply law-governed process. Not everything about our species is relevant to history. History is logical as well as temporal, and creative of human mind or spirit. History is limited to actions, which express thought or inner will. It is limited to human affairs only so long as we recognise humans as the only intelligent agents. The history of thought cannot be discovered by the methods of natural science, as if it were a mere event. A thought can only be discovered by thought. To discover again a thought that has already been enacted is to *re*-think the thought, or to *re*-enact it. History is not concerned with those elements of human affairs that are not actions. 'Impulses and appetites' may, in fact, determine human activity. In that case, the act is a part of a 'natural process.'[38]

What, in our species, is solely part of natural process and what is part of history? Many biological functions occur throughout our lives and we are never conscious of them. When we become conscious of them we may choose to act upon them in such a way as to make us healthier, stronger or more active. Such conscious acts are

[36] R. G. Collingwood, *An Essay on Metaphysics. Revised Edition With The Nature of Metaphysical Study; Function of Metaphysics in Civilization; Notes for an Essay on Logic. Edited with an Introduction by Rex Martin.* Clarendon Press, Oxford, 1998. pp. 285-343. See p. 285.
[37] Collingwood, 'Outlines of a Philosophy of History.' pp. 475-476. Chapter 4 of the present study, on the logic of question and answer, suggested some concepts such as 'development' and 'tradition' that are core to historical processes, in so far as there are historical processes at all. 'Progress' is also clearly a key concept of historical process.
[38] Collingwood, *The Idea of History. Revised edition.* p. 216.

part of history, even when the biological processes we are trying to influence are simply natural. Consciousness of the act being performed is a fundamental criterion for distinguishing historical processes from natural ones. But what form must this consciousness take to be part of history?

The philosophical tradition between Vico and Croce had maintained that human activity was creative of history and should be seen in its emotional origins, not simply rationalistically. In earlier chapters, we have seen that Collingwood held that reason is primarily concerned with choices, and that choice has its origin in desire. But, if history is reason, is emotion therefore part of nature? In Collingwood's philosophy, emotion seems to be a boundary case between history and nature. This is, however, to see history and nature in classificatory terms, and to seek to place emotion on one side of the boundary or the other. In the context of Collingwood's broader philosophy, we therefore need to ask whether there is another way to view emotion, in which emotion is wholly an activity of mind, but mind that is transformed in the process of becoming reason.

Human reactions, even to their own bodily functions, are emotional as well as rational, and they differ from instance to instance, across time and across cultures. Nevertheless, Collingwood's philosophy of history seems to explicitly exclude emotion from the subject matter of history. This opens his philosophy to charges that his theory of action was intellectualistic, and to charges of inconsistency between his theories of art and politics, and his thought about history. By contrast, Spinoza had given primacy to emotion in his account of human action, and Hegel had taken emotion as the wellspring of action. Dilthey had reacted against the intellectualism of Hegel's final theories in favour of a view that saw the whole person implicated in every action.[39] Collingwood, with his developmental and emergent theory of mind and historical process, held that the novel elements of each new level defined the processes, and existence, which first appear there. The whole person is involved in every act, but does not constitute every kind of process. In particular, not every element of being can enter historical processes of mind in such a way as to constitute history. The question for Collingwood's

---

[39] Dilthey rejected Hegel's account of history as being too focused on reason, and tried to substitute for reason 'life in its totality (experience, understanding, historical context and power of the irrational)'. W. Dilthey, *Selected Writings. Edited, translated and introduced by H. P. Rickman*. Cambridge University Press, Cambridge, 1976. p. 195.

theory was whether, and how, emotion becomes part of the historical process.

Collingwood remarked that the process of a 'merely immediate experience', or 'a mere flow of consciousness', 'is not an historical process.' This argument was the basis for his view that biography might contain history, but that biographies were 'constructed on principles that are not only non-historical but anti-historical', in the sense that they emphasised 'biological events' or 'natural process.'[40] That aspect of human being that is part of a natural process is properly studied by natural science. In *The New Leviathan*, Collingwood argued that if the natural sciences treat of human being, they treat the whole being as body. If human being is treated by reflection, then the whole of man is mind. There is, therefore, no 'body-mind' problem because there is no direct relation between body and mind. Rather, the relation is indirect, between the sciences of body and the sciences of mind, between the view of humanity in the natural sciences and the view of humanity in history.[41]

Collingwood's account of the relationship between body and mind, nature and history, was in sharp contrast to that of Dilthey, whose concept of life in its totality portrayed the structure of mind as primarily psychological rather than logical. On Dilthey's theory, psychology must be a legitimate and essential study of human affairs. Our understanding of other people through hermeneutic methods, therefore, has a psychological element; for Dilthey, we understand others through empathy with them. Applied strictly, the concept of empathy restricts our understanding of others to a limited sphere. Applied historically, the principle of empathy excludes from our knowledge all past societies, including our own, which differ significantly from our own experience. Taken strictly, Dilthey's criteria throw into doubt the possibility that people can ever understand each other. Yet, Dilthey's aim had been to set the study of human acts on a more secure foundation.

Dilthey's theory that the whole of human being forms part of every act provided a potent criticism of Hegel's rationalism. How, though, and in what way, does each aspect of human being form part of every act? The significance of an economic, political or moral act is not in our breathing, nor in many of the sensations and emotions which accompany our deeds. If the whole of human being is involved in every act, not every aspect of human being serves to constitute that act. When Collingwood emphasised the individuality of

[40] Collingwood, *The Idea of History. Revised edition.* pp. 302, 304.
[41] Collingwood, *The New Leviathan.* paras. 2.4-2.49.

an action he did not mean to include the particular tensing of each and every muscle; neither, though, did Dilthey. Rather, Dilthey operated with a somewhat narrower conception of the 'totality of life' and, in practice, defined the subject matter of the human studies as 'the objectification of life', while emphasising that objectification nevertheless involves an inner life.[42] Even in this more restricted form, Dilthey's theory lacked an explicit account of what constitutes human acts and, in particular, what constitutes historical acts. Dilthey's theory, then, did not provide a clear alternative to the distinction between historical and natural process.

In *The Principles of Art*, Collingwood, like Croce, developed a theory of art in which art is language, expressing emotion in an imaginative form. Art is therefore an element in every human activity. According to what is commonly referred to as the Croce-Collingwood theory, all language, however rarefied and rational, has its origin in the expression of emotion, and develops other functions out of that origin. Collingwood explicitly rejected the theory that language was symbolism because that theory could account only for the intellectualized forms of language. The intellect emerges only through the linguistic expression of 'emotions of consciousness'. Gesture and dance are the primary and original forms of language.[43] Extrapolating from the theory of language to the philosophy of history, all historical acts have an emotional content; they are in a real sense constituted out of the expression of emotion and the development of reason and choice from desire. The purposive characteristics of historical acts, together with the criteria by which they are judged successful or unsuccessful, therefore originate in relation to desire and emotion.

In his philosophy of history, Collingwood tended to discuss emotion, only to exclude it from history proper. In *The Idea of History*, he defined the subject matter of history as thoughts that made actions truly human actions and could be re-enacted. He there excluded from the theory of re-enactment emotions, sensations and thoughts that provide the immediate context for a particular action.[44] There was some basis for this argument in his discussion of emotions in *The Principles of Art*, where he wrote that

> emotions cannot be shared like food or drink, or handed over like old clothes. To speak of communicating an emotion, if it means anything,

[42] Dilthey, *Selected Writings*. p. 192.
[43] R. G. Collingwood, *The Principles of Art*. Clarendon Press, Oxford, 1938. pp. 225-6, 234, 244-247.
[44] Collingwood, *The Idea of History*. *Revised edition*. p. 298.

must mean causing another person to have emotions like those which I have myself.[45]

By contrast, it is the very same thought, shorn of its immediate context, that is shared in social life and re-enacted by historical thinking. Emotions may appear to be like one another but we can, in Collingwood's view, never have the same emotion in the way in which we can think the same thought. This point is surely right in the important sense that some emotions depend heavily on the particular state of our human organism and pre-rational psyche, but it cannot be complete. Since, on Collingwood's theory, language and intellect emerge only in and by the expression of emotion, the theory of re-enactment seems to create a yawning chasm between his philosophy of art and his philosophy of history.

Collingwood was not consistent in his discussion of emotion and history. In his unpublished work on folk tales, he argued for the importance of emotion in magic practices and therefore for the need for the historian to experience certain emotions when understanding magic.[46] Similarly, in *The Principles of History*, he argued that

> All history is the history of thought. This includes the history of emotions so far as these emotions are essentially related to the thoughts in question; not of any emotions that may happen to accompany them; nor, for that matter, of other thoughts that may happen to accompany them.[47]

The qualification made in this passage of *The Principles of History* was important because it did not distinguish between emotion and thought in defining history. Rather, it presented an apparent criterion for resolving the inconsistency — the idea that history includes whatever emotion or thought was relevant to the act we are studying and excludes whatever was irrelevant. All history is the history of thought and emotion, but this does not mean that all history is the history of all thought and emotion.

Collingwood's inconsistencies in relation to emotion in history can be remedied by reference to his broader philosophy of mind, in which emotion was crucial. The theories of mind and language presented in *The Principles of Art* and *The New Leviathan* are essentially the same. In each book, Collingwood emphasised the key role of the normal expression of emotion in healthy rational life. The failure to adequately express one's emotions would lead to a 'corruption of consciousness', and so an aberrant development of mental life, collective as well as individual. In order to resolve the apparent dis-

[45] Collingwood, *The Principles of Art*. p. 249.
[46] R. G. Collingwood, 'Fairy Tales: IV. Magic.' [Bodleian Library, Dep. 21.]
[47] Collingwood, *The Principles of History*. p. 77.

crepancies between these theories and those of *The Idea of History*, David Boucher at one stage introduced the idea of 'rational emotions', for which he found the basis in Collingwood's 1933 'Lectures on Moral Philosophy'.[48] 'Rational emotions' are emotions arising at the higher levels of reflective thought; because they relate to reflective thought, these emotions can be re-enacted. This possible solution gives appropriate emphasis to the transformative character of reflection, but does not take the transformative analysis far enough.

The theory of rational emotions begs the questions of, firstly, why any kind of emotion needs to be brought into the theory of rational mind at all and, secondly, how such emotions are re-enacted. If rational emotions are emotions, they are not thoughts, and while Collingwood was able to present a case that the sameness of thoughts makes it possible for them to be re-enacted, there seems to be no reason to reject his point that no two emotions are ever the same. An alternative to rational emotions is, however, conceivable if we take seriously the transformative character of expression. On this alternative view, an emotion expressed is an act, and acts have a thought element. Emotion exists in history, but not as simple emotion. Love, rage, shame, pride, fear and excitement may each occur in history but belong to history only to the extent that they are expressed through actions, and therefore thoughts.

In *The Principles of Art*, Collingwood recognised emotions of the intellect. Such emotions are expressed as intellectualised language, as when a scientific problem has been solved. In such cases, the expression of emotion is the expression of a particular thought. We may think through this thought for ourselves in so far as our experience allows.[49] This account can be generalised in such a way as to eliminate the apparent dichotomy between Collingwood's philosophy of art and language and his philosophy of history. The expression of emotion and desire are an essential part of the process by which choice becomes possible and reasoned choice begins to emerge. Yet, once these have emerged, they have a structure and dynamic of their own, no longer fully dependent on the particular emotional context in which they first appeared.

Emotion and intellect are each involved in the development of action. In a 'scale of forms', the lower forms of the concept survive into the higher forms. Applied to the problem of emotion and history, we can see that it is the rational element in the expression of

---

[48]   David Boucher, 'Editor's Introduction' to *The New Leviathan. Revised edition.* pp. xxxiv-xxxvi.

[49]   Collingwood, *The Principles of Art.* pp. 267-268.

emotion, that which involves alternatives, choice and ultimately reason, which forms the historical process and is known by historical thinking. On this interpretation, when Collingwood argued that 'all history is the history of thought' he did not mean that historical acts take place without emotion, nor that historical thought pretends that historical agents have no emotions. Rather, he meant that expression is required in order to constitute the object called history and that expression has a rational element. Emotion is preserved in history because it is the grounds of rational action, and so emotion is an object for historical knowledge.

As we have seen in this chapter, the theory of mind emerging in a world of process provided Collingwood with his account of the object of history. Since history is the process of mind, it is also the self-knowledge of mind. The historical process in turn develops through self-knowledge. In *The Idea of History*, Collingwood noted that, because 'knowing makes a difference to what is known', 'the historical development of the science of human nature entails a change in human nature itself.'[50] Whether and how the historical process can be known is therefore crucial to the significance of the historical consciousness. We need therefore to consider Collingwood's account of historical knowledge against this background, and in particular in the context of his account of reason.

[50] Collingwood, *The Idea of History. Revised edition.* p. 84.

CHAPTER 8

Knowing the Historical Object

Compulsive knowledge of human acts is compulsive historical knowledge, where history is constituted by acts. To gain historical knowledge is to act in a particular way, and such knowledge is possible because acts involve thought — choice and reason. If history is the self-knowledge of mind, the theory of historical knowledge is the theory of how self-knowledge is possible.

Collingwood was heir to a tradition that sought to vindicate the claims of history to provide genuine knowledge. Today, the claims of history to provide knowledge are themselves subject to challenge. The loosely defined tendency known as post-modernism typically shifts the emphasis from history as an object to the working of the historian's mind or to texts. The question then arises as to what ideologies or forces lie behind claims to historical knowledge. In Keith Jenkins' echo of Collingwood, post-modern history is '[n]ot so much "all history as the history of past people's minds" then, but "all history as the history of historian's minds".'[1] These minds are themselves taken to be the products of historical forces.

Collingwood's emphasis on the mind of the historian and his theory of the role of the history of history can be seen as in some sense the progenitors of post-modern themes. He would, however, have disputed the notion that such second-order history challenges the possibility of objective historical knowledge. On the contrary, it is only because problems have a history that we are able to frame questions that may be answered conclusively by historical inferences. Second-order history is not, as Jenkins has suggested, an

---

[1]   Keith Jenkins, *Re-Thinking History*. Routledge, London, 1991. p. 47.

activity that replaces first-order history of human acts.[2] Rather, second-order history gains its importance only because we continue to pursue history in its primary meaning.

Behind the post-modern shift to the study of historians as the primary historical activity lies scepticism about our knowledge of the human past. But, if we doubt knowledge of the past as a whole, we must also doubt our capacity to study the minds of historians. Similarly, if we assert that behind all written history there lie ideologies or power structures, we presuppose that complex features of the human past may be known truly. To the extent that post-modern theories emphasise the creative mind of the historian but fail to discuss the mind of all historical agents, they are incomplete versions of the theory that thought is objectified in history.

Ideas of historical process underpin any claim that historians are products of their own histories. The mind of the historian cannot be examined without an account of the object of history. Consequently, where sceptical writers would assert that changing circumstances and the exercise of power change readings of history, Collingwood would argue that knowledge changes circumstances because it changes our understanding of the situations in which we have to act. Where sceptics would assert that what we call knowledge is a technique for the mastery of other people, Collingwood would argue that the genuine growth of knowledge means a genuine growth in our capacity to act in our situations.

History is a process, a form of thinking and a kind of knowledge. Historical thinking is argument, and Collingwood's approach to logic was intended to reveal the character of historical knowledge at the same time as it clarified the historical process itself. In history and archaeology, as Collingwood practiced them, arguments are based on the interpretation of evidence and can lead to definite conclusions; this is what qualifies historical thinking as knowledge. Collingwood's theory of historical knowledge was grounded in his own practices. His approach to the question of how historical knowledge is possible can be briefly stated. For modern or 'scientific' history, knowledge is possible because its object is of a certain character and the attempt to know it partakes of this same character. As object, history is question and answer. As knowing process, history is the activity of question and answer about the historical object.

In Collingwood's terms, historical narratives are 'narratives of purposive activity'. There are other kinds of narrative, such as those of geology, but these narratives are only pseudo-history. History

[2]   Ibid. p. 70.

and pseudo-history are alike in that they are constructed by the interpretation of evidence in the form of relics of the past. An historian though, unlike a natural scientist, would interpret a relic in terms of purposive activity, or what the relics 'were for'. It was from this point that Collingwood drew the major conclusion that 'all history is the history of thought.'[3] Collingwood criticised those, such as the German historian Eduard Meyer, who defined history as being concerned with 'changes as such.' Meyer, and others, limited history 'by custom' to change in the field of 'human affairs.' Such arguments created a gulf between the theoretical basis of history and its practice. On Collingwood's view, the theoretical reason why history is limited to human affairs is that historians deal with actions, where actions are 'events brought about by the will and expressing the thought of a free and intelligent agent'. The historian can know a past thought by 'rethinking it in his own mind'.[4]

The practical obstacles to historical interpretation may appear to constitute a case against the possibility of historical knowledge, but Collingwood thought that they could be overcome. Firstly, we might lack evidence to interpret. Collingwood, however, argued that, because the present world has developed from the past, 'the whole present world consists of traces of the past, and of the whole past'. The implication is that the whole present world is potentially evidence for us, and that we may have all the evidence we need to know what we wish to know. Secondly, we might not recognise something as evidence until we interpret it. For Collingwood, this means that we cannot see evidence until we pose the questions we want to answer. Evidence, in short, exists only in relation to a question. The two sets of obstacles to historical knowledge mean that our reconstruction of the past can never be certain. But Collingwood argued that history was not, for all that, 'uncertain knowledge', or 'conjecture or imagination'. Rather our historical knowledge is as certain as is our capacity to show that 'the evidence in our possession points to one particular answer to the question we ask of it.'[5]

For Collingwood, practice preceded theory. His first major archaeological work was an excavation of the Romano-British fort at Ambleside, which he undertook from 1913 to 1915 and again in 1920.

[3]   R. G. Collingwood, *An Autobiography*. Oxford University Press, London, 1939. pp. 109-110.
[4]   R. G. Collingwood, *The Idea of History. Revised edition, with Lectures 1926-1928, edited with an introduction by Jan van der Dussen*. Clarendon Press, Oxford, 1993. p. 178.
[5]   R. G. Collingwood, 'Outlines of a Philosophy of History', printed in Collingwood, *The Idea of History. Revised edition*. pp. 426-496. See pp. 485-487.

In 1915, writing for a broad public to be reached through the magazine *The Antiquary*, he stated the historical and archaeological issues in terms of problems and solutions. The problem for a road builder in the north-west of England was to cross the 'Westmorland watershed; and the Lune valley has provided a solution' for Roman as well as more recent engineers. But for the Romans to take this route was to be liable to the attention of enemies in rough terrain. There was, therefore, a second problem — how to protect the road from these enemies. The solution possible from Roman experience was to occupy the rear and the front of the road. On this supposition, Collingwood suggested that the road between Ambleside and Ravenglass was a military road, and that it should yield to the archaeologist forts rather than civilian towns or villas. Since Ambleside was a central position for the Lake District, it 'would seem to be the best site at which to discover something of the history of our mountain-road'. Previous excavations, however, had revealed very little.[6] It was in this context that Collingwood undertook his own investigations, systematically excavating the site and determining its history.

The specific results of Collingwood's investigation are not at issue here, nor is their validity after a period of nearly ninety years. What is of interest is how, in one early, brief and popular piece, Collingwood implicated in his historical practices many ideas that were later the subject of his philosophy of history. In particular, the Romans were understood through their purposes, and these purposes were conceived in terms of problems and solutions. The issue for the historian was to think through what those problems were, and what solutions were possible. In light of that inquiry, other more specific questions could be framed and a specific field of interest demarcated — in this case, the history of the Roman fort at Ambleside. Earlier Roman history supplied the Romans with ways of solving their problems, and the earlier history of Romano-British studies in this area shaped Collingwood's historical inquiry. In both cases, the solution to one problem raised another. The logic of question and answer, the method of specific excavation, the principle of limited objectives articulated in *The New Leviathan* and the importance of second-order history were already apparent at this early

[6]   R. G. Collingwood, 'Roman Ambleside', *The Antiquary*. March, 1915. New Series, Vol. XI, No. 3, pp. 91-96. See p. 92. See also, R. G. Collingwood, 'The Exploration of the Roman Fort at Ambleside: Report on the Third Year's Work (1915)', *Transactions of the Cumberland & Westmorland Antiquarian & Archaeological Society*. (Henceforth cited as *TCWAAS*.) New Series, Vol. XVI, 1916, pp. 57-90.

stage in Collingwood's work.[7] He was not, however, to formulate them systematically in this way for two decades or more.[8]

Collingwood's major achievements were in the systematisation of thought about particular historical problems, more so than in field-excavation. Nowhere was this more pronounced than in the study of Hadrian's Wall, where Collingwood was in many ways the systematiser and populariser of the work of F. G. Simpson.[9] In 1920, Collingwood surveyed the history of attempts to understand the Wall. He undertook 'to tell a plain tale, the story of the process by which...the problem of the Wall has been attacked first in one way and then in another till finally, within the last generation, a complete solution seems to have come within the range of possibility.'[10] Although this had the air of one permanent problem, with only the ways of approach differing over time, the 'plain tale' turned out to be a developing problem, where methods as well as theories developed over time.

Collingwood surveyed six approaches to the Wall, focusing on the physical remains, the ancient authorities, the native British historians, surface inspection of the sites, early excavations and, finally, scientific excavation. Each of these approaches was subjected to scrutiny. Antiquarians, for example, had previously emphasised the 'ancient authorities', but Collingwood's chronological criticisms reduced six apparent authorities to one story continually repeated. Surface inspection led to theories which were more substantial and were undermined only as new discoveries were made; yet the method of surface inspection led to more problems than it answered, and it was the need for a way of 'removing difficulties' which led to a

[7]   R. G. Collingwood, *The New Leviathan, or Man, Society, Civilization and Barbarism.* *Revised edition, edited and introduced by David Boucher, with 'Goodness, Rightness, Utility' and 'What "Civilization" Means'.* Clarendon Press, Oxford, 1992. para. 31.61.

[8]   Returning to Ambleside in 1920, Collingwood noted that on Haverfield's interpretation of the Roman road system, questions would be raised which could be settled by examining certain pottery at Hardknot. Such an investigation would in fact 'solve' the problem beyond a 'shadow of doubt'. Examining Roman mortaria could lead to conclusions that were certain, yet every question solved led to other questions. R. G. Collingwood, 'Explorations in the Roman Fort at Ambleside (fourth year, 1920) and at other sites on the Tenth Iter', *TCWAAS.* New Series. Vol. XXI, 1921, pp. 1-42. See pp. 30-42.

[9]   For an account of Simpson's career see Grace Simpson's 'Editor's Introduction' to F. G. Simpson, *Watermills and Military Works on Hadrian's Wall: Excavations in Northumberland 1907-1913.* Titus Wilson, Kendal, 1976.

[10]   R. G. Collingwood, 'Hadrian's Wall: A History of the Problem', *The Journal of Roman Studies.* Vol. XI, 1921, pp. 37-66. See p. 37.

new method.[11] Early excavations provided that method, but also contradicted the 'ancient authorities'. Therefore, a more systematic and scientific reliance on excavation was necessary in order to piece together the story of the Wall.

Only in the period of scientific excavation were theories advanced in the form of hypotheses, which could be shaken by evidence. In this contemporary period, digging would be used to settle archaeological and historical questions. By reasoning along the lines of 'if x, then y', and so searching for y or corroborating the theory in the light of y, answers to questions could 'prove' their points. In Collingwood's view, material found by systematic digging could 'make it absolutely certain, quite apart from analogy with other sites' that, for example, the date of the wall was x. Only with the work of F. G. Simpson could the problem of the Wall be stated as three solvable problems, concerning the chronology of the stone Wall, the Vallum and the forts. The solution to each problem was to be had by digging and dating each type of site in a sequence. In this way, the history of the Wall itself could be shown as a series of stages, 'each new phase being not a new stage in the working-out of a plan, but a revision of the plan itself, an alteration of the design.' Modern excavation, then, could enable the historian to 'venture on a reconstruction of the events leading to the completion of the whole work.' This theory, which was essentially that of F. G. Simpson, could, for the first time, 'satisfy...all the terms of the problem.'[12] In this example, Collingwood was re-thinking the argument in Simpson's mind as a way of solving his own historical problem. When he understood that argument, and the history of the Wall, he was able to show that history as the story of problems and purposes in the thought of the Romans.

Collingwood's archaeological writings during the 1920s were explicitly and consciously stated in terms of arguments. Theories were given structure and rigour by a logic that was clear in Collingwood's historical practice, although it was relatively less developed in his philosophy. Collingwood sought to reason from evidence to conclusions, and digging, using the scientific method was the way to establish the evidence through which to draw his conclusions.[13] Where digging had not been conducted, or had not

[11]　Ibid. p. 53.

[12]　Ibid. pp. 62-64, 66.

[13]　His articles were typically punctuated with words and phrases such as: '[i]f so', 'conjecture', 'reconstruction', 'we may thus claim to have shown that', 'proved', and also 'leaves room for'. Other expressions which formed his writings in-

been undertaken in a modern and systematic manner, as at the Roman fort of Bewcastle, 'any suggestions must be taken as conjectural'. Nevertheless, evidence could still suggest certain conclusions and it would still be possible to argue for or against various possible interpretations and theories.[14]

One explicit example where Collingwood confronted an existing theory with his own approach to history as argument concerned J. B. Bury's proposal that the Roman occupation ended around 442 AD, and not 407-410 AD as was then commonly thought. I will not go into the subsequent history of this problem, only the way Collingwood addressed it in 1922. Collingwood attacked one theory in the light of other evidence and the inferences which could be drawn from it, and tested certain hypotheses along the way to reconstructing the story. He criticised Bury for examining literary sources only, rather than also examining archaeological sources. Even in terms of literary sources, Collingwood charged Bury with taking some documents literally, while others were given 'forced' interpretations or simply ignored.[15] The archaeological evidence which Collingwood brought to bear on the problem was principally coin-evidence, and he argued that the coin-evidence was

> overwhelmingly in favour of the view that Britain was lost by 410. It only fails of logical proof in the sense that no historical thesis can ever be logically proved; for on the side of archaeology no clearer and better proof could in the nature of the case ever exist.[16]

These were strong claims and vulnerable on many counts, not least because Collingwood relied upon a single kind of archaeological evidence. In his favour, Collingwood did point out that, in any given case, 'we must argue from the evidence which we possess', until we turn up more evidence, but this allowance did not, of itself, broaden the field of possible evidence.[17] Collingwood may well have been wrong to think that his criteria of proof were instantiated in this one particular case, but of more general interest are those criteria them-

cluded: '[i]t is hardly possible to arrange', '[t]o verify these inferences we dug to the southward, and found the missing guard-chamber', though some questions were left 'open pending evidence from other excavations', along with '[i]t follows that', and 'we can only say with certainty that'. These examples are taken from Collingwood, 'Explorations in the Roman Fort at Ambleside (fourth year, 1920) and at other sites on the Tenth Iter'.

[14] R. G. Collingwood, 'The Roman Fort at Bewcastle', *TCWAAS*. New Series, Vol. XXII, 1922. pp. 169-185. See p. 173.

[15] R. G. Collingwood, 'The Roman Evacuation of Britain', *The Journal of Roman Studies*. Vol. XII, 1922, pp. 74-98. See p. 87.

[16] Ibid. p. 83.

[17] Ibid. p. 79.

selves and the theory on which they rest. For Collingwood asserted that historical arguments are capable of proof, though not logical proofs such as proofs by definition or demonstrated axioms. Historical thinking could, however, attain the only sort of proof relevant to it.

What Collingwood understood to be the logical status of historical arguments can be seen in his 1938 account of the eighteenth-century field-archaeologist, John Horsley, and his work on Hadrian's Wall. In Collingwood's view, 'there has never been a writer on these subjects whose thought has been firmer or sounder in its logical structure.' By logical structure, Collingwood meant not only ' "linear inference" from premises to conclusions', but also the building up of a 'coherent whole of thought which, irrespective of its relation to the premises on which it rests, carries its credentials on its face, as a convincing or acceptable theory.' Each theory brings together different kinds of data. For example, a theory may relate archaeology and texts. In order to relate quite disparate data in this way it is necessary to 'supplement' what the texts 'tell us by reading into their words implications which are not expressed there.' If a text mentions some thing which cannot be seen, as an historian you 'must be allowed to reconstruct these remains in your head, in the hope that as so reconstructed they will tally with the statements and implications of the texts.' A consequence of this need for interpolation and reconstruction was that 'bad historical theories can seldom be logically refuted; but we can feel and locate the strains which they impose on the delicate organism of archaeological thought on the one hand or the scholarly interpretation of texts on the other.' Horsley's solution to the problem of the Wall seemed 'entirely adequate' to the evidence available to him, and was itself a 'logical and intelligible whole'. The new problem of the Wall had not been solved in so complete a manner. The problem, however, lay not in modern techniques but in 'our logic'. Only by a renewed emphasis on the logical adequacy of current thinking about the Wall could Horsley's achievement be equalled in the modern world.[18]

The theory that the Roman Wall was Hadrianic itself ran counter to the claims of the 'ancient authorities' that it was built by Severus. Indeed, the new theory could find no place for Severus, even as a rebuilder of the Wall. Instead, Collingwood offered a narrative of its rebuilding with Severus definitely excluded. He commented that

---

[18]   R. G. Collingwood, 'John Horsley and Hadrian's Wall', *Archaeologia Aeliana, or, Miscellaneous Tracts Relating to Antiquity.* Fourth Series. Vol. 15, 1938. pp. 1-42. See pp. 24, 26, 41-42.

This narrative is in part conjecture, and claims to be nothing more. To be either confirmed or refuted, it must await the results of much archaeological work that has not yet been even begun. Here it is only offered as an hypothesis easier than any other to reconcile with the facts as we know them.[19]

In this example, then, historical thinking was inferential, made use of hypothetical reasoning to reach a categorical conclusion, and allowed for the confirmation or refutation of a hypothesis in relation to the evidence. This process led to the reconstruction of history in a narrative form. The adequacy of the narrative, in light of Collingwood's view that truth is an activity, was determined by how well the narrative encompassed the available evidence.

A central feature of the theory already immanent in Collingwood's historical practices in the early 1920s was his account of digging as a way in which to test hypotheses through locating specific evidence. This was F. G. Simpson's method of selective excavation. As Collingwood applied it, the supposition that y was the case led the archaeologist to undertake the act x. More specifically, certain sections would be dug in order to establish the line of a particular rampart. Previous reasoning and information led to the initial hypothesis, which would be stated in the form 'if a happened, then b would have been the case, and so we shall search for b'; if b was found, it would be taken as evidence in confirmation that a happened.[20] The logical strengths of this approach may also be an archaeological weakness. The method depended on the questioning of a particular researcher with a certain purpose, at work at a certain time. Any digging disturbs and destroys sites, yet the number of researchers and their questions may be limitless. To use a site on Collingwood's principles is to destroy it for other purposes, although this is less likely than is the case with comprehensive excavations. A student of pre-Roman Britain might find that potential evidence had been destroyed by Collingwood's work, as would a student of the medieval period. The digging undertaken through Collingwood's methods might frustrate other Romano-British archaeologists, with different questions in mind. As an approach to digging, therefore, Collingwood's approach had limitations and, although more comprehensive recording of excavations would not provide knowledge, it would better meet the needs of generations of archaeologists and historians. But the importance of Collingwood's

[19] R. G. Collingwood, 'The British Frontier in the Age of Severus', *The Journal of Roman Studies*. Vol. XIII, 1923. pp. 69-81. See p. 81.
[20] R. G. Collingwood, 'Explorations of the Roman Fort of Burgh-by-Sands', *TCWAAS*. New Series. Vol. XXIII, 1923. pp. 3-12. See p. 8.

approach was as a method of achieving knowledge by sharpening hypotheses, bringing them to the test and, as he would have expressed it in later years, 'putting the evidence to the torture'.

Until now, I have tried to show some of the framework of Collingwood's approach to historical thinking. One important topic hinted at but not raised so far is the interpretation of evidence. Interpretation suggests possible hypotheses and clinches conclusions. To interpret physical remains, Collingwood maintained that it was necessary that they be 'brought into relation with others like them.'[21] Such comparisons might reveal parallels that would suggest a Romano-British connection for a certain site. But a suggestion could be 'converted into a certainty' if the site in question revealed, for example, typically Roman workmanship.[22]

Parallels between sites would prove useful up to a point, but the argument from workmanship also depends on comparisons and generalisations, moving from the known to the explanation of the unknown. It is in this sense that we should understand Collingwood's various attempts to systematise and generalise various elements of Romano-British history. His major contributions in this field were *The Archaeology of Roman Britain* (1930), his work on Roman inscriptions in Britain (first published in 1965) and a number of similar papers.[23] Each of these works classified and generalised over a large number of instances or sites, from towns and forts to smaller artefacts. Typologies were important in order to enable material to be brought into relation with other items. In the same vein, Collingwood's major historical work, *Roman Britain and the English Settlements*, involved narrative based upon extensive generalisation and analysis. In all of these cases, interpretation was dependent upon prior systematisation and generalisation, but the end was, as he put it elsewhere, 'a connected narrative' of the period.[24] Narratives made the human past intelligible, because an account of acts expressed the purposes of historical agents.

The idea of purpose was fundamental not simply to narratives but to all interpretation and classification. Sites and artefacts were classi-

[21]　R. G. Collingwood, 'Castle How, Peel Wyke', *TCWAAS*. New Series. Vol. XXIV, 1924. pp. 78-87. See p. 82.

[22]　Ibid. p. 84.

[23]　R. G. Collingwood, *The Archaeology of Roman Britain*. Methuen, London, 1930; R. G. Collingwood and R. P. Wright, *The Roman Inscriptions of Britain. Volume I, Inscriptions on Stone*. Clarendon Press, Oxford, 1965; R. G. Collingwood, 'A System of numerical references to the parts of Hadrian's Wall and the structures along its line', *TCWAAS*. New Series. Vol. XXX, 1930. pp. 108-115.

[24]　R. G. Collingwood, 'The Last Years of Roman Cumberland', *TCWAAS*. New Series. Vol. XXIV, 1924. pp. 247-255. See p. 247.

fied according to their use, their function or the ideas they expressed; a brooch was a brooch and not simply a piece of metal because of its purpose; a certain site was a fort and not a village because of the way it was used. In every case, the use was expressed in ways that left physical traces from which the historian or archaeologist could reconstruct the purpose. As Collingwood put the point when studying the famous Bewcastle Cross (also studied by his father, W. G. Collingwood)

> our first and chief duty [is to] read in it the thoughts which those who carved it expressed in their carvings: to understand how its interlaced patterns, with their subtle design and intense feeling, express here as elsewhere in early English and Celtic art a dark and brooding consciousness of eternity...[25]

Collingwood's historical researches were regulated, therefore, by the principle that history is an intelligible narrative of agents' acts and purposes. No historical narrative, and no interpretation, however conclusive the argument, can be definitive in the sense of no longer being open to revision. Rather, each history is 'only a bulletin reporting the present state of opinion.'[26] Not only does new evidence come to light, but history also depends on the capacity of the historian to examine a site and to 'reconstitute it in imagination'.[27] In another context, Collingwood wrote of being able to 'reconstruct the picture' of a certain fort.[28] This ability varies from historian to historian, and the historian's image will differ over time. The way in which the images differ is itself an important point in the history of history.

In the particular case of Hadrian's Wall, the ascription of the Wall to Hadrian and the narrative of its construction and reconstruction had led, by 1927, to further thinking which undermined the theory Collingwood had proposed in 1921. The Wall was still to be seen as an expression of Roman frontier policy, and as itself being 'the result of numerous experiments and adaptations whose history is exceedingly intricate'. The previous theory of the Wall, which held that the ditch, the forts and the Wall were all built under Hadrian, with the Wall itself being something of an 'afterthought', could now be seen

[25] R. G. Collingwood, 'The Bewcastle Cross', *TCWAAS*. New Series. Vol. XXXV, 1935. pp. 1-29. See p. 2.

[26] R. G. Collingwood, 'Hadrian's Wall', *History: The Quarterly Journal of the Historical Association*. New Series. Vol. X, 1925. pp. 193-202. See p. 194.

[27] R. G. Collingwood, 'Liddel Strength', *TCWAAS*. New Series. Vol. XXVI, 1926. pp. 390-397. See p. 394.

[28] R. G. Collingwood, 'Maiden Castle in Stainmore', *TCWAAS*. New Series. Vol. XXVII, 1927. pp. 170-177. See p. 177.

to have had 'very serious complications'. In particular, there was 'a Wall too many' where the Turf Wall was found between the Vallum and the Stone Wall. Furthermore, there was the added complication of a foundation for parts of the Stone Wall broader than the Wall itself. It also appeared that this foundation was contemporaneous with at least one fort, so that the previously accepted chronology was no longer sustainable.[29] Further work by F. G. Simpson showed that the broad-foundation was not an earlier wall, but simply an indication that the Stone Wall was originally intended to be wider than its most common width.[30] Collingwood's claim that Severus was not associated with the rebuilding of the Wall was similarly rejected within a matter of years.[31]

Hypotheses can be supported as well as rejected, and theories may be complicated as well as strengthened. Collingwood's work went through each process in his own lifetime. In thinking through his idea that the purpose of the Wall was as a 'chain of signal-stations', Collingwood was led to the logical consequence of his theory — there must have been further signal-stations extending along the coast of Cumberland. Pursuing his hypothesis, Colling-wood suggested a number of sites at which there could have been signal-stations, and invited others to investigate the areas in order to 'confirm or controvert the conjectures' he had put forward.[32] Famously, Collingwood's hypotheses were subsequently confirmed. Other work on the frontier served to restore some measure of importance to ancient authorities — as when evidence of the role of Severus in its restoration, or of Diocletian in its rebuilding, led Collingwood to put more reliance on those literary records.[33]

By 1931, Collingwood was able to revisit the full theory and history of the Wall, and show how the problem had developed and changed. Such revision in no way undermined the character of historical thought as leading to proven conclusions. To continue to question is to continue to seek proven conclusions, although as a consequence of such questioning we may come to see a particular answer as all that was possible in particular circumstances and

[29] R. G. Collingwood, 'The Roman Frontier in Britain', *Antiquity: A Quarterly Review of Archaeology*. Vol. I, No. I, March 1927. pp. 15-30. See pp. 19, 22, 23-24.
[30] R. G. Collingwood, 'Hadrian's Wall', *Antiquity: A Quarterly Review of Archaeology*. Vol. II, No. 6, June 1928. pp. 222-224.
[31] M. V. Taylor and R. G. Collingwood, 'Roman Britain in 1929', *The Journal of Roman Studies*. Vol. XIX, 1929. pp. 180-218. See p. 185.
[32] R. G. Collingwood, 'Roman Signal-Stations on the Cumberland Coast', *TCWAAS*. New Series. Vol. XXIX, 1929. pp. 138-165. See pp. 148, 164.
[33] R. G. Collingwood, 'Discoveries at Birdoswald, on Hadrian's Wall', *Antiquity: A Quarterly Review of Archaeology*. Vol. IV, No. 13, March 1930. pp. 102-103.

times. Collingwood reviewed earlier theories, examined them in their 'logical basis' and their 'assumptions' and tried to 'consider these presuppositions in turn'. At various points, details could be treated as 'provable' or at least as 'so probable that, in the present state of our knowledge it is the only working hypothesis open to a serious student.' The only way to 'construct a more or less satisfactory theory of the entire frontier-system' was, he said, 'on the hypothesis that the Vallum was the original *limes* [boundary]' and not otherwise. Of all the possibilities, only one was found to hold, only one possibility was 'realised in fact.' The new dating of the various periods in the history of the Wall, and the relationship between the disasters that occurred and events of the time, made clear that the Wall did succeed, and that its creators were both wise and skilled.[34] These are moral judgements, and they were made as reflections on acts that had been reconstructed from evidence. In this instance at least, Collingwood thought that the arguments were sufficiently secure as to warrant shedding any reticence to make such judgements.

In reflecting on the history of thinking about Hadrian's Wall, Collingwood was also led to comment on recent methodologies. He noted that comprehensive excavation was not possible on the Wall, if only because of its size. Only 'selective excavation' could yield results in this context. Surface inspections led to various tentative hypotheses and theories, 'and finally these were tested by bringing the problems to a focus at particular points where they could be solved, or at any rate advanced, by some quite small piece of excavation'. Collingwood noted that this approach differed radically from that of most professional archaeologists, who undertook more or less complete excavations of a site. The merit of the method of selective excavation was that it was appropriate to the site and the problem of the Wall as a whole. But there were other, more general, reasons for preferring selective excavations, namely that this was a 'method scientifically superior to that of complete excavation; demanding more constructive thought and, in consequence, yielding a richer return of knowledge in proportion to the expenditure of time and money.'[35] Selective excavation was, in other words, more rigorous and focused, and therefore more effective and efficient in yielding knowledge. It was not that only the one method could give

---

[34] R. G. Collingwood, 'Ten Year's Work on Hadrian's Wall: 1920-30', *TCWAAS*. New Series. Vol. XXXI, 1931. pp. 87-110. See pp. 91-92, 96, 107.

[35] R. G. Collingwood, 'Hadrian's Wall: 1921-1930', *The Journal of Roman Studies*. Vol. XXI, 1931. pp. 36-64. See pp. 37-39.

knowledge, but that one method was better suited to the final task. Whatever the limitations of selective excavation as an approach to digging in compact and layered sites, it was more specifically focused on ensuring that research would lead to knowledge rather than simply data.

Addressing the interests of his local antiquarian society in 1933, Collingwood urged that all practitioners interested in local prehistory adopt a policy of 'office-work, field-work, excavation and publication.' Office-work could include compilation, description, classification and generalisation, and particularly drawing conclusions and developing theories. Collingwood thought that there were few rules which could be stated concerning these last two activities; rather

> one has to ponder over the catalogue and the maps until some idea presents itself to the mind and then test the idea as best one can. But there is one rule; never form theories except on the broadest possible basis...better form no theories at all until he has brought his results into relation with those reached in adjacent districts...theories can be formed only by putting these bits together into a whole.[36]

Field-work was work on a site, but not yet excavation. To dig it was necessary to be able to draw, and field-work involved its own typical questions concerning the area and what could be found around it. Excavation, however, was the true test of archaeological theory, able to solve its specific problems, and only to be undertaken with an awareness of one's own training, and a respect for the advice of those more expert than oneself. Collingwood reminded his readers that excavation involved the destruction of a site. Finally, and arising out of the last point, it was a moral obligation firstly to dig with 'all possible care', and then to publish the results.[37] At least in this practical advice, Collingwood seemed to meet many of the criticisms that could be levelled against the method of selective excavation viewed solely as a narrow theoretical methodology, cut apart from any broader context of responsibility.

In this survey of the theory of history immanent in Collingwood's historical practice, it is appropriate to finish with his reflections on the purpose of historical researches. In 1931, he considered why the Wall was worth as much effort as had been expended upon it. He gave three answers. Firstly, because the Roman Empire was a phase

---

[36] R. G. Collingwood, 'An Introduction to the Prehistory of Cumberland, Westmorland and Lancashire north of the Sands', *TCWAAS*. New Series. Vol. XXXIII, 1933. pp. 163-200. See pp. 193-194.

[37] Ibid. pp. 195-198.

of history relevant to the contemporary world crisis. That Empire had been an 'experiment' in 'conscious political co-operation among peoples widely differing in race, language, traditions and civilisations.' How it succeeded and how it failed were issues of immediate contemporary relevance. Secondly, history should be 'so pursued as to win respect by the solidity of its logical structure', and the Wall had provided a field for the development of scientific historical methods.[38]

Thirdly, reason was that 'all science and all history depend, for their very possibility', on the assumption that ' "the real is the rational and the rational is the real".' In other words, unless nature and history are intelligible wholes with rational relations, 'then scientific and historical thought are folly'. Natural science was showing that 'no part of nature can remain finally impenetrable to human understanding.' The method of science was to take 'a special portion of nature' and to think about it 'until the object becomes, as it were, incandescent in the flame of thought, and is revealed as wholly intelligible.' History, too, must show that its subject-matter is rational:

> and this it must do, not by showing that certain points or tracts, scattered here and there in the abyss of time, shine with the light of rationality, but by showing that any tangle of human facts, patiently unravelled, makes sense....The more tedious the detail, the more apparently irrelevant the facts are to each other and to the whole, the more important it is to show that here...reason still reigns; there is still a thread, if one can find it; there is not chaos but order and intelligibility.[39]

Romano-British history, and the Wall in particular, was important in the sense that it represented a history not previously seen as fully intelligible. Research had made it intelligible. Only by making sense of historical data could one 'discover whether we are right, as historians, to assume that the real is rational and the rational real, or whether the story of human affairs is a tale told by an idiot, full of sound and fury, signifying nothing.'[40] In later years, Collingwood might well have written 'presuppose', rather than 'assume', for the idea of history he set out was a fundamental regulative idea which defined the end of historical research, but need not be consciously entertained in order to function in historical thought.

---

[38] Collingwood, 'Hadrian's Wall: 1921-1930', p. 62. Collingwood also emphasised the importance of the experimental dimension of Romano-British history when considering the place of Romano-British history in school-teaching. See the 'Report of the Discussion on "Roman Britain as a Subject of Teaching" held on January 12th, 1937', *The Journal of Roman Studies*. Vol. XXVII, 1937. pp. 251-253.

[39] Collingwood, 'Hadrian's Wall: 1921-1930'. pp. 62-63.

[40] Ibid. p. 63.

In his own time, Collingwood's practices and methodology were common in historical and archaeological scholarship. They were, however, stated systematically and transparently. In many ways, by reflecting on his own practice, Collingwood was reflecting on what was increasingly the norm of historical practice, and this is what gives his reflections their interest, because it underpins any claim to discuss the emergence and spread of an historical consciousness.

If the philosophy of history is, as Collingwood held, reflection upon practice and experience, then his theory of historical knowledge must be consistent with his practice. As we have seen, the main features of Collingwood's practice were that historical knowledge is argument to a conclusion that is drawn from the interpretation of evidence about the past. Such conclusions could be expressed in terms of narratives, and the narratives themselves concerned human agents and their thought, broadly conceived.

Collingwood's explicit theory of historical knowledge had three broad elements. Firstly, inference was at the centre of his theory. Secondly, the inferential process was governed by principles that could ensure secure knowledge. This account was grounded in his logic or theory of thought and, in the case of historical knowledge in particular, involved a key role both for generalisations, including those provided by specialist studies such as epigraphy or numismatics, and the idea of history as constituted by actions. Thirdly, the processes of historical inference had themselves developed, in conjunction with the idea of history.

Historical thinking can create a secure picture of the world in which we are interested only by virtue of its inferences. From day to day, we are usually willing to accept only short and unsophisticated inferences. By contrast, the complex of inferences by which we develop our understanding of history is, at its most refined, highly sophisticated and inter-locked. The strength and reliability of historical thinking — its claims to provide knowledge — consists less in the extent to which it has completed a picture of the entire human past, than in the capacity it offers to secure our inferences about those aspects of the world that concern human acts.

Hadrian's Wall does not exist. Nor does the Roman Fort at Ambleside. What exists are a certain number of stones, stories, objects and sites which have come to be the way they are. Part of our account of these particular objects, stories or documents is that they are relics of a particular place and time we call Roman Britain. The one stone is not simply a certain type of rock, but an object carved out in Roman times; it may have been used in a particular way during the building of a wall and perhaps re-used at a later stage. Transported from one decaying structure for use in another structure, such as a medieval house, and found in the nineteenth century by a builder who intended to re-use it to mend another part of a wall, the stone may have been recognised by a local antiquary as a Roman marker. A simple story of this type involves the reconstruction, through a process of interpretation and inference, of a series of acts and uses. Each element of the story is likely to be justified in different terms. At one stage in this development of our understanding of Roman Britain, the stone might attract us by the type of carving, and the appearance of an inscription. A further dimension will be inferred by the presence of the stone in the context of others, in what we take to be a structure of a particular type. Another element of the story will be inferred from the notes left by the antiquarian who found it and offered a series of arguments for why it was of Roman origin, and how it had been used. We can include certain phases in our historical reconstruction only if there is some reason for interpreting the stone as having been used in certain ways.

If Hadrian's Wall does not exist, still less does Roman Britain. A stone has physical existence, but Roman Britain existed only in the activities and thoughts of those who acted in certain ways in a certain place and time. In their organisation, commerce, beliefs, political and military endeavours, some people were Romano-British. That is, their activities had certain affinities with each other, and these affinities were recognised by the people concerned, in the way they dressed, ate, worshipped or conducted business. In parts of Britain, these very same activities, practices, institutions and beliefs were resisted and opposed. Whereas we can directly observe physical objects, and infer that they have been used for such and such a purpose in Roman times, we can infer the existence of Roman Britain only upon the basis of complexes of inferences concerning physical remains, stories, chronicles or the survival of certain practices.

In the 1920s, Collingwood emphasised the importance of interpretation to history. The importance of his theory lay in the philosophical construction he could place on his account of historical practice. On his account, the mind of the historian is active throughout every stage of the process by which historical knowledge develops. At no stage is there mere passivity or receptivity to ready-made fact. Historical thinking, therefore, involves taking responsibility for the assertions we make, for the way we handle material, and the way we conduct the process of historical thinking. Because historical thinking involves the exercise of the historian's freedom, the growth and development of scientific history is a growth in terms of responsibility taken and choice exercised.[41] In Collingwood's terms, the growth of responsibility and choice is the growth of freedom. It is precisely because historical thinking is free that it requires the discipline of explicit argument and logical structure if it is to remain knowledge.

In his 1930 pamphlet *The Philosophy of History*, Collingwood argued that the past is never known immediately, but only 'by interpreting evidence.' He drew attention to the fact that interpretation requires principles, and that 'the body of principles constitutes historical method or technique. He emphasised the importance of sciences such as archaeology or palaeography in supplying history with certain principles and techniques. Such principles he characterised as 'scientific', or those which concern specific kinds of evidence. Other kinds of principles were universal, applying 'to all evidence whatever'; this second group of principles 'compose the logic of historical method.'[42] Collingwood's distinction between two kinds of principle reflected his more general distinction between two kinds of concepts, or phases of concepts, the empirical and the philosophical. In that sense, his account of historical principles was consistent with his broader logic.

Archaeological generalisations, as in Collingwood's *The Archaeology of Roman Britain*, exemplified the empirical or scientific type of theorising, in that they grouped particular kinds of evidence. Other theories of this type concern, for example, written documents or photographs. Most such principles will be of limited application, and provide guidance in much the same way that rules guide action but do not fully determine it. Very often, the principles will not be made explicit until a particular inference is to be scrutinised critically. For example, we may infer from the content and style of a letter from one person to another the broad content and style of a letter to which the one we possess is a reply. Some of the principles we invoke in such a case will be as specific as the general phase of the relationship we are studying; others will be so general as to cover all written materials whatever. If a critic is to challenge our original inference, their criticisms will invoke a broad range of principles, but

[41] R. G. Collingwood, 'Lectures on the Philosophy of History' (1926), printed in Collingwood, *The Idea of History. Revised edition, with Lectures 1926-1928, edited with an introduction by Jan van der Dussen.* Clarendon Press, Oxford, 1993. pp. 359-425. See p. 375.

[42] R. G. Collingwood, *The Philosophy of History*. Historical Association Leaflet No. 79. Bell, London, 1930. pp. 13-14. [Reprinted in *Essays in the Philosophy of History: R. G. Collingwood.* (Edited by W. Debbins.) McGraw-Hill, New York, 1966. References are to the original publication.]

most likely focus on one particular principle. In the example of the letter, a critic may draw attention to the relationship between replies and the letters that prompted them. A reply need be a reply only to part of a fuller letter; part of a letter may deal with a particular topic, but we cannot infer that the whole letter concerned these topics. Alternatively, a critic may take a more general line, arguing, for example, that a writer may cast as a reply a letter that in fact replies to nothing.

Principles of the practical sort discussed above are indications of how we intend to proceed in our investigations. They are rational, not arbitrary, and their merits can be expressed in terms of how some such principles help the process of historical thinking to progress in a better way than others do. The principle that a written 'reply' is simply a literary device is a less successful principle in terms of making sense of history than is the principle that 'replies' do reply to some specific statement or action by another. By contrast, the principle that all replies reply to the full content and style of a previous letter is too general, though this principle does point towards a more qualified and successful principle of interpretation. Each and every one of these principles, however, presupposes further rational principles, such as that all written objects are written with a purpose, but this is not simply an empirical principle, it is a principle holding over all evidence whatsoever, in so far as it is historical.

It might be objected that a flake broken off in the course of making a stone tool does not reflect the principles of purpose discussed above, yet may be an important piece of historical evidence. The flake is a by-product of the process of making the stone tool, but it was not made in the same sense as the stone tool was made. Nevertheless, the toolmaker struck the original stone with purpose and this purpose is reflected in the shape of the flake; it too must be interpreted in the light of the maker's purpose. Agents' purpose is a universal principle of the idea of history itself, and the proper concern of the philosophy of history — philosophy oriented towards the problems of history.

Universal principles, in Collingwood's own theory of philosophical concepts, develop and transcend each other in a logical process. They exist, therefore, in less adequate forms and more adequate and complete forms. Historical practice in its own fullest form must be guided and regulated by universal principles of history in their most adequate and complete form. Every kind of history, if it is fully history, must exhibit certain characteristics that govern the practice of history from its conception to its subsequent communication and criticism. The body of universal historical principles is a canon for developing rigorous thought. How, then, should we interpret Collingwood's theory of re-enactment? Is it a universal historical principle, regulating history, or is it a methodology? W. J. van der Dussen, in his study of Collingwood, justly pointed out that re-enactment is 'undoubtedly the most discussed aspect' of his philosophy of history.[43] Nevertheless, most such discussions have tended to treat re-enactment as a theme that can be isolated from other elements of Collingwood's philosophy. Instead, I think we should see re-enactment as a corollary or consequence of Collingwood's views that thought is objectified in history, and that historical knowledge is inferential. Seen in this way, re-enactment is neither a mysterious doctrine, nor the most important element in Collingwood's philosophy of history.

The prominence that has been given to re-enactment reflects the difficulties Collingwood experienced in developing the theory, but overstates its place in his overall view of history. Separating re-enactment from its context within Collingwood's theory of action as constituting history need not lead to a mistaken view of what is involved in re-enactment, but it does lead to misunderstanding its significance. For example, W. H. Dray has interpreted Collingwood as holding that there is no understanding of an action unless there is critical re-thinking of it, including judgements of the validity of the argument. Understanding through re-enactment involves 'an historian eliciting from the performance of an action an implied practical argument which represents what was done as the thing to have done, given the agent's point of view.' Despite this formulation, which implies the concepts of individuality, reason and conclusiveness, Dray treated the concept of duty as an implausible extension of Collingwood's ideas of historical thought into the field of ethics.[44] By contrast, Gordon Graham criticised Collingwood, along with Oakeshott, for failing to explain what makes an historical explanation historical, as distinct from an explanation of action. Graham, indeed, argued that the philosophy of history does not deserve much attention, but, rather, 'the really difficult problems are to be found in the

[43] W. J. van der Dussen, *History as a Science: The Philosophy of R. G. Collingwood.* Martinus Nijhoff, The Hague, 1981. p. 96.

[44] William H. Dray, *History as Re-enactment: R. G. Collingwood's Idea of History.* Clarendon Press, Oxford, 1995. pp. 57, 66, fn 51 on p. 66, 323.

philosophy of action.'[45] Dray captured key elements of the theory of re-enactment but, without grounding this account in Collingwood's overall theory of action, he missed much of the underlying rationale for the theory. Graham, on the other hand, pointed to Collingwood's own interest, but without the recognition that Collingwood understood history within his overall theory of action.

Re-enactment has sometimes been seen as an important part of Collingwood's historical methodology, and sometimes as a principle of history; it has not generally been seen as a link between the theory of historical knowledge and universal historical principles.[46] The doctrine was initially interpreted methodologically, at least until Alan Donagan, W. H. Dray and others began to make substantial contributions to the study of Collingwood's thought. Later interpretations rejected the methodological view in favour of an analysis that saw the doctrine as part of 'Collingwood's analysis of the *a priori* characteristics of history.'[47] Margit Nielsen argued for a methodological interpretation of the doctrine, while David Boucher has pointed out that the re-enactment doctrine 'may be both a methodology and a condition of historical knowledge' — re-enactment disciplines the historical imagination.[48] Boucher's remark neatly points to the nub of the issue.

The methodological interpretation emphasises that an historian re-enacts thoughts as part of the whole process by which he comes to know the past. The non-methodological interpretation maintains that, unless the historian has re-enacted the thoughts of the agents he is studying, he has not fully understood their acts. The problem with calling re-enactment a methodology is that re-enactment is not a spe-

[45] Gordon Graham, *Historical Explanation Reconsidered.* Scots Philosophical Monographs, Number Four. Aberdeen University Press, Aberdeen, 1983. pp. 29-30, 63.

[46] The majority of commentators have limited their attention either to passages from Collingwood's writings in which the words re-enactment or re-thinking, or various cognate terms, can be found, or to a tightly defined conception of Collingwood's philosophy of history. This is true of even such a conscientious commentator as Margit Nielsen, who has given us a very comprehensive treatment of re-enactment as well as of the various interpretations which have been put forward by historians as well as philosophers. See Margit Hurup Nielsen, *R. G. Collingwood's Historiefilosofi: En undersoegelse af 're-enactment'-tesens interpretation.* Skrifter udgivet af det Historiske Institut ved Koebenhavns Universitet — Bind XI. Den Danske Historiske Forening, Koebenhavn, 1980. See also her article, 'Re-enactment and Reconstruction in Collingwood's Philosophy of History', *History and Theory.* Vol. XX, 1981.pp. 1-31.

[47] van der Dussen, *History as a Science.* p. 97.

[48] David Boucher, *The Social and Political Thought of R. G. Collingwood.* Cambridge University Press, Cambridge, 1989. p. 273, fn. 40.

cial tool or technique the historian keeps in his kit bag and produces at the appropriate time, when he has exhausted the possibilities of argument from evidence. The methodology of history is argument from the interpretation of evidence. Re-enactment takes place as part of that argument, not separately from the general movement of the historian's thought. The problem with calling re-enactment a necessary condition for historical knowledge is that it is never simply a criterion, against which the progress of the historian's work is to be judged. Rather, re-enactment is the grasping of past acts in the historian's own mind, the act by which the past is known better and more fully than before.

Elements of a re-enactment thesis were an important part of Collingwood's philosophy from a very early date, and were not confined to his writings on the philosophy of historical knowledge. In *Religion and Philosophy*, for example, Collingwood argued that it

> profits nothing to catalogue the heresies of early Christianity and get them off by heart, unless one enters with some degree of sympathy into the problems which men wished to solve, and tries to comprehend the motives which led them to offer their various answers.[49]

At a very early stage, Collingwood emphasised that the real interest of history lies in problems and motives for action. He noted that '[t]o speak of studying the mind of Jesus from within may seem presumptuous; but no other method is of the slightest value.'[50] By 1916, therefore, the idea of 'getting inside the mind' of a person was simultaneously a method, an ideal and a requirement in order to meet the purpose of studying an historical character.

More than a decade later, Collingwood analysed the work of Oswald Spengler, and argued that understanding of other cultures was possible only by 're-thinking for ourselves their thoughts, cherishing within us the fundamental idea which framed their lives; and in that case their culture lives on in ours'. In the same sense, 'Euclidean geometry lives on within modern history and Herodotean history within the mind of the modern historian.'[51] In another paper of the 1920s, which also dealt with Spengler, Collingwood claimed that the 'business of the historian is to discover what problems con-

[49] R. G. Collingwood, *Religion and Philosophy*. Macmillan, London, 1916. p. 42.
[50] Ibid. p. 43.
[51] R. G. Collingwood, 'Oswald Spengler and the Theory of Historical Cycles' (1927), reprinted in *Essays in the Philosophy of History: R. G. Collingwood*. pp. 57-75. See p. 71.

fronted men in the past, and how they solved them.'[52] They do this by thinking through the problems for themselves in the light of their situations. Long before he explicitly discussed re-enactment in *The Idea of History,* Collingwood saw 'entering into past thought' or 're-thinking past thought' as a goal of historical study, a condition of success in achieving historical knowledge and an historical practice. The thought which a historian 're-thinks' is a set of 'problems'.

A theory of re-enactment was also an important part of *An Essay on Philosophical Method.* In that book, Collingwood argued that philosophers aimed to 'solve or remove' the various 'difficulties and obscurities' with which they find themselves 'involved'; if the difficulties could not be removed they could at least be better understood. Philosophers, in that sense, addressed their writing primarily to themselves. The prevalent forms of philosophical writing throughout the history of philosophy have been, therefore, dialogues or meditations whose dialectic led to the modification of an initial position. Philosophical writing was fundamentally 'a confession, a search by the mind for its own failings and an attempt to remedy them by recognizing them.'[53]

How can a philosopher be read? Collingwood's answer was that to read a philosopher was to aim to ' "follow" them: that is, we understand what they think, and reconstruct in ourselves, so far as we can, the processes by which they have come to think it.' In his philosophy, a philosopher has expressed his experience, and in order to 'follow' or 'understand' him a reader must 'live through' the 'same experience'; Collingwood also described the same process as 'entering into the writer's mind with his own.' In order for this to happen, the same problem must have arisen in your mind as in the mind of the philosopher; that is the essential preparation for understanding a philosopher. Since the philosopher was engaged in a search for truth, the reader must share that concern, and therefore be a critic. From the base of a proper understanding of an earlier philosopher, which is achieved by thinking over again their thoughts in response to the problem with which they were concerned, the critic's true function 'is to develop and continue the thought of the writer criticized.'[54] The last point was the key theme of Collingwood's theory of progress.

---

[52] R. G. Collingwood, 'The Theory of Historical Cycles' (1927), reprinted in *Essays in the Philosophy of History: R. G. Collingwood.* pp. 76-89. See p. 85.

[53] R. G. Collingwood, *An Essay on Philosophical Method.* Clarendon Press, Oxford, 1933. pp. 209-210.

[54] Ibid. pp. 211-212, 215-217, 220.

A theory of re-enactment formed a major theme of another of Collingwood's most important works on the philosophy of mind, *The Principles of Art* (1938). Art, for Collingwood, was a universal activity of mind. Artistic activity expressed feelings or emotions in language. Artistic experience 'presupposes...psychical, or sensual-emotional, experience.' The activity of consciousness transmutes 'sense into imagination'. In turn, 'imaginative activity' expresses both 'purely psychical emotion' and a new 'emotion of consciousness', which is the original psychic emotion 'converted by the act of consciousness into a corresponding imaginative or aesthetic emotion.' In brief, art is a form of consciousness that translates sensation into imagination, which may then be transformed again, by consciousness, into intellect. 'Art proper', is both expressive and imaginative. To hear an artist express himself, and to understand him, is to 'have that same thing in...mind.' Art is also imaginative; a tune is an 'imaginative creation'. To study the notation written on a piece of music paper is to study something which enables an 'abstract or as yet unembodied plan' to be 'reconstructed in the mind of person who studies them.'[55] Imaginative reconstruction is necessary to obtain and understand the tune.

Part of Collingwood's argument for imaginative reconstruction in art proper was an analogy with more highly developed forms of thought. To hear a scientist lecture on a scientific theory is to hear noises, but it is also more than this. For the scientist is developing a 'scientific thesis', and the noises are simply a necessary element in fulfilling the purpose of going to hear a scientific speaker, namely, 'thinking this same scientific thesis for ourselves.' A lecture, therefore, is an occasion for 'a "reproduction" of the speaker's thought by the hearer, in virtue of his own active thinking.' To get anything out of either a piece of music or a lecture we have to 'reconstruct' something 'in our own minds'.[56] Communication is an activity on the part of both the speaker and the hearer.

The analogy between thought and feeling cannot, however, be total, for thinking is 'concerned with something that lasts, even if it does not last for ever; something that genuinely recurs as a factor in experience, even if it cannot recur to infinity.' Feeling, however, is a 'perpetual flux'. Even in the realm of thought, there can be no absolute assurance that we have understood another person. We can gain only 'an empirical or relative assurance' from, for example, the fact

---

[55] R. G. Collingwood, *The Principles of Art*. Clarendon Press, Oxford, 1938. pp. 118, 134-135, 272-273.
[56] Ibid. pp. 140-141.

that we are able to continue a conversation (a point which invites comparison with Davidson). An imaginative act of reconstruction is a key to that understanding; but we could not perform such an act of reconstruction unless we were already 'equipped for it' by our own previous experience.[57] Collingwood's argument was that intellectualised language is accessible to a hearer first through the peculiar kinds of emotion it expresses. The object to be reconstructed must have been expressed, and, therefore, even intellectual language conveys its own emotions. Specialized language carries a charge of specialized emotion, and Collingwood argued that the traditional account of 'the proposition', to the extent that it was said to convey thought and not emotion, is a purely 'fictitious entity.'[58] There is, consequently, also an analogy between art and the intellect, reflecting their common character as activities of mind. We cannot gain access to intellectual thought simply through the peculiar characteristics of intellectual language. A purely technical, methodological account of the reconstruction of past thoughts is erroneous. The root of the error, on Collingwood's account in *The Principles of Art*, would be the attempt to purge understanding of emotion, and therefore of the need to prepare the understanding mind.

On the account given in *The Principles of Art*, there is only one way to reconstruct a thought, and this involves going through the special emotional aspect it expresses. As we have seen earlier, the particular emotion of desire sets up the need for choice amongst alternatives. We would have no access to an intellectualised thought unless we had ourselves undertaken the activity of re-thinking the choices that a thinker has made, and this means understanding the rational element in their emotions. Since *The Principles of Art* was written later than the original (1936) draft for *The Idea of History*, and presented re-enactment in the context of a broader philosophy of mind, we should be wary of interpreting re-enactment solely in the light of isolated statements from *The Idea of History*. Similarly, we should be wary of any interpretation of *The New Leviathan* that claimed that Collingwood no longer believed in re-enactment, because the philosophy of mind sketched in *The New Leviathan* is essentially that of *The Principles of Art*.[59]

---

[57] Ibid. pp. 159, 251.
[58] Ibid. pp. 266, 268-269.
[59] Such a view of *The New Leviathan* was held by David Boucher in *The Social and Political Thought of R. G. Collingwood*. p. 119.

When seen against the background of Collingwood's theory of mind and action, it is clear that many interpretations of re-enactment are simply erroneous. The erroneous interpretations include the idea that re-enactment involves intuitive access to past thoughts, or simple empathy with historical characters.[60] Nor is there any basis for the idea that re-enactment can give certain knowledge of past thoughts, a view put forward by W. H. Walsh.[61] Another interpretation of re-enactment aligned the theory with debates about 'covering law' explanations and the 'rational explanation' of history. The rational explanation theory of history was most closely associated with Alan Donagan and W. H. Dray, who introduced the discussion partly in order to make Collingwood's views more intelligible. Other philosophers, such as R. F. Atkinson, have criticised the rational explanation model for neglecting the historical importance of what could not be 'the object of anybody's rational endeavour.' Atkinson aligned Collingwood with the 'rational explanation' model because, in Atkinson's view, Collingwood treated reasons and intentions as causes of action. In line with his criticism of the 'rational explanation' model, Atkinson criticised Collingwood for 're-fusing to face the obvious' by denying that the effects of the eruption of Vesuvius are of interest to the historian, only the actions of those affected.[62]

Atkinson's criticisms may have merit in terms of the theories of Donagan or Dray, but Collingwood's argument was that thoughts are the reasons for action, which constitute them as acts and thereby constitute the historical process.[63] Atkinson's approach begs the question of what constitutes the historical process. As an interpretation of re-enactment, the rational explanation theory neglects the important role of re-enactment as both a condition for historical knowledge and an act that occurs in trying to understand the human past. To echo Gordon Graham's comment noted earlier, if explanation is to be logically distinguished from the process of ascertaining historical facts, Collingwood did not offer any theory of historical

[60] There is a useful discussion of such theories in van der Dussen, *History as a Science*. pp. 93-96.

[61] W. H. Walsh, *An Introduction to Philosophy of History. Third edition.* Hutchinson, London, 1967. pp. 44-45.

[62] R. F. Atkinson, *Knowledge and Explanation in History: An Introduction to the Philosophy of History.* Macmillan, London, 1978. pp. 26, 102, 148.

[63] For Collingwood's treatment of cause in history as reason, see R. G. Collingwood, *An Essay on Metaphysics. Revised Edition With The Nature of Metaphysical Study; Function of Metaphysics in Civilization; Notes for an Essay on Logic. Edited with an Introduction by Rex Martin.* Clarendon Press, Oxford, 1998. See Part IIIc: Causation, pp. 285-343.

explanation at all, instead he argued that to know what happened is to know why it happened.

Rex Martin has argued that the idea of an historical process makes problematic the idea of re-enactment.[64] Specifically, Martin's argument was that the 'fact of differentiation' in time makes re-enactment 'problematic'; historical processes and re-enactment are in some way incompatible. This is a key issue, because I have argued both that Collingwood saw history as a process of action, and that re-enactment is a corollary of that view. Martin rightly argued that historical processes involve differentiation. The people of another time and culture to our own may have differed greatly from us. In fact, the idea of self-knowledge as self-creation presupposes such changes, because it involves the view that we become different by virtue of understanding actions we did not ourselves perform. At some point, the difference between those we try to study and ourselves may be vast and fundamental. Collingwood's folk-manuscripts address precisely such a problem, on the subject of magic.[65] The answer to this problem is, however, not to deny the theory of re-enactment, but to remain wary of how readily we can understand other people who differ greatly from ourselves.

We can understand people with magical beliefs only to the extent that we can experience some of the same emotions as they, and therefore understand the choices that arose for them. If we do not find we can have such experiences, we will not be able to understand their belief in magic.[66] This is the reverse of what occurs when there is historical progress, for in such cases we retain earlier solutions. A similar argument easily leads to relativism, particularly in morality, as when those who have suffered claim not to be understood by those who have not, or when those who have confronted moral dilemmas are studied by those who have never doubted the right

---

[64] Rex Martin, 'Collingwood's claim that Metaphysics is a Historical Discipline', *The Monist*, Vol. 72, No. 4, October 1989. pp. 489-525. See p. 506.

[65] R. G. Collingwood, 'Fairy Tales: IV. Magic'. [Bodleian Library, Dep. 21.]

[66] It is important that the restrictions of experience be seen to apply to inference generally, not simply to emotion. In his 1930 pamphlet, *The Philosophy of History*, Collingwood argued that data and interpretation exist in conjunction. Anything may be data to the historian, if he can find the way to interpret it. The activity of investigation limits and defines the range of the historian's data. Logically, the historian's problem comes first — the question he is trying to answer. But he can answer only those questions which his own previous thought and experience allow him to pose rigorously; in Collingwood's terms, the question must 'arise' for him out of his 'previous thoughts'. The activity of posing questions leads the historian to select, specialise and periodise; such concepts of historical understanding relate entirely to the activity of posing questions. Collingwood, *The Philosophy of History*. p. 14.

course of action. Their own history prepares people to understand some experiences, but others remain beyond them. As we have seen, however, Collingwood held that thought is common property and that to come to know ourselves is at the same time to know others. The process of civilising is an educative process whereby people come into possession of the power to understand their own experiences through their knowledge of others, and thereby to see anew their own situation and choices. As we come to have more experiences, to understand more people and actions, we understand better the acts we already understood in some sense before. There are likely always to be acts that remain beyond our grasp. That is not, however, a reflection on re-enactment. Rather, it is a reflection on the conditions and boundaries of knowledge.

CHAPTER 9

Historical Self-Consciousness

In the 'Introduction', I drew attention to a variety of commonplace forms of historical consciousness, particularly those that involve narratives about individuals and their deeds. These may be criticised as being incompletely historical. Indeed, in an earlier chapter, we saw that one consequence of Collingwood's focus on action was that inadequacy — particularly the inadequate expression of emotion, alternatives and choices — could become a powerful concept for historical criticism. Criticism against a standard or goal that already exists in some sense in our civilisation cannot, however, be purely negative. Nor can the basis for criticising commonplace historical consciousness simply be academic or professional. Rather, the focus must be on the idea of history as it has developed to the present time. Collingwood argued that

> When we think of history as merely a trade or profession, a craft or a calling, we find it hard to justify our existence as historians. What can the historian do for people except turn them into historians like himself? And what is the good of doing that? Is it not simply a vicious circle, whose tendency is to overcrowd the ranks of the profession and to produce and underpaid 'intellectual proletariate' of sweated teachers? This may be a valid argument against the multiplication of historians, if history is merely a profession, but it cannot be if history is a universal human interest; for in that case there are already as many historians as there are human beings, and the question is not 'Shall I be an historian or not?' but ' How good an historian shall I be?'[1]

---

[1]   R. G. Collingwood, *The Philosophy of History.* Historical Association Leaflet No. 79. Bell, London, 1930. p. 3. (Reprinted in *Essays in the Philosophy of History: R. G. Collingwood.* (Edited by W. Debbins.) McGraw-Hill, New York, 1966.)

An account of historical consciousness, therefore, must begin from the view that existing activities already involve elements of a more fully developed idea of history, even when these are found at a relatively low level of elaboration. The role of criticism is to draw out how human activities would be more adequate if we adopted a more explicit, self-conscious, approach to the historical elements in our civilisation.

In earlier chapters, we have seen how Collingwood characterised the world in terms of process. Action is a specific type of process that constitutes history, and determines what historical knowledge must be. Historical consciousness, is, therefore, consciousness of the world as having such characteristics. The key to the human capacity to act more rationally and adequately is, however, self-consciousness. The emerging practice of choice for the reason of duty, where duty could be known through the compulsive knowledge of acts and situations provided by the practice of history, was reflected in the development of the concepts of history and duty. The development of the ideas of duty and history could therefore be seen to represent a development in the moral history of humanity. Historical consciousness is, then, the self-consciousness of people who come to know their own capacity for self-creation. In this chapter we will see that the historical consciousness is constrained in two ways — by the sense of responsibility that must attach to historical thought, and by what Collingwood termed the '*a priori* historical imagination'.

Collingwood's philosophy of history and moral philosophy culminated in the idea of self-knowledge. In his theory of rational action, we come to know who we are through our actions and our choices. History provides this self-knowledge.[2] The obverse of Collingwood's theory of rational action is that we shape what we are capable of by coming to know ourselves. When we understand our situation historically, we shape the alternatives between which we must choose. It is not enough that history be for self-knowledge, it must be self-knowledge for the sake of choice, action or, in brief, self-creation. In complete contrast to many common views of history (and also in the uncommon views of Michael Oakeshott), which see history as concerned with the past with no application to the present, history must be, on Collingwood's account, about the present, and about practice.

---

[2]   R. G. Collingwood, *The Idea of History. Revised edition, with Lectures 1926-1928*, *edited with an introduction by Jan van der Dussen*. Clarendon Press, Oxford, 1993. p. 10.

On Collingwood's theory, the goal of historical thought is knowledge of the present. He maintained that the past is not actual, and so it is not anything with which we can be directly acquainted. The past never exists ready to hand, but is understood only through interpretive acts. What we interpret is something that presently exists, and our questions and reasons for posing them are founded in the present. There is no past as such to understand, yet we cannot simply dispense with the concept of the past in favour of the concept of the present. Past thought is not really past, because it can again become present thought. It is essential that, in a world conceived as process, the present has come to be; understanding the present is therefore inseparable from understanding how it has come to be. In pursuing historical inquiries, therefore, we are investigating the present as it has come to be — as an outcome of the past. If history is knowledge, it is knowledge of how the present has come to be what it is.[3]

By 1939, Collingwood had come to the radical conclusion that 'all genuine historians interest themselves in the past just so far as they find in it what they as practical men, regard as living issues.'[4] Not all stories about the past are histories, because they are not all stories of actions. Similarly, there need not be a 'living issue' behind each and every story of the past, in the light of which we seek clarification through historical knowledge. Myths and fictions form part of art or religion. We can seek to understand the past in these terms, but if we end with these ours will be a poorer understanding than if we had approached the past historically. If the issue through which we look to myth and fiction for understanding is a 'living issue', by failing to understand it historically we would thereby leave ourselves less able to act.

For Collingwood, people are what they have become. This is a specific application of the fundamental idea of the world as process and action. People have become what they are by virtue of their actions. This principle does not mean that there are no other 'happenings', but simply points out that it is the way in which 'happenings' are understood and integrated into a person's actions that makes the world of actions, or *res gestae*. Implicitly, people are only what they have become. There are, therefore, no other options for self-knowledge; the only knowledge of what people are is knowl-

[3]   Collingwood, *The Philosophy of History*. p. 16.
[4]   R. G. Collingwood, 'Notes on Historiography written on a voyage to the East Indies', (1938-1939), printed in R. G. Collingwood, *The Principles of History: and other writings in philosophy of history. Edited with an introduction by W. H. Dray and W. J. van der Dussen*. Oxford University Press, Oxford, 1999. pp. 235-250. See pp. 239-240; entry dated 5.2.39.

edge of what they have been. What people can become depends on what they are. Human history is the movement of people understanding the situations in which they find themselves, and acting as they can; they act in the ways in which they are capable of acting. Only what people are can shape what they will do — there are no sources of human capacity outside the world of process and action. We can never know the future, because the future is never a fact that can be known; we can only hint at what does not exist. The only hint of what we could do is what we have become. Knowing what human beings have done is the only thing that enables us to hint at the possibilities for future action.

An account of past actions is necessary because everything has come to be as it is. The specific subject of our inquiries is determined by our 'living interests', and knowledge of past acts becomes possible only when we make past thoughts into present thoughts. Our sense of obligation or duty arises in the historical process, and is therefore objective, but is understood as such only when we reconstruct the history of thought on the basis of the evidence available to us. In this sense, obligation is also subjective. We come under the obligation to perform a specific act because acts are individual, and so the obligation arises only in a specific form, and can be discharged only in a specific way. Agents belong to the process of thought that we call history; they know their obligations only by historical thinking.

If history is concerned with the present, it is concerned with values. Since, for Collingwood, value is equated with the good, and good with choice, historical agents act for reasons and therefore cannot avoid attempting to realise certain values. There is, however, a common argument that historian's values distort their understanding of history. On one extreme of this argument, the very fact that historian's have values, and exercise these in their work, must distort the understanding of historical actions. Values, like emotions, may differ significantly between people and over time. Unlike emotions, however, values may change explicitly in the historical process. The values of past agents and those of the historian may therefore differ significantly. Is it therefore inevitable that the historian's values will dominate the values of historical agents? If so, then any inferential reconstruction of history is an unavoidable falsification.

In the 1920s, Collingwood had advocated reticence in moral judgements about history.[5] This early account was, however, inadequate in the context of Collingwood's developing account of action and history. Firstly, if the subject matter of history always concerns values, and historians are required to be reticent about such issues, the practice of history must fall far short of its object. The problem is less that a reticent historian would fail to mention agents' values in his work, but that he would fail to recognise the significance of actions in the light of agents' values. Secondly, Collingwood's early account of values in history stemmed from the idea that it is a matter of will to determine whether and how we pass judgement. Collingwood's historian is reticent because he obeys his conscience. What he did not consider was the possibility that it is necessary that historians pass judgement on others when they ought (on his early theory) to be reticent for lack of knowledge. The issue of values in history goes beyond explicit praise and blame, and includes the processes by which investigations are shaped. An historian's values themselves affect his sense of historical significance, and how well he understands an action.

On Collingwood's account of history as action, historian's values are essential to the process of developing questions and conceptions of the past, thereby advancing historical knowledge. In his 1936 lecture 'Can Historians be Impartial?' he argued that history is not value neutral in any sense, and that the attempt to make it so can only diminish the status of history.[6] In response to the criticism that the lack of value neutrality in history hinders genuine knowledge, Collingwood's view was that it is only through choice in historical inquiries, and therefore through the expression of value, that we can come to know anything at all. It is a fact that investigators do prefer some answers over others, and emphasise or neglect the evidence

[5]   In the 1920s, Collingwood advocated reticence in passing judgement on the acts of others. He proposed an ethic of 'perpetual reservation' that would recognise the difficulty of putting oneself in a position to know enough about the acts of others to be able to pass judgement on them. Historians who saw their roles in terms of praising or blaming others were said by Collingwood to represent 'an end of all proper historical study.' In so far as an historian understands what an agent has done, he also justifies the action, because he thereby shows that the agent chose the act as good. To show what others have considered good, however, is also to show the limitations of their choices. But, even when history 'is in a position to praise or blame, [it] can never do either unreservedly.' R. G. Collingwood, 'Lectures on Moral Philosophy for M[ichaelmas]-T[erm]-1921: written at various times, May — October, 1921.' [Bodleian Library, Dep. 4.] pp. 114, 118.

[6]   R. G. Collingwood, 'Can Historians be Impartial?', printed in Collingwood, *The Principles of History.* pp. 209-218.

Action as History

for each answer accordingly, but this does not mean that someone who recognises various possible answers will completely fail to test various hypotheses. Not to see alternatives is simply blindness (stemming, on Collingwood's view, from a failure to express emotion), rather than prejudice. Not to conceive of the possibility of alternatives is a failure to think, rather than a failure of thinking. It would be possible, on his analysis, to desire that one answer be the right answer, and yet to consider others. Prejudice is not the same as failing to conceive of the possibility that there might be other answers. The issue is how carefully a particular historian would treat the various possibilities. The appropriate injunction to the historian is not, therefore, to be reticent but to be more fully a self-critical historian — how good an historian shall I be?

Collingwood's later account of values in history reflected his broader theory of reasoned choice. The reasons we have for our choices — utility, rightness and duty — represent values in each and every action. The historical acts we reconstruct, and the act of reconstructing them through historical thought, in this respect, are alike. In keeping with his general approach of not erecting different concepts into separate entities, we do not need to separately reconstruct values, where values are seen as in some sense standing alongside acts. Rather, values are integral both to the object of history and to the act of historical inquiry. Collingwood characterised historical studies as a series of interim reports, and was readily aware of the fallibility of individual historians. In any particular case, we may indeed falsify our account of history, but he aimed to show under what condition history would not be falsified, even when our values and those of the agents we study may differ. If an historical reconstruction is valid, it is valid in terms of the values of the historical agents involved.

One might object that Collingwood's views on value mean that 'anything goes' in history as long as values are expressed. On this line of thinking, and adapting Oakeshott's terminology, what Collingwood did was to import 'politics' into 'history', to the detriment of 'historical science'. This objection does not, however, tell against Collingwood. In the first instance, he would reject the idea that history and practice could exist apart from each other. Instead, his argument was that thought is primarily practical, and that there can be no dichotomy between theory and practice. There can be no sense in which 'anything goes' in history, for historical inquiries are governed by criteria of inference from evidence that are themselves open to criticism; progress is achieved only through a critical assessment of earlier problems and solutions. There is no need to advocate reticence, therefore, because the activity of history is governed by the need for responsible claims and judgements. Collingwood, however, was not content simply to defend history against criticism. Rather, he sought to turn a point that might well be thought a limitation of history into a point of strength. He could see no threat to historical thinking from the fact that values change. Rather, he took such changes in values to indicate that there is 'not a mere advancement of knowledge' but 'an advancement in the whole moral attitude of humanity.'[7]

On Collingwood's account, it is necessary that we pass judgement. Only in his later work did he clearly articulate that passing value judgements is a responsibility that historians have to face, although with a sense of the gravity of their acts. In 'Can Historians be Impartial?' Collingwood stated that historians are people who take up a 'serious task, not only of discovering what actually happened, but of judging it in the light of our own moral ideals.' The twin aspects of this responsibility cannot be separated. As he put the point in concluding his paper

> If we feel that we cannot shoulder [the responsibility], we ought to drop historical studies and do something else. What we cannot do, is to continue playing with historical research [and] yet shirk the responsibility of judging the actions we narrate: saying this was wise, that foolish; this courageous, that cowardly; this well done, that ill.[8]

To understand an action is not to avoid the moral issues of the action, but to enable immanent criticism of the purposes of the agent — this gives it gravity. To undertake historical work is, therefore, to be governed by a sense of moral responsibility. But this sense of responsibility is not the only guide to the historical consciousness, because historical work is governed, more generally, by the idea of history. As we have seen earlier, for Collingwood historical facts are concrete — 'this' — yet historical objects are never here and now, never perceptible. History can be knowledge only if it is a wholly reasoned account of transient and concrete events.[9] But what principles regulate the process by which historical inferences take place?

F. H. Bradley, in *The Presuppositions of Critical History* (1874) focused attention upon the way in which historians bring their own

[7] Ibid. p. 218.
[8] Ibid.
[9] R. G. Collingwood, *The Historical Imagination. An Inaugural Lecture delivered before the University of Oxford on 28 October 1935.* Clarendon Press, Oxford, 1935. p. 5. (Reprinted, with changes, in Collingwood, *The Idea of History.* pp. 231-249. References are to the original publication.)

criteria to the process of judgement and interpretation of historical statements.[10] These criteria were peculiar to history and enabled history to be a serious discipline, rather than simply arbitrary in the mind of each individual historian. Building on Bradley and Croce, Collingwood proposed that the 'historical imagination' had an *a priori* structural function in historical knowledge. That is, in history imagination organises and interpolates between otherwise isolated incidents, allowing continuous 'historical narrative or description' to emerge. Modern historical practice involves the historian taking responsibility for the picture he presents of the past, thereby becoming his own authority rather than the purveyor of other people's claims about the past. This responsibility does not simply encompass the historian's interpolations, but his interpretation of the actions or occurrences that he connects in his imagination. Since there are no fixed data, there are no fixed points from which the historical imagination strikes out. Instead, the imagination is involved at every phase of the process.[11]

A first order realist philosophy of history seeks some means by which to refer an account of history to history itself. Once we reject a first order realist account of historical knowledge, because the past no longer exists, then we lose the possibility of disciplining historical thought along realist lines. If history involves imagination, it might seem, then, that history is no better placed than fiction. Indeed, Croce had closely aligned history with art, and Collingwood himself held that art is an element in every human activity. But whereas the novelist need not claim truth for his works, historical work does involve a claim to truthfulness.[12] For Collingwood, the *a priori* characteristics of the historical imagination provide the means by which historical reconstructions can be justified.

Since the criteria of truthfulness in history cannot involve an external reference, they relate solely to the instantiation of certain principles. In his inaugural lecture, *The Historical Imagination*, Collingwood identified three specific criteria that he took to distinguish history from fiction in terms of truthfulness.[13] These rules gov-

---

[10] F. H. Bradley, 'The Presuppositions of Critical History', reprinted in F. H. Bradley, *Collected Essays*. Clarendon Press, Oxford, 1935. pp. 1-70.
[11] Collingwood, *The Historical Imagination*. pp. 13, 16.
[12] Ibid. pp. 17-18.
[13] Ibid. pp. 18-19. In his work on folk-tales, Collingwood identified other rules, which he called 'Bishop Butler's maxim' and 'Spinoza's rule'. (R. G. Collingwood, 'Fairy Tales: III. The Historical Method.' [Bodleian Library, Dep. 21.]) The first held that everything is what it is and not another thing. The second called upon us to understand rather than to deride or condemn human actions.

ern the workings of the historical imagination, providing it with its specific character and focus. Firstly, the historical picture must be concerned with particular places and times. A work of fiction may also be focused in this way, but need not be. Collingwood's point was that an historical work must have such a basis, but his point is by no means obvious. Historical narratives of detailed events in one country or region, over a limited period, seem to instantiate this principle particularly well. But where does this leave comparative approaches to history, non-narrative descriptions and explanations, analogies or histories of ideas and concepts? None of these types of historical thinking seem to instantiate the principle at all well, yet each was a common part of historical practice even in Collingwood's time. Indeed, Collingwood himself was an exponent of each of these forms of historical thinking and writing.

Comparative methods deliberately cross boundaries of space and time. Descriptions and explanations in a non-narrative form often involve only broad indications of space and time. Analogies are drawn almost despite space and time location. Histories of concepts, such as *The Idea of History*, often make only cursory references to space and time. To take Collingwood's argument literally, therefore, is to exclude each of these varieties of historical understanding. To make sense of the principle, then, we need to take it in a different sense, as pointing to the presuppositions of history rather than to the products of historians. Interpreted in this way, comparative methods, descriptions, and analogies all presuppose events and actions with definite space and time locations, even where they do not explicitly focus upon them. We compare and describe concrete historical situations, and our analogies are built upon our prior understanding of concrete situations. The same principle applies to the history of ideas or concepts, because each thinker comes to a prob-

On first inspection, Bishop Butler's maxim seems to represent the commonplaces that Collingwood had rejected in 'Truth and Contradiction'. Spinoza's rule would seem to apply to anthropology as much as to history, and was as much a moral injunction as an element of historical methodology. Yet, both principles were relevant to the task of differentiating history from naturalistic sciences. Bishop Butler's maxim points to the concrete character of historical fact, as opposed to the classificatory approach of the naturalistic sciences. In that sense, the maxim is a statement of the special character of historical thought, because it points to the logical characteristics of the historical object. Spinoza's rule involves a similar rejection of naturalistic science because it points to the special problem of knowing the historical object. History is not known simply from the outside, but by a mind like enough to the object as to be able to understand past actions. The attitude of condemnation and denigration involves a perspective outside the agent's purposes. Spinoza's rule therefore invokes the moral caution of the historian.

lem in the light of the previous history of the concept, and their contribution is specific to that situation. Narrative history differs from other kinds of history in taking location in space and time as an explicit subject, but it is a presupposition of all forms of history.

The second principle to which Collingwood drew attention in his inaugural lecture was that of the consistency of the historical picture with itself in the 'one historical world'.[14] Fiction needs no such claims to consistency, for the artist is entirely free to abandon one imaginary world in which he is no longer interested for a new one which interests him more. This principle seems more clear-cut than the first, yet why do we assume that there is only one historical world? Historians differ greatly about what has happened in the past, why should we not assume that they are thinking about different historical worlds? Once we abandon the realist conception of history, there is no longer a firm anchor for historical thinking in reality. If the historical picture is anchored and disciplined, we must search for those elements in the notion that truthfulness is an activity of achieving comprehensiveness, and the idea that history is based upon inference from interpreted evidence. Two historians may have different views of history, because they find themselves in different situations, asking different questions, with different determinants of evidence, and different ways of interpreting evidence. Nevertheless, in order for either view to have credibility, each must be committed to a critical approach that forces them to consider everything as potentially evidence, and to consider as secure only a view that can make sense of what others take to be evidence. The historical world is one not because historians fail to differ about it, but because the activity of history cannot avoid critically harmonising the whole picture of the human past.

The third principle that Collingwood saw as governing the historical imagination, and differentiating it from the novelistic imagination, was that historical pictures are justified in terms of evidence. This, rather than his first two principles, is central to the disciplining of the historical imagination. Indeed, it lies behind the other two. Historical accounts, to qualify as such, must be justified in terms of an inferential and interpretative process. Fictional accounts may also be justifiable, but what makes them fictional is precisely that they need not be justifiable, that in large measure they cannot be so justified. Evidence is whatever can be used in justifying the historian's picture of the past. The enabling factors are the historian's prior conceptions of the past, and the questions he asks. Part of being

[14] Collingwood, *The Historical Imagination.* p. 18.

a good historian is to find new ways in which to use evidence. To use evidence, and find new forms of interpretation, the historian must call upon his entire knowledge of the historical world and so, as Collingwood maintained, 'historical knowledge can only grow out of historical knowledge.'[15]

Historical self-consciousness, then, is a self-regulating activity, independent of natural science. But Collingwood's approach to the regulation of historical self-consciousness in *The Historical Imagination* was too narrow. Collingwood came to define his goal as the development of 'a complete philosophy conceived from an historical point of view.'[16] Each of the key concepts we have seen in earlier chapters is an element of the modern idea of history that is part of that 'complete philosophy'. The cornerstone of Collingwood's approach was his focus on activity, particularly the concept of action and the idea of the world as process. Within this world, action objectifies thought in history, and historical knowledge requires conclusive inferences from evidence to agents' thoughts. The full determination of individual action by thought is possible only with action according to duty, which requires compulsive answers to questions about alternatives and situations that are themselves historical. Finally, because historical thought is a self-conscious activity it carries with it a sense of responsibility for the way in which it is conducted.

Together, the concepts that form the modern idea of history regulate the activity of history. They do this in a permissive and not simply a restrictive sense. That is, they articulate standards and goals by which to judge the relative success or adequacy of any particular activity of the historical consciousness to the modern idea of history. Therefore, the modern idea of history permits both aspiration and criticism. Historical practice becomes more adequate by the conscious pursuit of each element of the modern idea of history.

Should, though, historical consciousness play the role that Collingwood assigned to it in relation to present and future action? Collingwood's account of self-knowledge and self-creation seems conservative — it sets the boundaries and possibilities of action alike in terms of the present and the past. By contrast, it does not explicitly seek to open up entirely new possibilities for the future; similar criticisms could be made of Croce. Indeed, in large measure, Collingwood and Croce's thought could be read as forming a philosophy of limits to human possibility, which sits oddly alongside

[15]   Ibid. pp. 18-19.
[16]   Collingwood, *The Idea of History.* p. 7.

Collingwood's vision of 'solutions to the problems' of human life. We might well ask how Collingwood's theory differs from a theory of human action as habit. If we maintained that habit is the dominant element in human action, we would also conclude that the future must be much like the past, because it seems that people do only what they can, and can do only what they have already done. Nevertheless, it would be wrong to say that Collingwood's view amounts to no more than this. What distinguished his view from the theory of habit was precisely the element of self-consciousness. For self-knowledge itself involves self-creation, and to understand one's own actions is thereby to make oneself in some sense a different person, one whose actions are not simply habitual, but self-determining.

An alternative way to interpret the apparently conservative elements in Collingwood's view is that these forestall the idea that human beings can create themselves *ex nihilo*. Instead, human self-creation is a concrete achievement of labour; human creativity means that solutions can be found to human problems, but the limitations on creativity ensure that this can only be by sustained and concerted effort of a particular type. Whereas the theory of habitualism is defeatist, Collingwood's theory justifies sustained work on real human problems. As David Roberts has said of Croce, the world is constantly remade, but always 'in the same laborious, tragic, never-ending process. There is no deliverance from this labor.'[17]

One might object that Collingwood unduly limited the possibility of human action by not doing justice to various kinds of historical activity. If there are forms of history outside that envisaged by Collingwood, the boundaries of human action must be redrawn. A second objection would be to argue that the possibilities of action are determined by the natural scientific consciousness in our civilisation, and that the possibilities of action are greater in so far as the natural scientific elements are not dominated by the historical. Finally, we could question whether there are elements of reason in our current civilisation which are neither natural scientific nor historical reason, but some third form not reducible to the others, and which gives rise to an enhanced capacity to act. These are important objections. Nevertheless, in considering them, we must note, at the outset, that Collingwood's oppositions were never absolute in the way that any of these types of objection would require. Rather, his account of

---

[17] David D. Roberts, *Benedetto Croce and the Uses of Historicism*. University of California Press, Berkeley, 1987. p. 124.

opposition focused on the transcendence of one form by another. Unchanged elements of the earlier forms survive in the later forms, so that there could not be, for example, an 'historical civilisation' unless there were elements of a 'scientific civilisation' within it.

At what level could a substantial objection be launched by the argument that Collingwood's account of history as the self-knowledge of mind is too narrow? The principle that history is based on inference from evidence seems as secure as any principle could be; the alternative view would be that history is based on observation, but historical practice goes well beyond this limitation. Provided that we are trying to tell a story about the past, and not simply a story set in an imaginary past, we have no choice but to argue from evidence.[18] The kinds of evidence we use, and the arguments we are able to put forward, will differ as we acquire new skills, but this reinforces the importance of the principle, rather than taking away from it.

Since Collingwood's time historians have found new ways of using evidence and new ways of arguing with old evidence. Similarly, many more groups of people are commonly accorded agency in today's historiography than was commonly the case in Collingwood's time. These are important facts about the development of historiography over the past fifty years. It is, however, more productive to see in what ways movements such as feminism, advances in archaeology, or in the analysis of action into practical inferences, have added clarity and richness to ideas which Collingwood set out more briefly.[19] Such developments would not challenge his account of history. Rather, they can be justified in terms of that account. We can argue, then, that the principles that Collingwood discerned at work in his own time have been instantiated more broadly in current practice. This would also add weight to his argument that historical

---

[18] Collingwood contrasted the modern conception of history based upon evidence with the earlier style of 'scissors-and-paste' history, which relied exclusively on testimony. C. A. J. Coady, *Testimony: A Philosophical Study*. Clarendon Press, Oxford, 1992, Chapter 13, based his criticisms of Collingwood's approach to testimony on the assumption that Collingwood made an absolute distinction between the earlier and later forms of history. As with all of Collingwood's seemingly clear-cut distinctions and oppositions, it is necessary to remember that his own analysis of concepts, and of the 'idea of history' meant that modern scientific history developed from and transcended the achievements of earlier forms of history. Testimony had a place in scientific history, as something to be used as evidence in the historian's own recreation of the past. By being used in this manner, scissors-and-paste history based upon 'testimony' was transcended.

[19] On practical inference, see Rex Martin, *Historical Explanation: Re-enactment and Practical Inference*. Cornell University Press, Ithaca, 1977.

understanding involves the coming of a new civilisation. Each instance of sophistication in historical argument, or of a broadening of the range of topics which can be treated historically, or of greater clarity in historical concepts, can be seen as an instance of the advance of an historical civilisation.

The idea that history is the realm of action, *res gestae*, seems, however, less secure. Many historians have sought to reduce the emphasis on human agency, or to deny it altogether, in favour of the work of God or of various kinds of impersonal forces and structures that are believed to drive history. Such accounts might lead us to very different views of what action is possible in the future, although they are likely to be more conservative than Collingwood's in the sense that human agents are less responsible for history. Viewed in isolation, we cannot object to the search for forces or structures that do not depend on human action. The difficulties arise, however, in terms of how such forces or structures relate to reason. If there is reason there is a process created out of reason and it is necessary to give an account of this process. The process of mind brings together natural and other structures as objects of knowledge; they are thereby taken up into history as objects of thought and action. How, then, can such structures determine reason?

Part of the motivation behind a theory that assigns a lesser role to human agency in history is scepticism about the human capacity for reason. This sort of scepticism is salutary if it is used to show that human history does not always take the course that particular participants intend, but that point takes nothing away from the idea of agency itself. Rather, such scepticism points to the complex course of history when there are multiple agents. Theories that seek to replace human agency with the workings of vast impersonal forces fall into three further difficulties. Firstly, they may be simple positivistic generalisations, and thereby fail to deal with the concrete individuality of historical fact. Secondly, they may emphasise some element of reasoned choice, such as utilitarian value, but falsely erect this element of human reason into a force that operates independently of other forms of reason. Thirdly, they may fail to make any distinction between mere processes and changes and a process comprised of reasoned choices, thereby confusing history with an account of whatever has happened in the past. Any specific instance of an impersonal theory of history, such as a strict economic determinism, is likely to show each of these failings. This undermines the prospect that a coherent view of history could be developed completely outside the concept of agency.

If we accept the concept that history is argument from evidence about agency, Collingwood's theory of re-enactment follows with relative ease — the historian must argue to that which made the action an act rather than a mere event. Since action has a thought element, knowing the action involves knowing the thought. The only way in which a thought is known is by thinking it through for oneself. To know a past action, therefore, the historian must re-enact past thoughts in his own argumentative processes. Re-enactment occurs not because the historian thinks that he must re-enact thoughts, but because he must understand actions, and can do so only in a certain way. We could write a work and not argue to the thoughts of agents, but such a work would be incompletely historical. We cannot aim to find practices that are simultaneously historical and run directly counter to the principle of re-enactment.

The real alternative to re-enactment in history would be a theory holding that thought is not the distinctive element of action. What, though, is not thought, but can make something an action? We could not simply point to some logical feature that holds an act together, if such a feature is likely also to apply to other kinds of events and occurrences. (The argument that history is concerned with individuality points to a logical feature of action, but the claim is that this logical feature belongs to history alone.) Nor could we point to some other element of consciousness such as feeling, because as soon as there is reflection upon feeling we are dealing with a process distinguished by thought. Re-enactment, therefore, should be regarded as a principle of history alongside those of action and evidence.

The idea that history is the self-knowledge of mind follows on from the idea that history involves argument from evidence to the thought element of an act, which is thereby re-enacted. If the same thought is thought by the historian as by the original actor, the past, which comprises deeds done in the past, is never completed or dead, for it lives again in the mind of the historian, who is therefore the living heir of human history. We are, then, back with the concepts with which the objection started. It would be no objection to say that this or that kind of history fails to deliver self-knowledge, because this amounts to saying no more than that it somehow fails to be fully history. Most likely, as with the theories of impersonal historical forces, the reason a certain kind of history fails to deliver self-knowledge is that it fails in some way adequately to exemplify the concept of action. If Collingwood unduly limited his conception of the possibilities of human action, it was not because there are forms of history outside those he envisaged.

The second broad objection to Collingwood's account of action as dependent on the self-knowledge of mind in history turns to natural science. To have force, the objection must be more than a claim about technology, for technology has to be conceived and used, and the capacity of technology to shape our scope for future action is therefore dependent on the historical capacities of conceivers and users. Rather, the objection relates to how we can view our world if we view it through natural science. The differentiation of science from history, on which this objection depends, was one that Collingwood himself made. We can see the grounds for the objection within Collingwood's view of the difference between natural science and history, but we can also see how he rejected it, by arguing that natural science was itself dependent on history.

On Collingwood's view, the differences between history and natural science mean that neither can simply be reduced to the other. In the first instance, Collingwood maintained that history was not natural science, and so not reducible to the terms and methodology of naturalistic science. On this point, Collingwood was the heir of the nineteenth-century revolt against positivism in the study of human history. The emphasis which thinkers such as Rickert and Croce placed on the individuality of historical fact had drawn them to distinguish the proper study of history from all forms of generalised abstraction from fact. Collingwood was not, however, prepared (as Alexander at one stage seemed to be) to resolve all knowledge into historical knowledge. To do so would be to fail to recognise the distinction between natural process and a process of actions. Naturalistic sciences treat the world as generalisable, whereas for history the world comprises individual concrete fact. History and the naturalistic sciences were not excluded arbitrarily from studying the subject matter of the other; rather, they involved different conceptual and logical elements.

As we have already seen, in *The New Leviathan*, Collingwood argued that the 'sciences of body' study humanity, but as body. The historical 'sciences of mind' study humanity as mind. Two ways of viewing sciences (firstly, through their logic and, secondly, through their subject matter), are brought together in the idea that the world exists as concrete individual fact only within a particular sphere, the sphere of mind. The facts of geology are facts only incompletely, because naturalistic sciences and geological change are each indifferent to what makes this syncline precisely *this* syncline. Similarly, it does not matter whether it is this or that instance of a specific gene that is reproduced, but that the gene itself, a thoroughly general form, survives through reproduction. But it is essential to history that Oliver Cromwell was a definite individual, and the beheading of Charles I a unique and individual act undertaken by certain people at a certain time. History as the study of individual concrete fact can study only mind because only mind exists in such a way.

In *The Idea of Nature*, as he intended to do in *The Principles of History*, Collingwood pointed to the dependence of natural science on abstraction from concrete historical fact. The concrete fact to which he drew attention was not the natural fact itself, because this is never fully concrete, but rather the historical fact that an observation was made by someone in certain circumstances. Natural science is abstraction from the fact of observation to generalised processes. The naturalistic and historical sciences therefore serve, in Collingwood's approach, as poles towards which any particular inquiry would tend or aim. Fascination with the sheer beauty of one particular natural phenomenon takes us away from the ideal of abstract generalisation, yet we can never be fully concerned with the individual fact of this phenomenon because it does not exist in such a way.

Generalisation and abstraction also serve history, particularly in fields such as archaeology, but the only way to treat *this* particular prehistoric settlement as a phenomenon to be generalised is to cease to treat it as the outcome of specific human actions. As long as we recognise the settlement as the outcome of human endeavour, we leave outstanding the questions of who settled there, when they did so, how they used it, and when and why the settlement was abandoned or destroyed. To answer those questions is to be an historian. The relationship between history and other human sciences is, therefore, that the human sciences either serve history or are history. The human sciences are not a genuine third group between the naturalistic and historical sciences; in so far as they are sciences at all, they are sciences in the process of becoming history.

The third broad line of criticism of Collingwood's theory of modern history suggests that there may be elements of reason in our present civilisation that go beyond both scientific reason and historical reason. The objection reduces to the issue of whether there is an activity whose logic is neither the abstract generality of science, nor the concrete individuality of history. (But if law is equivalent to generality, and history equivalent to particularity, what then of means and ends?) Such an activity must be one of reason, and itself not transcended by science or history. To put the issue in other language, there can be no alternative grounds of reasoned action unless there is a logic that is neither abstract nor concrete, neither general nor individual. Given the difficulty surrounding the emergence of the concept of historical individuality, we could expect a similarly long period of emergence for any further logical concept. But, unless such a concept becomes apparent, we can say with certainty that there are no activities based upon such logic, and therefore no other nascent civilisations within our modern Western cultures. One implication of this counter argument is that we can work only within the scientific and the historical cultures. This reinforces the criticisms of the idea that the human sciences are a third type of study distinct from both natural science and history.

The third type of objection, in particular, also needs to be justified in terms of an historical account of reason; if we could produce the requisite account, we would be left to wonder whether historical thought was not, after all, more fundamental to the determination of action. In the absence of the necessary historical account, it is not possible to make specific comments around this type of objection. It is, however, possible to see how the objection could originate in Collingwood's own work, and how he could reject it.

On Collingwood's arguments in *Speculum Mentis*, we cannot point to art or religion for our alternative activities, because these are prior to science and history in the movement of mind. Nevertheless, during the 1920s, Collingwood would clearly have pointed to philosophy as an activity beyond scientific and historical thinking. (I will return to the relationship between history and philosophy in the next chapter.) The key point to consider here is that, when Collingwood wrote *Speculum Mentis*, his conception of history was significantly less developed than it later became. The objection cannot simply be founded on that earlier conception of history. Rather, the objection is itself open to the criticisms that led Collingwood to revise his concept of history and proffer an historical account of metaphysics. In light of such criticisms, philosophy could no longer be considered as an independently existing activity in the terms that are at stake in this kind of objection.

None of the three broad types of objection I have considered can be readily sustained. Rather, they can be turned into restatements of and arguments for Collingwood's views. We should, then, reconsider the premise that Collingwood's account closes off possibilities for human action. Instead, we may do better to see his philosophy as opening up ways of understanding problems and choices that have not previously been possible. A natural science of the human past would first generalise about 'human nature' and subsequently develop rules by which to approach human behaviour. These rules can themselves influence future human action when we seek to make behaviour conform to those rules. By doing so, however, we close off the possibility of determining action by a rational and dialectical process, in which people can participate who nevertheless start out from different positions. Acts can be understood, but to understand them is to participate in creating individual solutions to individual problems. Far from being conservative, an historical approach to self-knowledge and self-creation presents radical possibilities for creating ways of life based on reason, discussion, shared effort and common enterprise. If such a civilisation is possible, it is because we understand ourselves as self-creative people in individual historical situations.

In what sense can we have a civilisation that both builds on the historical consciousness and reinforces it? Earlier in this chapter, in discussing the role of values in history, we saw that Collingwood claimed that changes in values represent not merely an 'advance of knowledge' but 'an advance in the whole moral attitude of humanity'. This claim draws attention to the relationship between knowledge and moral attitudes, moral philosophy and history, and historical practice and the development of human abilities, but it begs the question how such an advance could occur. In one important sense, there can be no moral progress or advancement. For Collingwood, morality has to do with how we face the situations in which we find ourselves. We face our problems better or worse, and it is not necessarily true that we face them better simply because we face them later. Collingwood also held that a problem is what we understand it to be; a change in the problem therefore implies a change in our understanding. For Collingwood, an advance in the nature of the problems we face is possible only if there is also an advance in how we face them.

In Collingwood's view, in modern Western civilisations, we are able to understand and face our situations in a more rational and morally adequate way; this is the key meaning of 'an advance in the moral attitude of humanity'. As our conceptions of choice and action develop and become more self-conscious, our acts and answers become more adequate to our problems. We can articulate more adequately the choices we face. We answer our questions with acts that we choose from reason, rather than capriciously. Our decisions can be made from duty rather than mere utility or right.

Since a problem is what we understand it to be, the history of history (what Collingwood called history of the second order) is fundamental both to the problem and to how we face it. We can preserve the valuable elements of old solutions and offer genuinely new solutions only when our inquiry has arisen through the development of a specific problem. The history of how others have developed our problem is a key to understanding what that problem is. We need, therefore, to be able to self-consciously re-evaluate our history. But it is important that genuine re-evaluations take place within the same scale of values, and not simply through the expression of different values from different scales. The expression of different values would simply be part of achieving different knowledge, and not the advance of knowledge.

On Collingwood's account, it makes no sense to distinguish between private capacity and the capacity of Western civilisation. Thought is inherently public and is objectified in acts which include, but are not limited to, linguistic expressions. In so far as we enter into the thoughts of others, we enter into the thought of our civilisation. Indeed, on this view, our civilisation exists only in so far as we are able to enter into the thought of others. The moral advance of humanity must also be the moral advance of our civilisation.

CHAPTER 10

Historical Civilisation

Michael Oakeshott distinguished between the 'civil condition', in which members relate to each other through 'common recognition of the rules which constitute a practice of civility', and instrumental, 'enterprise associations' focused on utility.[1] Oakeshott argued that theories of what he called the modern European state tended towards the two poles of 'civil association' or 'enterprise association', although politics was constituted out of the tension between each pole. The tension between the two poles of civil or enterprise association also reflected self-understanding, which was itself contingent or historical.[2]

Oakeshott's account rested on a theory of action similar to Collingwood's. In *On Human Conduct*, Oakeshott described the conduct of agents as 'performances whose imagined and wished-for outcomes are performances of other agents or other performances of himself'.[3] For Oakeshott, doing begins in an agent's understanding of a situation, where understanding 'is a diagnosis: that is, a verdict in which it is recognized to be in some respect unsatisfactory', and to which he should respond. As we saw in an earlier chapter, in outline, this was also Dewey's conception of the origins of logic. Oakeshott, whose theory in this respect closely resembled Collingwood's, argued that the agent's response takes form in an 'action or an utterance equivalent to an action', and is therefore a chosen 'answer or rejoinder'. The intention of the agent is in the decision, not prior to

[1]   Michael Oakeshott, *On Human Conduct*. Clarendon Press, Oxford, 1991. p. 128.
[2]   Ibid. pp. 320, 326.
[3]   Ibid. p. 36.

it.[4] It follows that human conduct is an inheritance of practice through understanding, learning and re-enacting.[5] To theorise about substantive action is therefore to develop an historical understanding of the contingent. Evidence makes contingent history intelligible, and the historical understanding takes a narrative form. Oakeshott differed from Collingwood principally by denying that historians re-enact actions.[6]

When once we begin to focus on subjectivity, we face the problem of what kinds of relations are possible between agents. Oakeshott usefully drew attention to the way in which self-understanding shapes agency, and therefore how agents associate. If self-understanding changes and we reject a fixed or single concept of 'man', the ways in which agents may associate will also change. For Collingwood, as we shall see, the character of a civilisation depends on what constitutes agency, and therefore on how the agents understand themselves and each other. When seen against the background of Collingwood's account, Oakeshott was right to argue that self-understanding is contingent or historical, and right to argue that action is understood historically. His account of civil association and enterprise association, however, were accounts of association based on rule and utility, respectively. What Oakeshott did not consider was the possibility that historical self-understanding was a different way of understanding action that included rule and utility, but was not reducible to either. He could not, therefore, consider the possibility that historical self-understanding must lead to different forms of association between agents.[7]

For Collingwood, historical civilisation is not the only kind of civilisation, but is a development with distinctive characteristics that derive from the modern idea of history. An historical civilisation is one in which civilising occurs through the acts of people who self-consciously understand themselves historically, and where historical reason determines action. In the 'Introduction', I quoted Collingwood's plan for the third book of *The Principles of History*. In his plan, Collingwood stated that an historical civilisation had not yet emerged. He also maintained that it was possible to characterise such a civilisation, 'without difficulty', by working out

[4]　　Ibid. p. 39.
[5]　　Ibid. pp. 86-87.
[6]　　Ibid. pp. 105-107.
[7]　　More recently, the emergence of the field of 'law and economics' has also sought to relate two forms of reason for action. Nevertheless, this does not exhaust the reasons for action. Concrete accounts of individual actions remain historical accounts.

the idea that history is enacted and, consequently, is not an object in the sense that natural science has an object. Collingwood took this argument to mean that, in the case of history, there cannot be a distinction between theory and practice, a point on which his theory diverged radically from Oakeshott's.

In the 'Introduction', I also noted that Jose Ortega y Gasset based his concept that radical reality takes the form 'I am I and my circumstance' on the idea that the act alone is the unmediated datum of thought in the act of living. Ortega's goal has been characterised as the ' "reimplantation" of reason in life'.[8] A similar comment could be made about Collingwood's focus on action and the way in which he used that concept to overcome the distinction between the logical and the actual. Ortega conceived of persons without the category of substance. If 'I am I and my circumstance', to be I is not to characterise 'being', but to consist of a life-project, in terms of which I had to do x, and in terms of which I will have to do y tomorrow.[9] For Ortega, 'Man has no nature; what he has is history' (a point that Collingwood would say held only of man as mind). Ortega's underlying thought was that we are as we now are because of what we were; to understand what we are today is to relate what it is that we were. In his lectures of 1940 and 1944 Ortega proclaimed that the 'hour of the historical sciences is at hand', and that 'Pure reason...must be replaced by narrative reason.' He added: 'This narrative reason is "historical reason".'[10]

It is possible to find in Ortega's work elements that relate to Collingwood's concern with the emergence of an historical civilisation, as well as to his concept that 'duty' is the determination of action by historical reasoning. The terminology of 'historical reason' was, perhaps, happier than Collingwood's choice of the word 'duty' to explain choices made in light of an historical understanding of a situation. Collingwood's account of action and history, however, enables an immanent criticism of contemporary practices. Ortega's account, by contrast, gives rise to a strong distinction between those who live in a particular way, and those who do not. Those who do not are the 'mass-men'. Those few who do are the 'innovators'.

---

[8] Antonio Rodriguez Huescar; *Jose Ortega y Gasset's Metaphysical Innovation: A Critique and Overcoming of Idealism.* Translated and edited by Jorge Garcia-Gomez. State University of New York Press, Albany, 1995. p. 152.

[9] Jose Ortega y Gasset, *Historical Reason.* Translated by Philip W. Silver. W. W. Norton, New York, 1984. p. 91.

[10] Ibid. p. 118.

In Ortega's philosophy, living is deciding what to do next, and this is to decide what to be.[11] I have always to do something, to make choices amongst possibilities; I am 'having to be and...having to be thus and so and not otherwise'.[12] Self-projection involves anticipating my actions, valuing them, deciding which project is to be mine, 'inventing' my project, and 'taking into account my circumstance and vocation'.[13] Societies, however, may seek to plan social conduct, and in doing so they aim to reach ever deeper into the levels of personality or 'life-projects'; this gives rise to 'mass-man'. The emergence of 'mass-man' involves the destruction of possibilities for 'life-projects'.[14] Society is always an interplay between masses whose lives are 'unoriginal' and a minority that is 'innovative, fruitful', although even the unoriginal invent their lives in some sense.[15] If Oakeshott's account can be criticised as neglecting duty, Ortega's is liable to the charge that it resolves all reason, including utility and right, into the equivalent of duty, or condemns that which is not duty as the activity of 'mass-man'.

In a less encompassing way, many of the elements of what Collingwood and Ortega meant by an historical civilisation have been key concerns of later philosophers. As we saw in the 'Introduction', contemporary thinkers such as Alasdair MacIntyre have embraced a narrative conception of action. Analytical philosophers have sometimes noted that narrative has become a dominant theme of thought about history.[16] The emphasis on narrative, however, also reflects other movements, including the tendency towards scepticism and in favour of literary analysis of historical work. Collingwood would recognise these later tendencies, although he would see the purely literary analyses of historical thought as falling far short of an adequate conception of history and action. In turn, he might consider that much of the reluctance to address his claims about civilisation stems from the contemporary deflationary account of language, which makes words like 'civilisation' sit uncomfortably in current debates.

Much of the unease with terms like civilisation may be attributable to the fear that a civilisation is a mysterious kind of entity, in much the same way as a society has been treated as an entity by

[11] Huescar, *Jose Ortega y Gasset's Metaphysical Innovation*. p. 106.
[12] Ibid. p. 122.
[13] Ibid. p. 140.
[14] Ibid. p. 142.
[15] Ibid. pp. 146-147.
[16] Raymond Martin, *The Past Within Us: An Empirical Approach to Philosophy of History*. Princeton University Press, Princeton, 1989. p. ix.

much social and political theory. On Collingwood's usage in *The New Leviathan*, which he took to be both traditional and proper, civilisation and society are, however, concepts that relate to action. Collingwood traced his account of action through to accounts of society and civilisation. By following that account we can see how he brought to bear many of the concepts we have seen earlier in this study. In brief, an historical civilisation is one in which the free members of a social community, aware (through historical thinking) that they are free, decide to understand themselves and each other historically, and to determine their acts according to duty. In doing so, they recognise each other's freedom, agreeing on their common duty. They will to be civil, and seek to convert their disagreement to agreement — this is achieved through historical understanding, including in the field of politics.

For Collingwood, neither society nor civilisation is a class concept. Rather, the members of a society effect that society through '*their joint activity as free agents*'.[17] Society is not brought into being by a 'consensual social contract', but by the decision or will of free agents to initiate the contract. Free persons, who seek to 'immanently rule themselves', bring society about. Society differs from a simple community, where members merely have something in common, because the members of a society share the 'social consciousness' of those 'who are free and know themselves to be free.'[18] Social consciousness is practical, rather than theoretical, and can be characterised as 'an act of deciding to become a member and to go on being a member: a will to assume the function of partnership with others in a common undertaking, and a will to carry out that function.'[19]

There is a continual dialectic by which communities that are not societies become societies.[20] This is effectively the dialectic to civilise because, for Collingwood, '*to civilize is to socialize*.'[21] The dialectic can, however, work in two directions. Civilisation is created by will:

> The members of any non-social community who, awaking to free will, decide no longer to drift with their emotions, but to take charge of the situation in which they corporately find themselves and do something

[17] R. G. Collingwood, *The New Leviathan, or Man, Society, Civilization and Barbarism. Revised edition, edited and introduced by David Boucher, with 'Goodness, Rightness, Utility' and 'What "Civilization" Means'*. Clarendon Press, Oxford, 1992. para. 19.8. (Emphasis in original.)
[18] Ibid. paras. 20.2, 20.23, 20.36, 20.63, 20.65, 29.11.
[19] Ibid. para. 20.21.
[20] Ibid. paras. 24.71, 21.5.
[21] Ibid. para. 37.22. (Emphasis in original.)

with it, whatever in particular they decide to do, have embarked on the process of civilizing themselves.[22]

By contrast, there is also a 'will to barbarism', that is, 'a will to do nothing, a will to acquiesce in the chaotic rule of emotion which it began by destroying.'[23]

To act civilly is to turn disagreement into agreement and to banish violence from relationships with other persons. To be civilised, therefore, is to live in such a way as to 'endeavour to convert every occasion of non-agreement into an occasion of agreement.'[24] People have emotions of friendliness and unfriendliness towards others. They may seek to hurt others and to gain power over them (to live 'eristically'), or they may choose to form themselves into societies of common purpose, where purposes are discussed in terms of situations and possible solutions (to live 'dialectically').[25] For Collingwood, agreement comes in a community

> whose custom is that everybody who has anything to teach to anyone else who wants to know it shall teach it; and that everybody who does not know a thing that may be useful for the betterment of living shall go frankly to one who knows it, and listen while he explains it or watch it while he shows it, confident by custom of a civil answer to a civil question.[26]

When the members of a social community make practical decisions, they may choose to do so for reasons of utility, right and duty. To the extent that they decide for reasons of utility, they choose means that will achieve particular ends. Collingwood described such action as determining a '*policy*'. To decide on a course of action in terms of right, was to follow law.[27] As we have seen in earlier chapters, Collingwood argued that choices from utility or right were free, but insufficient to determine concrete, historical acts. Decisions made in terms of utility or right therefore retained an element of caprice. To fully determine a free act through choice is to understand the uniqueness of a situation in such a way that only one alternative course of action is open. To choose in this way is to choose from 'duty'. In *The New Leviathan*, Collingwood described duty as the 'in-

---

[22]	Ibid. para. 36.93.
[23]	Ibid. para. 36.94.
[24]	Ibid. para. 39.15.
[25]	Ibid. paras. 36.82, 36.83, 36.84, 36.89.
[26]	Ibid. para. 36.46.
[27]	Ibid. paras. 28.5, 28.6. (Emphasis in original.)

telligible necessity to which a free man bows, and in bowing shows himself free'.[28]

In Chapter 6, I argued that there were two sources of compulsion in Collingwood's account of duty. Firstly, there is compulsion because a choice is the conclusion to a process of reasoning, where we have to reason to a concrete action. We must accept the conclusion of our own argument, or risk being blown in many different directions by our competing emotions and desires. Secondly, there is compulsion because we risk a deep form of insincerity, where we are no longer the person we have become, or understand ourselves to be. The members of a social community or civilisation face these compulsions just in so far as they choose to pursue a common undertaking, seeking to convert disagreement into agreement by discussion and the custom of teaching and learning. Viewed in this way, what Collingwood called a 'body politic' makes decisions out of duty because

> having the traditions it has, it would repudiate all but one as ways of life in which it will not acquiesce; or because, living in the conditions in which it does live, all but one are ways it would be chimerical to pursue.[29]

The members of a social community have made a choice to 'immanently rule themselves'. They have, therefore made a choice to determine their corporate acts by reason. Where it becomes possible to fully determine their acts, rather than to leave some element to caprice, the members of such a society develop an obligation to do so, at the risk of ceasing to pursue the undertaking they have chosen in common. On Collingwood's argument as I have presented it in this study, historical understanding has made it possible to fully determine acts, where concrete and unique situations require concrete and unique solutions or answers. The members of the social community who have chosen to determine their acts by reason face both the possibility and the obligation of doing what they have chosen; when they choose to do so, through historical understanding, they become an historical civilisation.

If, as Collingwood thought, the members of a social community reach agreement through the customs of discussion, teaching and learning, the strength of an historical civilisation must reside in the degree to which these customs reflect the practice of historical understanding. Bringing about an historical civilisation simply means being in the practice of thinking in historical terms, that is,

[28] Ibid. para. 28.84.
[29] Ibid. para. 28.89.

understanding oneself and one's situation in terms of the concepts and methods of modern history. For the members of a social community that thinks historically, bringing about an historical civilisation means thinking about the actions of others in terms of the utility, right and duty of their free choices. The explanation of the act of another will be regarded as incomplete until it is seen as being done for the unique reason that Collingwood called 'duty'.[30] In the sphere of politics

> A man who accustoms himself to think historically about political questions that confront him in the present will ask, not how he and others can attain certain ends or obey certain rules, but how they can do the one thing which is open to them as self-respecting men, conscious of their several freedom and each other's, agreeing upon a joint action in doing which each will be doing his duty.[31]

The process of civilising can never be complete, for elements of a non-social community, or of the will to barbarism, are always present within any society. Indeed, on Collingwood's account of mind, we choose rationally only because we face the dilemma of competing emotions and desires. Socialisation and civilisation arise only by choosing not to live in such a way. Similarly, disagreement is not abolished by the determination to convert it to agreement; rather, that determination exists only in virtue of a choice about how to handle future situations where such disagreement will occur. Conversely, some degree of civility and understanding are necessary before, in Collingwood's language, we can seek to convert eristical relationships into dialectical relationships.

Oakeshott saw a continuing tension between the poles of 'civil association' and 'enterprise association'. On Collingwood's account, there are continuing tensions between social and non-social elements in a community, civilisation and barbarism, eristical and dialectical relationships, choices made for reasons and capricious choices.[32] To be rational and civil are achievements and aspirations, but to achieve them is never to have reached a completion. David

---

[30] Ibid. para. 28.9.
[31] Ibid. para. 28.91.
[32] Collingwood was not a relativist in discussing relations between civilisations. In his view, civilisation was an activity not simply an achievement; the concept develops as a scale of forms. Collingwood at one point argued that our own civilization and that of, for example, the traditional Bantu, are different, but this does not make one a civilisation and the other something else. Each is a civilisation, and the members or adherents of each see it as good. It does not, however, follow that the two cannot be compared and judgements reached that one is more civilised. Rather, the standard of civility used in the comparison must be

Boucher has noted that Collingwood, in common with his friend Guido de Ruggiero, conceived of freedom as rationality, but saw that freedom could exist only in a society whose institutions support the progress of consciousness towards liberty, thereby enabling dialectical rather than eristical relationships.[33]

For there to be an historical civilisation, it must become one. For a society to support a civilisation that could become historical in character, it must first be such as to advance the growth of thought and rationality. The society's institutions and means of education must value and promote critical rational traditions. The members of such a society must recognise the distinctiveness of human agency, and a fundamental feature of their debates will concern who is an agent and in what their agency consists. As the society becomes historical, it will resolve the questions about agency into accounts of what acts have made individual agents become as they are. The pursuit of self-knowledge must already be essential to the development, sharing, interpretation and critical application of the standards of such a society. In such a society the members must already value and cultivate self-knowledge, and they will come to realise that they can achieve this by understanding themselves and others through the methods of history. Principles, rules and laws will be important as ways of defining and conveying possible responses to situations, but they will be seen as increasingly inadequate unless both situations and possible solutions are conceived historically. In societies where such conditions are met, there are the beginnings of an historical civilisation. Because historical self-consciousness will be the development of elements that are already in some sense present within

---

one that is seen as such by each. (R. G. Collingwood, 'Notes on 'Barbarism''. n.d. [Bodleian Library, Dep. 24.] pp. 2-3, 21-22.)

In a later paper, Collingwood argued that our concept of civilisation had come to allow for genuinely different ideals; there is not simply one ideal realised to different degrees, nor is there simply one scale. Rather, it is necessary to ask in what ways a society is civilised. Nevertheless, the different ideals pursued by different civilisations are also in one sense 'convergent'. Each is an ideal 'of civilised conduct' and, in that sense, 'the same ideal': '[t]he plurality of civilizations does not exclude a sense in which civilization is one.' Beyond the ideal which any actual civilisation has achieved, and that at which it aims, is a 'third order ideal', 'the ideal of civility as such'. All civilisations converge towards this level of ideal, though they differ at the first and second levels. (R. G. Collingwood, 'What "Civilization" Means', printed in *The New Leviathan. Revised edition*. pp. 480-511. See pp. 487-490, 494-495.)

[33] See David Boucher's 'Introduction' to R. G. Collingwood, *Essays in Political Philosophy. Edited with an introduction by David Boucher*. Clarendon Press, Oxford, 1989. pp. 10-13.

the society, the emergence of an historical civilisation will represent a genuine progress or 'advance in the moral attitude of humanity'.

Although Nietzsche thought that modern Western societies were already historical civilisations, it is easier to say that, in the late twentieth and early twenty-first centuries, Western societies were psychologising or sociologising civilisations, becoming historical.[34] Alasdair MacIntyre, for example, has suggested that the characters of the aesthete, therapist, manager or bureaucratic expert have crucial roles in our cultures, which are no less important for being based on 'moral fictions' such as predictive effectiveness and control.[35] Such cultures become historical not by adding the dimension of time or ideas of change to psychological or sociological categories, nor even by limiting the claims made on behalf of these ways of thinking. Rather, they become historical in those moments when generalisations and ideas of human nature are transcended by the analysis of concrete situations, which leads to unique solutions for unique problems. These moments may involve the acts of the members of a body politic, but they may also involve personal lives. We are historical particularly at those times when we go beyond our memories in order to reconstruct our pasts. Such reconstructions can compel us to see what we did not see and could not have experienced at the time. Our reconstructed pasts can make sense of our lives for us.

As both Collingwood and MacIntyre would maintain, the historical dimension of our modern civilisation is neither manipulative nor managerial, neither predictive nor legislative. It does not focus on behaviour, but instead focuses upon reasons for actions. Historical civilisation involves people offering each other reasons for choices. This does not eliminate disagreement or differences between people or their purposes, but it does provide them with the capacity to reason through to common solutions. We improve human affairs, therefore, not by technical mastery of people, but by better understanding those situations in which we find ourselves. If many of our problems are yet to be solved, we need to look first at how we have stated them. If we have yet to state a problem in terms of human action, it is because we have been incompletely historical. Seeing our situation, and our problem, historically makes it soluble not in the sense that the historical record provides the answers, or the concrete

---

[34] For a stimulating discussion of the similarities between the metaphysics of Nietzsche and Collingwood, see Michael Hinz, *Self-Creation and History: Collingwood and Nietzsche on Conceptual Change*. University Press of America, Lanham, 1994.

[35] Alasdair MacIntyre, *After Virtue: A Study in Moral Theory. Second edition*. Duckworth, London, 1985. pp. 73, 75.

examples of how to go forward, but because we will no longer mistake our situation for what it is not. The issue is what actions are open to us. The question of what limitations confront us, a question that arises particularly within a scientific framework, needs to be replaced by questions about what alternative actions are possible for us.

Historical thinking makes the problems of men and their relationships soluble in another sense too. The historical consciousness is a consciousness of processes of which we ourselves are a part and which, far from being 'a tale told by an idiot, full of sound and fury, signifying nothing', involve rational action and the successful attempt of past agents to state and solve their own problems. As the inheritors of this process, made so by historical consciousness, we inherit the knowledge that problems can be solved, and the capacity to state our problems in a soluble way. These are the foundations for a rational faith that human problems are soluble, and a challenge to act as rationally as we now can. In effect, the problems of men and their relationships become soluble by the choice of a life in which they are recognised as such. This may seem as if it goes too far, that it represents the closed circle of an imaginary world, where we choose to live as we choose to imagine the world to be. But such a comment neglects the role of self-criticism in the emergence of such a world.

As we have seen in this study, for Collingwood, the world brought into being by rational mind differs dramatically from the world of natural process. The historical world is created by living as rational consciousness, and understood only as concrete reason or history. The emergence of historical consciousness transforms the rational world, and this transformation can properly be called the emergence of an historical civilisation. Our civilisation is genuinely historical precisely to the extent that these ways of understanding ourselves and determining our actions are elements in every act. Model building and sheer speculation about possible futures have little role in achieving or further developing historical civilisations. Rather, societies achieve such civilisations by their concrete efforts in addressing their own problems, and this concrete effort must build on a practical faith that solutions can be found. The vision of such a civilisation must be an historical tale told about values and achievements immanent in that society.

Since Ancient Greece, Western civilisations have enjoined an examined life for their rational members. Only the self-critical exercise of reason can bring human life to its full potential. The meaning of the examined life has itself changed greatly. Reason is no longer attuned primarily to 'eternal verities', nor is it focused on the exercise and maintenance of a fixed role in an ordained social and political structure. Subjectivity is a fundamental element in the modern Western world that has necessarily transformed the lives we are to examine as much as it has changed the way in which such examination may take place.

Once we begin to doubt the existence of unchanging truths, particularly of the moral kind, and once we admit the historical nature of human life, we must seek a new and different content for the examined life. In modern Western cultures, only mind can create moral value, and yet the most prevalent conceptions of self barely allow that we can transcend the ordinariness of our psyches. The only content we can give to the examined life under such conceptions is that it means that we come to know our wants. To say this is to say more than merely to express capricious wishes, but it is to say very little about the life we are to examine, what it is to examine it, and what it is to lead such a life.

Collingwood's account of action as history enables us to provide the ideal of the examined life with a more specific content. The life we are to examine is mind as action, which creates a special type of process, history or (appropriating Ortega's language) the process of narrative reason. This life is based upon the expression of desire, but the peculiar importance of action and processes of reason lies in their emergent qualities and their self-generating and self-referring properties. Mind as psyche is creative of mind as reason, but our focus belongs on mind as reason. Mind as action constitutes history, and therefore the proper way to examine a life is through the methods of history. Whereas, since the Ancient Greeks, the examined life has been epitomised by contemplation, in the modern historical world the emphasis should be on self-creative action. In the modern world, to lead an examined life is to reason concretely to all one's actions and to eliminate the element of caprice in choice.

The concept of an historical civilisation, and the new content it gives to the idea of an examined life, reinforce the notion that moral philosophy was an arena in which Collingwood could broach and develop the ideas that influenced other areas of his philosophy. His attempt to orientate philosophy in the direction of history was an attempt to show how philosophy was to be remade, rather than the finished philosophy itself. The systematic conception that would sum up this re-orientation cannot simply be assembled from the books he lived to write, but it can be seen by following the development of key aspects of his thought. His books left many ideas implicit in order to focus more clearly upon the issues he wished to examine. Any scholar of his work is necessarily engaged in re-stating both implicit and explicit ideas.

There is a coherent view running through Collingwood's work that can be seen as developing earlier traditions and contemporary insights. This view is best seen emerging dialectically through his various attempts to apply his emerging concepts of action and history across several fields of philosophy.

Collingwood's theory and cosmology of process, for example, took shape through his encounters with the work of Alexander and Whitehead. He came to see action as a special kind of process, characterised by rationality. On this view, human beings are rational only intermittently. This is not because people are already rational and then fall away from rationality. Rather, it is because they become rational and becoming rational is work accomplished only intermittently. To the extent that they fail to express their emotions (and suffer a 'corruption of consciousness'), and thereby fail to articulate the alternatives between which they must choose, they will fail to accomplish the work of becoming rational. Collingwood took the need for a theory of thought from this general orientation and the immanent reason tradition, which saw thought as objectified in history. He brought this theory into relation firstly with historical knowledge and secondly with the historical process. He gained his conception of historical knowledge in his own maturing practice as an archaeologist and historian.

For Collingwood, the theory of action illuminated the object of history and the theory of historical knowledge. Uniting these two themes brought into focus the moral and civilising importance of historical practices. On this view, our lives are going on in a world which itself goes on, but (to again use Ortega's language) they are a radical reality within that world. We are people who have done certain things and will do others and thereby create a unique narrative drama. There is a unity in history, but it is not the unity of a single theme or idea; rather, history has an emergent unity which operates first at the level of the day-to-day and upon that basis organises actions into other narratives or unities. Theories such as these are the grounds for a rational faith in the self-creativity of human being. They are also the basis for an ideal of life and civilisation which has modern historical thought at its core.

Collingwood's variety of liberalism placed a distinctive emphasis upon reason and criticism. Since thought was, for Collingwood, primarily a corporate activity, his variety of liberalism avoided the restrictive and artificial individualism of many other liberal theories. In Collingwood's philosophy, there was an important role for tradition and for the conversion of antagonism into agreement. *The New Leviathan* was his account of politics prompted by a time of crisis, but the concepts it deployed can equally describe the civilisation and functions of modern, relatively stable and peaceful societies. Such societies require reasoned accounts of the problems they face, the choices they have to make, and therefore to what they can aspire. They require accounts of the non-social elements in their communities, of how far they fail in rationality and in the expression of emotion, and of the bases of their civility. On Collingwood's argument, to give such accounts is to undertake historical work.

What Collingwood took the relationship of history and philosophy to be is, perhaps, the second most discussed aspect of his thought — behind only the theory of re-enactment. Most commonly, the question that has been asked is whether Collingwood became an historical relativist and, if so, how this might detract from his overall achievement. The relationship between history and philosophy was to be the subject of the third part of Book Two of *The Principles of History*. The period when he worked on that unfinished draft was when he was at his most radical in his interpretation of the relationship between history and philosophy, arguing that philosophy was 'liquidated' by being converted into history.[36]

It is clear that, as his conception of history was enriched, Collingwood came to see history as the most important activity in the structure of what he termed (in *The New Leviathan*) 'the modern European mind'. He was not concerned with history as it had existed but as it existed in his own time, and its potential future importance. If the self-knowledge of mind is history, the highest form of history must take many of the traditional functions of philosophy. Collingwood did not, however, simply abandon philosophy for history. Rather, if the world was to be treated through the concepts of process and action, and thought was to be seen as objectified in history, the necessary and proper object of philosophy is history.

On Collingwood's conception, the object of philosophy is revealed in the process of history. History cannot, therefore, eliminate philosophy. Nor is religion eliminated by the emphasis on his-

[36] R. G. Collingwood, 'Notes on Historiography', printed in Collingwood, *The Principles of History: and other writings in philosophy of history. Edited with an introduction by W. H. Dray and W. J. van der Dussen.* Oxford University Press, Oxford, 1999. p. 238. The section is titled 'That History is the Only Kind of Knowledge'. See also T. M. Knox, 'Editor's Preface', in the first edition of R. G. Collingwood, *The Idea of History.* Clarendon Press, Oxford, 1946. p. x.

tory as the self-knowledge of mind. Rather, such an emphasis means that theology and history can be grasped only together. As Gordon Graham has recently put a similar point, history is not theology, and theology is not history, but the theological meaning of Jesus' life can be grasped only historically.[37] It is fundamental to Christianity that Jesus was an historical figure whose life can be understood historically, rather than, for example, metaphorically. Philosophy, then, must be seen to have a content different to what has previously been conceived. Collingwood dramatically expressed this point in the field of metaphysics when he claimed that metaphysics is an historical study of that which is presupposed absolutely by thought or action. Philosophy cannot be 'liquidated' in the sense of no longer existing in any form, but liquidated in an outdated form by being given a new and more specific character consistent with the overall conception of process and action and with the development and practice of history.[38]

Western cultures share an historical consciousness; they may or may not share that consciousness with other cultures, but Collingwood might argue that we can only judge that we do so by investigating their concepts of choice and civility. What we take to be examples of an historical consciousness — including our self-understanding, our approach to teaching and learning, our stories about others and the other forms of commonplace historical consciousness — can be criticised as being more or less adequate to the modern concept of history. Where there are views that see history as a product of structural and impersonal elements, we can provide reasons to prefer those that emphasise persons and their deeds. Where studies based on means towards ends, or on regularity and law, offer no more than manipulation and control, we can aspire to wisdom and understanding.

In the movement from Hegel to Croce and then to Collingwood, the historicisation of philosophy and the subjectivisation of modern thought have become the same thing. Collingwood sought to resolve several difficulties faced by earlier versions of the immanent reason tradition, particularly the divide between the logical and the actual. Whereas earlier thinkers in this tradition had depended upon concepts outside history, Collingwood overcame these distinctions

---

[37] Gordon Graham, *Evil and Christian Ethics*. Cambridge University Press, Cambridge, 2001. (New Studies in Christian Ethics, No. 20.) esp. pp. 69-70.

[38] David Boucher has therefore seen *The New Leviathan* as Collingwood's own last attempt to practice history and philosophy in the new form he envisioned for both. David Boucher, 'Editor's Introduction' to Collingwood, *The New Leviathan. Revised edition.* p. xviii.

by locating reason and logic in history conceived as a process of action. Seen in this way, the practices of history are animated by a rational faith in the self-creative role of historical knowledge. Each of the earlier thinkers in the tradition saw that the emergence of an historical consciousness is an important event in Western societies. Collingwood showed the greater possibilities that arise when historical consciousness becomes self-consciousness.

Bibliography[1]

Works by R. G. Collingwood

Collections of unpublished writings

Bodleian Library, Oxford.

Oxford University Archives, Oxford.

Mrs Teresa Smith, Oxford.

Published writings, by year of publication[2]

'Roman Ambleside', *The Antiquary*. March, 1915. New Series. Vol. XI, No. 3. pp. 91-96.

Religion and Philosophy. Macmillan, London, 1916.

'The Exploration of the Roman Fort at Ambleside: Report on the Third Year's Work (1915)', *TCWAAS*. New Series. Vol. XVI, 1916. pp. 57-90.

'Hadrian's Wall: A History of the Problem', *The Journal of Roman Studies*. Vol. XI, 1921. pp. 37-66.

'Explorations in the Roman Fort at Ambleside (fourth year, 1920) and at other sites on the Tenth Iter', *TCWAAS*. New Series. Vol. XXI, 1921. pp. 1-42.

'The Roman Fort at Bewcastle', *TCWAAS*. New Series. Vol. XXII, 1922. pp. 169-185.

---

[1] This bibliography is restricted to works cited in the text — for general bibliographies, see C. Dreisbach, *R. G. Collingwood: A Bibliographic Checklist*. Philosophy Documentation Center, Bowling Green State University, Bowling Green, Ohio, 1993, and Ruth A. Burchnall, 'Catalogue of the papers of Robin George Collingwood (1889-1943), (Dep. Collingwood 1-28).' Bodleian Library, Oxford, 1994. Additional bibliographical resources can be found in *Collingwood and British Idealism Studies*, formerly *Collingwood Studies*, published annually by the R. G. Collingwood Society.

[2] References to *The Transactions of the Cumberland & Westmorland Antiquarian & Archaeological Society* are abbreviated as *TCWAAS*.

'The Roman Evacuation of Britain', *The Journal of Roman Studies*. Vol. XII, 1922. pp. 74-98.

'The British Frontier in the Age of Severus', *The Journal of Roman Studies*. Vol. XIII, 1923. pp. 69-81.

'Explorations at the Roman Fort of Burgh-by-Sands', *TCWAAS*. New Series. Vol. XXIII, 1923. pp. 3-12.

Speculum Mentis, or The Map of Knowledge. Clarendon Press, Oxford, 1924.

'Castle Howe, Peel Wyke', *TCWAAS*. New Series. Vol. XXIV, 1924. pp. 78-87.

'The Last Years of Roman Cumberland', *TCWAAS*. New Series. Vol. XXIV, 1924. pp. 247-255.

'Hadrian's Wall', *History: The Quarterly Journal of the Historical Association*. New Series. Vol. X, 1925. pp. 193-202.

'Liddel Strength', *TCWAAS*. New Series. Vol. XXVI, 1926. pp. 390-397.

'Maiden Castle in Stainmore', *TCWAAS*. New Series. Vol. XXVII, 1927. pp. 170-177.

'The Roman Frontier in Britain', *Antiquity: A Quarterly Review of Archaeology*. Vol. I, 1927. pp. 15-30.

'Hadrian's Wall', *Antiquity: A Quarterly Review of Archaeology*. Vol. II, 1928. pp. 222-224.

'Roman Signal-Stations on the Cumberland Coast', *TCWAAS*. New Series. Vol. XXIX, 1929. pp.138-165.

(with M. V. Taylor), 'Roman Britain in 1929', *The Journal of Roman Studies*. Vol. XIX, 1929. pp. 180-218.

The Archaeology of Roman Britain. Methuen, London, 1930.

The Philosophy of History. Historical Association Leaflet No. 79. Bell, London, 1930.

'A System of numerical references to the parts of Hadrian's Wall and the structures along its line', *TCWAAS*. New Series. Vol. XXX, 1930. pp. 108-115.

'Discoveries at Birdoswald, on Hadrian's Wall', *Antiquity: A Quarterly Review of Archaeology*. Vol. IV, 1930. pp. 102-103.

'Ten Year's Work on Hadrian's Wall: 1920-30', *TCWAAS*. New Series. Vol. XXXI, 1931. pp. 87-110.

'Hadrian's Wall: 1921-1930', *The Journal of Roman Studies*. Vol. XXI, 1931. pp. 36-64.

An Essay on Philosophical Method. Clarendon Press, Oxford, 1933.

'An Introduction to the Prehistory of Cumberland, Westmorland and Lancashire north of the Sands', *TCWAAS*. New Series. Vol. XXXIII, 1933. pp. 163-200.

'The Present Need of a Philosophy', *Philosophy*. Vol. IX, 1934. pp. 262-265.

The Historical Imagination. An Inaugural Lecture delivered before the University of Oxford on 28 October 1935. Clarendon Press, Oxford, 1935.

'The Bewcastle Cross', *TCWAAS*. New Series. Vol. XXXV, 1935. pp. 1-29.

(Author unknown; R. G. Collingwood as Chair), 'Report of the Discussion on "Roman Britain as a Subject of Teaching" held on January 12th, 1937', *The Journal of Roman Studies*. Vol. XXVII, 1937. pp. 251-253.

'Review of R. Klibansky and H. J. Paton eds., *Philosophy and History: Essays presented to Ernst Cassirer'*, *The English Historical Review*. Vol. LII, 1937. pp. 141-146.

The Principles of Art. Clarendon Press, Oxford, 1938.

'John Horsley and Hadrian's Wall', *Archaeologia Aeliana, or, Miscellaneous Tracts Relating to Antiquity*. Fourth Series. Vol. 15, 1938. pp. 1-42.

An Autobiography. Oxford University Press, London, 1939.

The Idea of Nature. (Edited by T. M. Knox.) Clarendon Press, Oxford, 1945.

The Idea of History. (Edited by T. M. Knox.) Clarendon Press, Oxford, 1946.

(with R. P. Wright), *The Roman Inscriptions of Britain. Volume I, Inscriptions on Stone*. Clarendon Press, Oxford, 1965.

Essays in the Philosophy of History: R. G. Collingwood. (Edited by W. Debbins.) McGraw-Hill, New York, 1966.

Essays in Political Philosophy. Edited with an introduction by David Boucher. Clarendon Press, Oxford, 1989.

The New Leviathan, or Man, Society, Civilization and Barbarism. Revised edition, edited and introduced by David Boucher, with 'Goodness, Rightness, Utility' and 'What "Civilization" Means'. Clarendon Press, Oxford, 1992.

The Idea of History. Revised edition, with Lectures 1926-1928, edited with an introduction by Jan van der Dussen. Clarendon Press, Oxford, 1993.

An Essay on Metaphysics. Revised Edition With The Nature of Metaphysical Study; Function of Metaphysics in Civilization; Notes for an Essay on Logic. Edited with an Introduction by Rex Martin. Clarendon Press, Oxford, 1998.

The Principles of History: and other writings in philosophy of history. Edited with an introduction by W. H. Dray and W. J. van der Dussen. Oxford University Press, Oxford, 1999.

Works by other authors

Published work

Agassi, J., 'Questions of Science and Metaphysics', *The Philosophical Forum.* New Series. Vol. 5, 1974. pp. 529-556.

Alexander, S., *Space, Time, and Deity. With a new foreword by Dorothy Emmet.* Two volumes. Macmillan, London, 1966. (First published in 1920.)

Atkinson, R. F., *Knowledge and Explanation in History: An Introduction to the Philosophy of History.* Macmillan, London, 1978.

Ayer, A. J., *Philosophy in the Twentieth Century.* Unwin, London, 1984.

Ayer, A.J., *Language Truth and Logic.* Gollancz, London, 1936.

Belnap, Jr., N. D., 'Questions: Their Presuppositions, and How They Can Fail to Arise', in *The Logical Way of Doing Things.* (Edited by K. Lambert.) Yale University Press, New Haven, 1969. pp. 23-37.

Belnap, Jr., N. D. and Steel, Jr., T. B., *The Logic of Questions and Answers.* Yale University Press, New Haven, 1976.

Berlin, I., *Vico and Herder: Two Studies in the History of Ideas.* Chatto and Windus, London, 1980.

Bosanquet, B., *The Essentials of Logic.* Macmillan, London, 1895.

Boucher, D., *The Social and Political Thought of R. G. Collingwood.* Cambridge University Press, Cambridge, 1989.

Boucher, D., 'Overlap and Autonomy: The Different Worlds of Collingwood and Oakeshott', *Storia, Antropologia e Scienze Del Linguaggio.* Vol. IV, No. 2/3, 1989. pp. 69-89.

Bradley, F. H., *The Principles of Logic. Second edition.* Oxford University Press, Oxford, 1922.

Bradley, F. H., *Ethical Studies. Second edition.* Clarendon Press, Oxford, 1927.

Bradley, F. H., *Collected Essays.* Clarendon Press, Oxford, 1935.

Buchdal, G., 'Logic and History. An Assessment of R. G. Collingwood's *Idea of History*', *Australasian Journal of Philosophy.* Vol. 26, 1948. pp. 94-113.

Buchdal, G., 'Has Collingwood been unfortunate in his critics?', *The Australasian Journal of Philosophy.* Vol. 36, 1958. pp. 95-108.

Bultmann, R., *History and Eschatology, The Gifford Lectures 1955.* Edinburgh University Press, Edinburgh, 1957.

Burke, T., *Dewey's New Logic: A Reply to Russell.* University of Chicago Press, Chicago, 1994.

Campbell, R., *Truth and Historicity.* Clarendon Press, Oxford, 1992.

Clark, M., *Speaking Out of Turn: Lectures and Speeches, 1940-1991.* Melbourne University Press, Melbourne, 1997.

Coady, C. A. J., *Testimony: A Philosophical Study.* Clarendon Press, Oxford, 1992.

Croce, B., *The Philosophy of Giambattista Vico.* (Translated by R. G. Collingwood.) (1913). Reprinted by Russell & Russell, New York, 1964.

Croce, B., *Philosophy of the Practical, Economic and Ethic.* (Translated by Douglas Ainslie.) Macmillan, London, 1913.

Croce, B., *What is Living and What is Dead of the Philosophy of Hegel.* (Translated by Douglas Ainslie.) (1915). Reprinted by Russell & Russell, New York, 1969.

Croce, B., *Logic as the Science of the Pure Concept.* (Translated by Douglas Ainslie.) Macmillan, London, 1917.

Croce, B., *History: Its Theory and Practice.* (Translated by Douglas Ainslie.) (1921). Reprinted by Russell & Russell, New York, 1960.

Croce, B., *History as the Story of Liberty.* (Translated by Sylvia Sprigge.) Allen and Unwin, London, 1941.

Davidson, D., *Essays on Actions and Events.* Clarendon Press, Oxford, 1980.

Davidson, D., *Subjective, Intersubjective, Objective.* Clarendon Press, Oxford, 2001.

Dewey, J., *Logic: The Theory of Inquiry.* John Dewey, The Later Works, 1925-1953. Volume 12: 1938. Southern Illinois University Press, Carbondale, 1991.

Dilthey, W., *Selected Writings. Edited, translated and introduced by H. P. Rickman.* Cambridge University Press, Cambridge, 1976.

Dixon, R., *Prosthetic Gods: Travel, Representation and Colonial Governance.* University of Queensland Press in association with the API Network, St. Lucia, 2001.

Donagan, A., 'The Verification of Historical Theses', *The Philosophical Quarterly.* Vol. 6, 1956. pp. 193-208.

Donagan, A., *The Later Philosophy of R. G. Collingwood.* Clarendon Press, Oxford, 1962. Reprinted, 'with a new preface and corrections', by University of Chicago Press, Chicago, 1985.

Dray, W. H., *Laws and Explanation in History.* Oxford University Press, London, 1957.

Dray, W. H., 'Comment', in *Objectivity, Method and Point of View: Essays in the Philosophy of History.* (Edited by W. J. van der Dussen and L. Rubinoff.) E. J. Brill, Leiden, 1991. pp. 170-190.

Dray, W. H., *History as Re-enactment: R. G. Collingwood's Idea of History.* Clarendon Press, Oxford, 1995.

Dummett, M., *The Logical Basis of Metaphysics.* Harvard University Press, Cambridge, 1991.

Dummett, M., *Origins of Analytical Philosophy.* Harvard University Press, Cambridge, 1993.

Dussen, W. J. van der, *History as a Science: The Philosophy of R. G. Collingwood.* Martinus Nijhoff, The Hague, 1981.

Dworkin, R., *Taking Rights Seriously. New impression with a Reply to Critics.* Duckworth, London, 1978.

Emmet, D., *The Passage of Nature.* Temple University Press, Philadelphia, 1992.

Evans, R. J., *In Defence of History.* Granta, London, 1997.

van Fraassen, B., *The Scientific Image.* Clarendon Press, Oxford, 1980.

Gardiner, P., *The Nature of Historical Explanation.* Oxford University Press, London, 1952.

Goldstein, L. J., *Historical Knowing.* University of Texas Press, Austin, 1976.

Graham, G., *Historical Explanation Reconsidered.* Scots Philosophical Monographs, Number Four. Aberdeen University Press, Aberdeen, 1983.

The Shape of the Past: A Philosophical Approach to History. Oxford University Press, Oxford, 1997.

Evil and Christian Ethics. Cambridge University Press, Cambridge, 2001. (New Studies in Christian Ethics, No. 20.)

Haack, S., *Philosophy of Logics.* Cambridge University Press, Cambridge, 1978.

Hamblin, C. L., *Imperatives.* Basil Blackwell, Oxford, 1987.

Hegel, G. W. F., *Phenomenology of Spirit. Translated by A. V. Miller, with analysis of the text and foreword by J. N. Findlay.* Oxford University Press, Oxford, 1977.

Hegel, G. W. F., *Philosophy of Right. Translated with notes by T. M. Knox.* Clarendon Press, Oxford, 1942.

Hegel, G. W. F., *Lectures on the Philosophy of History. Translated by J. Sibree.* Bell, London, 1890.

Hegel, G. W. F., *Introduction to the Lectures on the History of Philosophy. Translated by T. M. Knox and A. V. Miller.* Clarendon Press, Oxford, 1985.

Hintikka, J., 'Questioning as a Philosophical Method', in *Principles of Philosophical Reasoning.* (Edited by J. H. Fetzer.) Rowman and Allenheld, Totowa, 1984. pp. 25-43.

Hinz, M., *Self-Creation and History: Collingwood and Nietzsche on Conceptual Change*. University Press of America, Lanham, 1994.

Hodder, I., *Reading the Past: Current Approaches to Interpretation in Archaeology. Second edition*. Cambridge University Press, Cambridge, 1991.

Hodder, I., *The Archaeological Process: An Introduction*. Blackwell, Oxford, 1999.

Huescar, A. R., *Jose Ortega y Gasset's Metaphysical Innovation: A Critique and Overcoming of Idealism*. (Translated and edited by Jorge Garcia-Gomez.) State University of New York Press, Albany, 1995.

Jenkins, K., *Re-Thinking History*. Routledge, London, 1991.

Joachim, H. H., *The Nature of Truth: An Essay*. Clarendon Press, Oxford, 1906.

Jones, H., 'Idealism and Epistemology (I)', *Mind*. New Series. Vol. II, 1893. pp. 289-306.

Kant, I., *On History. Edited, with an introduction, by Lewis White Beck*. Library of Liberal Arts, New York, 1963.

Knox, T. M., *Action*. George Allen & Unwin, London, 1968.

Leonard, H. S., *Principles of Reasoning. An Introduction to Logic, Methodology, and the Theory of Signs*. Dover, New York, 1967.

Lucas, G. R., Jr., *The Rehabilitation of Whitehead: An Analytic and Historical Assessment of Process Philosophy*. State University of New York Press, Albany, 1989.

Lyons, W., *Matters of the Mind*. Edinburgh University Press, Edinburgh, 2001.

MacIntyre, A., *After Virtue: A Study in Moral Theory. Second edition*. Duckworth, London, 1985.

Martin, Raymond, *The Past Within Us: An Empirical Approach to Philosophy of History*. Princeton University Press, Princeton, 1989.

Martin, Rex, *Historical Explanation: Re-enactment and Practical Inference*. Cornell University Press, Ithaca, 1977.

Martin, Rex, 'Collingwood's Claim that Metaphysics is a Historical Discipline', *The Monist*. Vol. 72, No. 4, 1989. pp. 489-525.

Martin, Rex, 'Collingwood's *Essay on Metaphysics* and the three conclusions to the *Idea of Nature*', *British Journal for the History of Philosophy*. Vol. 7, No. 2, 1999. pp. 333-351.

McCullagh, C. B., *The Truth of History*. Routledge, London, 1998.

McFee, G., 'Bradley, Possibility and a Question-and-Answer Logic', in *Perspectives on the Logic and Metaphysics of F. H. Bradley*. (Edited by W. J. Mander.) Thoemmes Press, Bristol, 1996. pp. 269-287.

Milne, A. J. M., *The Social Philosophy of English Idealism*. George Allen and Unwin, London, 1962.

Milne, A. J. M., 'Collingwood's Ethics and Political Theory', in *Critical Essays on the Philosophy of R. G. Collingwood*. (Edited by M. Krausz.) Clarendon Press, Oxford, 1972. pp. 296-326.

Mink, L. O., *Mind, History, and Dialectic: The Philosophy of R. G. Collingwood*. Indiana University Press, Bloomington, 1969. Reprinted by Wesleyan University Press, Middletown, 1987.

Morris, C. R., *Idealistic Logic: A Study of Its Aim, Method and Achievement*. Macmillan, London, 1933.

Nielsen, M. H., *R. G. Collingwood's Historiefielosofi: En undersoegelse af 're-enactment'-tesens interpretation*. Skrifter udgivet af det Historiske Institut ved Koebenhavns Universitet — Bind XI. Den Danske Historiske Forening, Koebenhavn, 1980.

Nielsen, M. H., 'Re-enactment and Reconstruction in Collingwood's Philosophy of History', *History and Theory*. Vol. XX, 1981. pp. 1-31.

Oakeshott, M., *On Human Conduct*. Clarendon Press, Oxford, 1991.

Ortega y Gasset, J., *Historical Reason*. (Translated by Philip W. Silver.) Norton, New York, 1984.

Passmore, J., *A Hundred Years of Philosophy. Second edition*. Penguin, Harmondsworth, 1980.

Patrick, J., *The Magdalen Metaphysicals: Idealism and Orthodoxy at Oxford, 1901-1945*. Mercer University Press, Macon, 1985.

Pettit, P., 'The contribution of analytical philosophy', in *A Companion to Contemporary Political Philosophy*. (Edited by Robert E. Goodin and Philip Pettit.) Blackwell, Oxford, 1993. pp. 7-38.

Popper, K., *Objective Mind: An Evolutionary Approach*. Revised edition. Clarendon Press, Oxford, 1979.

Prichard, H. A., *Moral Obligation, and Duty and Interest: Essays and Lectures*. Oxford University Press, London, 1968.

Roberts, D. D., *Benedetto Croce and the Uses of Historicism*. University of California Press, Berkeley, 1987.

Ross, W. D., *The Right and the Good*. Clarendon Press, Oxford, 1930.

Rubinoff, L., *Collingwood and the Reform of Metaphysics: A Study in the Philosophy of Mind*. University of Toronto Press, Toronto, 1970.

Rubinoff, L., 'History and Human Nature: Reflections on R. G. Collingwood', *International Studies in Philosophy*. Vol. XXIII, No. 3, 1991. pp. 75-89.

Ryle, G., *Philosophical Arguments: An Inaugural Lecture, Delivered before the University of Oxford, 30 October 1945*. Clarendon Press, Oxford, 1945.

Searle, J. R., *The Construction of Social Reality*. Penguin, Harmondsworth, 1996.

Simpson, F. G., *Watermills and Military Works on Hadrian's Wall: Excavations in Northumberland 1907-1913*. (Edited by Grace Simpson.) Titus Wilson, Kendal, 1976.

Somerville, J., 'Collingwood's Logic of Question and Answer', *The Monist*. Vol. 72, No. 4, 1989. pp. 526-541.

Strawson, P. F., *Introduction to Logical Theory*. Methuen, London, 1964.

Vico, G., *Vico: Selected Writings*. Edited and translated by Leon Pompa. Cambridge University Press, Cambridge, 1982.

Walsh, W. H., *An Introduction to Philosophy of History*. Third edition. Hutchinson, London, 1967.

Whitehead, A. N., *Process and Reality: An Essay in Cosmology* (1929). Reprinted by Free Press, New York, 1969.

Whitehead, A. N., *Adventures of Ideas*. (1933). Reprinted by Macmillan, New York, 1952.

Wisniewski, A., *The Posing of Questions: Logical Foundations of Erotetic Inferences*. Kluwer Academic Publishers, Dordrecht, 1995. (Synthese Library, Volume 252.)

Young, R. A., 'Collingwood's Logic of Questions and Answers', *Bradley Studies*. Vol. 3, No. 2, Autumn 1997. pp. 151-175.

Yovel, Y., *Kant and the Philosophy of History*. Princeton University Press, Princeton, 1980.

Unpublished thesis

Modood, T., 'R. G. Collingwood, M. J. Oakeshott and the Idea of a Philosophical Culture.' PhD, University College, Swansea, 1984.

Index

A

action, vii, viii, 2, 5, 7-8, 10-12, 14-17, 24-25, 27-29, 32, 35, 44-45, 57, 59, 62-63, 71-72, 75, 79, 89, 96-97, 101-146, 150, 152, 154, 156-157, 176-180, 184-193, 197-222

action and history , viii, 17, 24, 27, 45, 101, 191, 209, 219

theory of action, 8, 62, 119, 179

activity, vii, 1, 2, 5, 7, 10, 14, 27-31, 35-36, 42, 44-45, 48-54, 60-61, 66-69, 77, 79, 82, 84-85, 88-89, 91, 93, 99-100, 104, 106, 111, 123-124, 133, 139, 141, 143-144, 148-149, 151-152, 154, 160-161, 167, 182-183, 185, 193-198, 203-204, 210-211, 214, 219-220

Agassi, J., 86

agency, vii, 3, 95, 199-201, 208, 215

agent, 7, 10-11, 14, 36, 43-44, 50, 57-59, 95, 106-107, 115-119, 121, 127, 129, 130-132, 137, 150-151, 161, 169, 174, 178-179, 190-194, 197, 200-201, 207-208, 211, 215, 217

Alexander, Samuel, 18, 51-59, 61-63, 148, 202, 219

Ambleside, 161-164, 174

Anselm, 61

appetite, 20, 65

archaeology , 3, 17-18, 21-22, 24, 73, 75, 77, 160-167, 172, 174, 176, 199, 203

selective excavation, 167, 171-172

signal-stations, 170

Aristotle, 34, 38, 41, 42, 44, 61, 70, 75, 99

art , 29, 32, 35-36, 97, 144, 152, 154, 169, 182-183, 189, 194, 204

Atkinson, R. F., 184

Ayer, A. J., 42, 81

B

Bayou, H. P., 42

becoming, 27, 32, 34-35, 41-42, 48, 52-53, 123, 148, 152, 194, 203, 216, 219

Belnap, N., 85-87, 98-99

Bergson, H-L., 123

Berkeley, 42, 124, 198

Berlin, Isaiah, 12, 50

Bewcastle, 165, 169

Bosanquet, B., 67-69, 79, 102

Boucher, David , ix, 23, 35, 101-102, 156, 179, 183, 215, 221

Bradley, F. H., 7, 18, 23, 52, 67-69, 79-80, 85, 102, 110, 112, 193-194

Buchdal, G., 130

Bultmann, R., 135, 136

Burke, T., 91

Bury, J. B., 165

Butler, Bishop, 194

C

Campbell, R., 2

Cassirer, E., 21

categorical imperative, 110-111, 116, 117

causality, 42, 150

choice (*See also utility, right, duty*), 66, 91-93, 95, 101-102, 105, 107, 109, 117, 120, 122, 127, 129, 130-137, 152, 183, 185-188, 191-192, 200, 204-205, 209-210, 212, 214, 216, 220

capricious, 102, 106, 120, 130, 214, 218

rational choice, 101, 108, 119, 120

civilization, (*See also historical civilization*) viii, 4-7, 24-25, 28, 30, 43, 53-54, 97, 122, 137, 147, 187-188, 198-200, 203, 205-206, 208-220

Clark, Manning, 144

Coady, C. A. J., 199

Collingwood, R. G.

An Autobiography, 4-5, 17, 19, 21-23, 29, 32, 35, 41, 52, 73, 77-78, 80, 83-85, 98, 115, 161

An Essay on Metaphysics, 17, 19, 21, 24, 27, 38, 41-43, 59, 66-67, 77, 81-83, 85, 95, 150-151, 184

An Essay on Philosophical Method, 19-20, 23, 27, 37, 39, 41, 55, 59, 61, 64, 94, 128, 181

'Can Historians be Impartial?', 191, 193

'Fairy Tales', 155, 185, 194

'Goodness, Rightness, Utility', 23, 109, 115-116, 126-127, 130, 135

'Human Nature and Human History', 58

'Lectures on Moral Philosophy', 102, 104, 107, 110, 114, 127, 135, 191

'Lectures on the Philosophy of History', 14, 176

'Libellus de Generatione', 22, 27-28, 31-32, 34, 41, 73

'Note for an Essay on Logic', 95

'Notes on Historiography', 74, 189, 220

'Outlines of a Philosophy of History', 140, 142, 150, 151, 161

'Prolegomena to Logic', 71, 72

Religion and Philosophy, 27, 28, 32, 180

Roman Britain and the English Settlements, 168

Speculum Mentis, 19-22, 27-28, 35-37, 125, 143, 204

The Archaeology of Roman Britain, 168, 176

The Historical Imagination, 193-194, 196-197

The Idea of History, 11, 17-19, 22-24, 35, 57, 103, 115, 124, 126, 129, 139, 141-144, 146-149, 151, 153-154, 156-157, 161, 176, 181, 183, 188, 193, 195, 197, 220

The Idea of Nature, 1, 5, 24, 28, 55-56, 60, 62, 104, 146-149, 203

'The Nature and Aims of a Philosophy of History', 125, 140

The New Leviathan, 6, 9-10, 20, 21-23, 28, 33, 54, 57, 63-64, 66, 77, 83, 108-109, 121-122, 126-129, 147, 153, 155-156, 162-163, 183, 202, 211-212, 214, 220-221

The Philosophy of History, 176, 185, 187, 189

The Principles of Art, 11, 17, 20, 28, 97, 154-156, 182-183

The Principles of History, 4-6, 10, 28, 52, 56-57, 62, 74, 144, 149, 155, 189, 191, 203, 208, 220

'Truth and Contradiction', 22, 27-33, 71, 83-84, 194

Collingwood, W. G.169

consciousness (*See also historical consciousness, self-consciousness*)

corruption of, 94, 97, 219

forms of consciousness, 64

moral, 113, 120, 141, 147

constructionism, 48-50

Cook Wilson, J.51, 67

Croce, vii, 10, 12, 15-18, 34-35, 38-39, 51, 102, 106, 119, 121, 123, 152, 154, 194, 197-198, 202, 221

D

Davidson, Donald, 11, 57, 61, 111, 120, 183

de Ruggiero, G.18, 56, 215

Descartes, 2, 9, 61, 147

desire, 20, 38, 65-66, 82-83, 98, 102, 105-106, 112, 115, 133, 140, 145, 152, 154, 156, 183, 192, 218

Dewey, John, 18, 67, 75, 78, 88-91, 95-96, 99, 207

Dilthey, W.15, 18, 152-154

Dixon, Robert3

Donagan, Alan19-21, 32, 66, 84, 130, 179, 184

Dray, W. H. 19, 49, 131-132, 178-179, 184, 189, 220

Dummett, Michael9

Dussen, W. J. van der 18, 22, 178-179, 184

duty (*See also choice*), 25, 35, 38, 66, 97, 102, 106-137, 139, 141, 144, 147, 150, 169, 178, 188, 190, 192, 197, 205, 209, 210-214

Dworkin, Ronald, 109-110

E

economics, 110, 208

education, 215

Emmet, D.52, 54, 59

emotions, 13, 16-17, 28, 54, 97, 105, 135, 140, 152-157, 182-183, 185, 187, 190, 192, 211-214, 219-220

empathy, 153, 184

epistemology of history, 51, 58

ethics, 74, 103, 130, 178

Evans, Richard, 48-49

evidence, 31, 78, 83-84, 89, 118, 127, 130, 133, 135, 160-161, 164-171, 174, 176-177, 180, 190-192, 196-197, 199, 201

evolution, 54, 70, 147-149

F

Fackenheim, E. L.21

folklore, 18, 21, 155

Foucault, M., 7, 18, 43

freedom, viii, 4, 8, 35, 106-107, 114, 126, 130, 144, 175-176, 211, 214-215

French Revolution, 52, 118, 129-130

G

Gadamer, H. G., 18

Galileo, 146

Gardiner, Patrick19

generalisations, 52, 133, 168, 174, 176, 200, 216

Gentile, G.,18

geology, 124, 146, 160, 202

Goldstein, L. J., 50

Graham, Gordon, 80, 145, 178-179, 184, 221

Green, T. H., 18, 23

H

Haack, Susan, 69

Hadrian's Wall, 163-166, 168-171, 173-175

    Diocletian, 170

    Severus, 166-167, 170

Hamblin, C.85-86

Hamilton, W.68

Hammurabi, 126, 128

Hegel, vii, 2, 10, 12-16, 18, 21, 34, 42, 56, 61, 63, 70, 94-95, 140, 147-149, 152-153, 221

Heidegger, M., 18, 21, 42

Herder, J. G., 12, 148

Hintikka, J., 86

Hinz, Michael, 5, 216

historical agents, vii, 19, 114, 127, 128, 136, 149, 157, 160, 168, 190, 192

historical imagination *(See also imagination)*, 194, 196

historical practice, viii, 25, 47-48, 50-51, 73, 75, 78, 84, 104, 164, 172, 174-175, 181, 194-195, 199, 205

historical reconstruction, 175, 192

historical self-consciousness, 197, 215

historical understanding, 118, 134, 185, 195, 208-209, 211, 213

history

    historical civilization, 6, 7, 200, 208, 211, 213, 215, 216

    historical consciousness, viii, 1-4, 17, 24-25, 125-126, 157, 174, 187-188, 193, 197, 205, 217, 221-222

    historical inquiry, 162, 192

    historical knowledge, 5, 7-8, 12, 25, 49, 55, 101, 132-133, 137, 139, 141-144, 146, 149, 157, 159-161, 174-175, 178-181, 184, 188-189, 191, 194, 197, 202, 219, 222

    historical process, 55, 141-143, 146, 149, 150, 153, 157, 160, 184, 219

    historical reason, viii, 4, 198, 203, 208, 209

    history of history, 159, 169, 205

    metaphysics of history *(See also history: object of history)*, 7-10, 51

    modern history, 59, 129, 147, 180, 203, 214

    object of history, viii, 7, 25, 57, 122, 137, 139, 140, 143, 146, 157, 160, 192, 219

    scientific history, 15, 126, 176, 199

history of thought2, 4, 57, 69, 149, 151, 155

Hodder, Ian, 3

Huescar, Antonio Rodriguez, 9, 209-210

human nature, 4, 6, 133, 141-143, 149, 157, 204, 216

Hume, 32-33, 42, 124, 141

Husserl, E.21

I

idealism, 19, 33-35, 67-68, 70, 72, 79, 142

imagination *(See also historical imagination)*, 20, 106, 154, 161, 169, 179, 182-183, 188, 194-196

immanent reason, vii, 10, 12, 219, 221

individualism, 220

individuality, 6, 36, 114, 117-120, 122-124, 129-130, 154, 178, 200-204

inference, 38, 67, 87, 166, 174-176, 185, 192, 196, 199

intelligence, 13, 142, 147

interpretation, 3, 7, 11-12, 16-17, 21, 33, 48-49, 61, 84-85, 99, 114, 118, 124, 130, 141, 157, 160-161, 163, 166, 168-169, 174-177, 179-180, 183-185, 194, 197, 215, 220

J

James, W., 67, 81, 123

Jenkins, Keith, 159

Joachim, H. H., 30, 68-69, 79

Jones, Henry, 29, 72

K

Kant, 12-13, 16, 18, 38, 42, 79, 102, 108-111, 113, 116-117, 126, 128-130, 140, 148-149

Knox, T. M., 14, 19, 109, 143, 220

Kuhn, T. S., 18, 43

L

Leibniz, 38

Leonard, H. S., 90, 99

liberalism, 7, 24, 219

life, viii, 2, 4-5, 11, 15, 27, 53, 56-58, 63, 74, 90, 106, 108, 133-134, 136-137, 142, 145, 147-149, 152-156, 198, 205, 209-210, 213, 217-219, 221

Lloyd-Morgan, C., 53

Locke, 38, 124

logic, 3, 14-15, 17, 21, 24-25, 28-29, 32-33, 36, 41, 52, 63-81, 83-86, 88-91, 93-102, 122, 124, 128, 140, 151, 160, 162, 164, 166, 174, 176, 202-204, 207, 222

concept of logic, 71

idealist logic, 67, 80

presuppositions, 19, 21, 24, 42-44, 56, 58, 60-61, 83, 84, 90, 150, 171, 195

propositional logic, 10, 29, 38, 54, 65-67, 70, 79, 83-84, 86, 96, 183

question and answer, 21, 24, 29, 33, 42-43, 63-66, 69, 70, 73, 75, 77-88, 90-100, 106, 122, 132, 151, 156, 159-164, 167, 170, 172, 185, 189, 191, 196-197, 203, 205, 214-215, 217

Lotze, R. H., 67

Lucas, G. R, Jnr, 53

Luther, 114

Lyons, W., 2

M

Mach, E., 123

MacIntyre, Alasdair, 3, 210, 216

Martin, Rex, 41, 62, 84-85, 185, 199

Martin, Raymond, 210

matter, 17, 39, 40-42, 52-56, 70, 74, 81, 88-89, 99-100, 106, 116, 132, 134, 136, 148, 152, 154-155, 170, 173, 191, 202

McCullagh, C. B., 49

McFee, Graham, 80

metaphysics, 5, 7-10, 17, 28, 33, 41-42, 44, 51-52, 67-68, 70, 83, 97, 122, 204, 216, 221

Meyer, E., 161

Milne, A. J. M., 23, 120

mind, 2, 8-10, 12-14, 18-21, 28-29, 32-33, 35-37, 43, 48, 51, 53-57, 62-64, 66-70, 72-75, 78-80, 82-83, 85-86, 89, 91, 95, 98-99, 101-102, 105, 107, 112, 118, 127, 132-133, 139, 141-143, 146-149, 151-153, 155-157, 159-161, 164, 167, 172, 175, 180-184, 194, 199-204, 209, 214, 217-218, 220-221

Mink, Louis, 18, 20-21, 85

Modood, Tariq, 35

Moore, G. E., 18, 67

moral philosophy, viii, 1, 4, 6, 17, 23-25, 29, 101-108, 110, 113, 115, 118-122, 125-126, 128-129, 131, 134-137, 144, 156, 188, 205, 218

moral judgements, 104, 171, 191

moral responsibility, 193

Morris, C. R., 67, 68, 79, 80

N

narrative, 2, 3, 19, 148, 160, 166-169, 194-195, 208-210, 218-219

natural science, 1, 4, 19, 44, 49, 62, 89, 139, 140, 147, 150-151, 153, 197, 202-204, 209

Newton, 94, 147

Nicholas of Cusa, 34

Nielsen, M., 179

Nietzsche, 5, 216

O

Oakeshott, M. J., 7, 18, 35, 178, 188, 192, 207-210, 214

ontological argument, 58-59, 61-62

Ortega y Gasset, Jose, 9, 11, 18, 61, 90, 209, 210, 218-219

P

passion, 14, 16, 65

Passmore, John, 18, 67

Patrick, James, 19, 67

Peirce, C. S., 18, 67

Pettit, P., 108-109

philosophical concepts, 28-29, 31, 37-39, 41, 64, 94, 101, 128, 177

philosophical knowledge, 38

philosophy of art, 17, 55, 155-156

philosophy of history, viii, 4, 8, 13-19, 22, 24-25, 32, 45, 47, 51-52, 55-57, 61, 74, 101, 113, 121-122, 130, 137, 139, 149, 152, 154-156, 162, 174, 177-179, 188-189, 194, 220

philosophy of language, 8-10, 61

philosophy of religion, 17

Plato, 34-35, 38, 61, 72

political philosophy, 17-18, 21, 23-24, 101

Popper, K., 18, 86

practical reason, 65-67, 107, 109, 120, 125, 132

Prichard, H. A., 51, 131

process (*See also* history: historical process), 1-2, 7-8, 10, 12, 16, 21-22, 24-25, 27-29, 32, 34-36, 40,

44-45, 47-48, 51-63, 65-67, 70-74, 78-79, 82, 85, 87, 89-95, 98-99, 101-103, 105, 109, 117, 121-123, 129, 133-136, 141-154, 156-157, 160, 163, 167, 170, 174-175, 177, 179, 181, 184-186, 188-191, 193-194, 196-198, 200-203, 205, 212-214, 217-222

natural, 55-56, 132, 149, 151, 153

progress, viii, 5, 8, 40-41, 44, 126, 132, 144-147, 177, 180-181, 185, 192, 205, 215-216

psyche, 73, 132, 155, 218

psychology, 67-75, 80, 89, 99, 102, 153

R

realism, 23, 29, 32-33, 35, 40, 48-52, 56, 58, 62, 67-68, 71, 75, 97, 131, 194, 196

re-enactment, 19, 48, 114, 130, 149, 151, 154-155, 178-186, 201, 208, 220

religion, 13, 18, 28, 32, 35-36, 97, 112, 145, 189, 204, 220

Rickert, H., 21, 202

right (*See also choice*), 30, 38, 66, 85, 96-97, 104, 108-113, 116-117, 121-123, 125-126, 136, 147, 150, 155, 173, 185, 192, 205, 208, 210, 212, 214

rules, 6, 48-49, 88, 102, 104, 110-118, 120, 122, 127-128, 130, 132-133, 135, 141, 150, 172, 176, 194, 204-205, 207, 214-215

Roberts, D., 198

Roman Britain, 18, 128, 167-168, 170, 173-175

Ross, W. D., 109, 112, 116

Rousseau, J. J., 102

Rubinoff, Lionel, 19-21

Russell, Bertrand, 12, 15-16, 59, 67, 80, 91

Ryle, G.,18-20

S

Saint Augustine, 114

Saint Paul, 114

scale of forms, 24, 31, 37-42, 44, 56, 95, 101, 106, 109, 117, 119, 128, 156, 214

science, 1, 4, 28, 32, 35-38, 40-44, 49, 59-60, 64, 68, 71-72, 74-75, 81, 86, 110, 115, 121, 123-124, 133, 145-147, 157, 173, 194, 202-204

Searle, John, 58

self-consciousness, 122, 130-131, 188, 197-198, 222

self-knowledge, viii, 4, 14, 17, 25, 97, 106-107, 131-133, 135-137, 139, 141-144, 146, 157, 159, 185, 188-189, 197-199, 201-202, 205, 215, 220-221

Simmel, G., 149

Simpson, F. G., 163-164, 167, 170

social community, 5, 211-214

society, 4, 6, 28, 50, 172, 210-211, 213-217

Somerville, James, 81-82

Spengler, O., 48, 180

Spinoza, 34, 61, 113, 152, 194

Steel, T., 86-87

Strawson, P. F., 98

subjectivity, 2, 33, 35, 121, 208, 221

T

theoretical reason, 21, 66, 73, 107, 125, 161

thought, vii-ix, 1-13, 17-22, 24-25, 27-35, 37-43, 44, 47-48, 52, 56-63, 65-67, 69-75, 78-82, 87, 89-91, 95, 97-101, 103, 106, 108, 111, 113, 117-118, 121-125, 130-137, 139-146, 148-152, 155-157, 159-161, 163-166, 170-174, 178-183, 185-186, 188-190, 192-194, 197, 200-201, 204, 206, 209-210, 213, 215-216, 218-221

movement in thought, 69-70

truth, 21, 28-31, 35, 39-40, 49-50, 54, 65, 67, 71, 73, 79, 83-85, 90, 96, 98, 105, 116, 120, 149, 167, 181, 194

Y

Young, R. A., 85

Yovel, Y., 13

U

universals, 37, 42, 111, 128

utility (*See also* choice), 66, 102, 106-110, 113, 116-117, 120-123, 125-127, 129-130, 136, 192, 205, 207-208, 210, 212, 214

V

values, 7, 85, 190-193, 205-206, 217

van Fraassen, Bas, 86

Vico, vii, 10, 12, 16, 18, 121, 152

W

Walsh, W. H., 184

Whitehead, A. N., 18, 51-63, 67, 70, 148, 219

will, 10, 13, 17, 20, 28, 57, 72, 78, 102, 105, 107-108, 112-115, 117, 121, 126, 135, 151, 161, 191, 211-214

Wisniewski, A., 87-88, 98-99

Wittgenstein, L., 18